COMPLETE
MEDITERRANEAN
DIET COOKBOOK
for Beginners

2000+ Days
of Effortless, Healthy,
and Budget-Friendly Recipes

Quick & Easy 30-Minute Dishes
and a No-Stress 30-Day
Meal Plan

Lara Mare

Table of Contents

Table of Contents

Table of Contents

Introduction: Welcome to the Mediterranean Diet
The Origins and Evolution of the Mediterranean Diet

The Mediterranean diet is more than just a way of eating; it is a **vibrant tapestry** woven from centuries of **history, culture, and tradition**. Originating in the ancient civilizations of **Greece, Rome, and Egypt,** this diet is deeply rooted in the daily lives and rituals of the people who lived around the Mediterranean Sea.

The Natural Bounty of the Mediterranean

From the bustling markets of Athens to the terraced vineyards of the Amalfi Coast, the Mediterranean diet has been shaped by the **natural abundance** of the region. The **warm, sun-drenched climate** and **fertile soil** gave rise to a diet rich in:

- **Fresh fruits and vegetables**
- **Whole grains and legumes**

These foods are not only delicious but also **packed with nutrients. Olive oil**, often referred to as "liquid gold," became the **cornerstone** of this diet, valued both for its **flavor** and **health benefits**.

The Influence of Great Civilizations

The history of the Mediterranean diet is intertwined with the rise of some of the world's most **influential civilizations**. The **ancient Greeks and Romans**, renowned for their **philosophical, artistic, and scientific** advancements, also recognized the importance of a **balanced diet**. Meals were celebrated as a **communal experience**, where food was not only sustenance but also a way to:

- **Foster social bonds**
- **Promote physical health**
- **Cultivate mental clarity**

Evolution Through Cultural Exchange

Throughout the Middle Ages, the Mediterranean diet continued to evolve as it absorbed influences from the **Byzantine Empire**, the **Arab world**, and the various cultures trading across the Mediterranean. These cultural exchanges enriched the diet with **new flavors** and **techniques**, adding diversity to its ingredients and cooking methods. For example:

- **Spices from the East** enhanced traditional dishes.
- Citrus fruits from Persia **introduced a refreshing brightness to Mediterranean cuisine.**

Resilience and Adaptability

What makes the Mediterranean diet particularly remarkable is its **resilience and adaptability.** Despite the waves of change that have swept through the region over the centuries—**wars, migrations**, and the **rise and fall of empires**—the **fundamental principles** of this diet have remained intact. Today, the Mediterranean diet continues to be celebrated for its:

- **Simplicity**
- **Sustainability**
- **Proven health benefits**

Proven Health Benefits

Modern science has confirmed what the ancients seemed to know instinctively: the Mediterranean diet is one of the **healthiest ways to eat**. Research consistently shows that those who follow this diet experience:

- **Lower rates of heart disease**
- **Longer life expectancy**
- **Better overall health**

But beyond the statistics, the Mediterranean way of life has a deeper appeal. This diet encourages us to **slow down, savor each bite**, and appreciate the connection between **food, family, and community**.

A Celebration of Life and Well-Being

In embracing the Mediterranean diet, you are not merely adopting a set of dietary guidelines—you are stepping into a **living tradition** that has nourished both **body and soul** for millennia. This is more than just a diet; it is a **celebration of life**, a testament to the enduring **wisdom of ancient cultures**, and an invitation to enjoy a **healthier, happier**, and more fulfilling way of living.

Health Benefits of the Mediterranean Diet: Heart Health, Longevity, and Weight Management

The Mediterranean diet is more than just a collection of delicious recipes; it's a **scientifically-backed gateway to a healthier, longer, and more fulfilling life**. Imagine a diet that not only delights your taste buds but also **fortifies your heart, helps you maintain a healthy weight**, and even **adds years to your life**. This isn't a fantasy—it's the reality for millions who embrace the Mediterranean way of eating.

Heart Health: Protecting Your Most Vital Organ

At the core of the Mediterranean diet lies its **profound impact on cardiovascular health**. Numerous studies have shown that this diet **significantly reduces the risk of heart disease**, which remains the leading cause of death worldwide. The secret to its success is found in its emphasis on **heart-friendly fats**, particularly those found in:

- **Extra virgin olive oil**: Rich in monounsaturated fats
- **Fatty fish** like salmon and mackerel: High in omega-3 fatty acids

These healthy fats work to:

- **Lower bad cholesterol (LDL) levels**
- **Reduce blood pressure**
- **Prevent the formation of dangerous blood clots**

The result is a heart that's **strong, resilient**, and ready to take on life's challenges.

Longevity: Adding Years to Your Life and Life to Your Years

The Mediterranean diet is also a proven ally in the **fight against aging**. In regions like the Greek island of Ikaria, known as a **"Blue Zone"** where people routinely live past 100, the diet is a **cornerstone of longevity**. The key to its anti-aging effects lies in the diet's **abundance of antioxidant-rich foods**, such as:

- **Fruits and vegetables**: Packed with antioxidants
- **Whole grains**
- **Healthy fats**

These foods help to **combat inflammation**, a key factor in the aging process. By reducing chronic inflammation, the Mediterranean diet **adds years to your life** while keeping you **active and vibrant** well into old age.

Weight Management: A Sustainable, Enjoyable Approach

For those looking to manage their weight, the Mediterranean diet offers a **sustainable and enjoyable solution**. Unlike restrictive diets, this way of eating is all about **abundance**—filling your plate with a variety of **nutrient-dense foods** that satisfy your hunger and nourish your body. The diet's focus on:

- **Whole, unprocessed foods**
- **Balanced blood sugar levels**

Helps to:

- **Prevent spikes and crashes** in blood sugar
- Naturally promote a healthy weight, **without the need for counting calories or eliminating entire food groups**

It's a lifestyle that encourages **mindful eating** and makes weight management a **natural byproduct** of a healthy way of life.

A Holistic Approach to Well-being: More Than Just Food

Perhaps one of the most compelling aspects of the Mediterranean diet is its **holistic approach to well-being**. This is not just a diet; it's a lifestyle that promotes **mindfulness, community, and balance**. The Mediterranean way of eating invites you to:

- **Slow down** and savor each meal
- **Enjoy the company** of loved ones
- Focus on the **joy of food** and its role in daily life

It's a reminder that health is not just about the food we eat but also about **how we live our lives**.

A Path to a Healthier, Happier Life

In embracing the Mediterranean diet, you're choosing more than just a way to eat—you're choosing a **path to a healthier, happier, and more vibrant life**. It's a decision that promises not only to **transform your body** but also to **enrich your soul**, one delicious meal at a time.

How the Mediterranean diet fits into a modern lifestyle, even for beginners.

In today's fast-paced world, finding a diet that aligns with our **busy lifestyles** while promoting **health and well-being** can seem like an impossible task. Yet, the **Mediterranean diet**, with its rich history and time-honored traditions, seamlessly fits into even the most hectic of modern lives. Whether you're a seasoned cook or a beginner, this diet offers a **flexible, sustainable**, and **delicious way** to nourish your body and soul.

Simplicity and Ease of Preparation

One of the most remarkable aspects of the Mediterranean diet is its **simplicity.** You don't need to be a gourmet chef or spend hours in the kitchen to enjoy its benefits. Many iconic Mediterranean dishes are incredibly **easy to prepare,** often requiring just a handful of **fresh, wholesome ingredients.**

For example:

- **Greek salad** with tomatoes, cucumbers, olives, feta cheese, olive oil, and lemon juice
- **Grilled fish,** seasoned with herbs, served with a colorful array of roasted vegetables

These meals are not only **quick to prepare** but also **burst with flavor and nutrition,** making the Mediterranean diet accessible even for those with the busiest of schedules.

Mindful Eating: Nourishing Body and Mind

The Mediterranean diet embraces the concept of **mindful eating,** encouraging us to slow down and savor each bite. In a world where we're often rushing from one task to the next, taking the time to enjoy a meal becomes an act of **self-care**. This diet invites us to:

- **Reconnect with our food**, appreciating its colors, textures, and aromas
- **Eat mindfully**, reducing stress and improving digestion
- Foster a deeper connection to the present moment through the sensory experience of eating

Eating mindfully nourishes not only the body but also the mind, helping to reduce **stress** and enhance overall **well-being.**

A Balanced, Enjoyable Approach to Eating

For beginners, the Mediterranean diet offers a refreshing break from the restrictive, **calorie-counting** approaches that dominate much of today's diet culture. Instead, it promotes **balance and variety,** allowing you to enjoy a wide range of foods that are both satisfying and good for you. Key components include:

- **Whole grains and lean proteins**
- **Fresh fruits and vegetables**

There's no need to deprive yourself or follow complicated meal plans. The Mediterranean diet celebrates the **joy of eating well,** combining health with flavor.

Adaptable for Any Lifestyle

The Mediterranean diet is inherently **adaptable,** making it easy to fit into any lifestyle. Whether you're:

- **Cooking for a family**
- **Dining solo**
- **Entertaining friends**

The Mediterranean diet can be tailored to your needs. It also aligns with the growing trend toward **sustainable, eco-friendly eating** by focusing on **seasonal, locally sourced ingredients.** It's a diet that respects the **earth** as much as it nourishes the **body.**

Small Changes, Big Health Benefits

Incorporating the Mediterranean diet into your daily routine doesn't mean completely overhauling your life. Instead, it's about making **small, meaningful changes** that lead to **lasting health benefits.** Simple ways to get started include:

- **Swapping processed foods** for whole, natural ingredients
- **Experimenting with new recipes** that highlight Mediterranean flavors
- **Making the dishes your own**, customizing them to your taste

Most importantly, **enjoy the process.** The Mediterranean diet is about more than just food—it's a **celebration of life, community**, and the simple pleasures of sharing a meal with those you love.

A Lifestyle for Modern Living

Even for beginners, the Mediterranean diet is a **natural fit for modern living**. It's a lifestyle that honors tradition while embracing the needs of today's world—a way of eating that is as **flexible and diverse** as the people who enjoy it. By choosing the Mediterranean diet, you're not just adopting a new way of eating—you're embracing a **way of life** that promises to enrich your **health, happiness**, and **well-being** for years to come.

What Makes the Mediterranean Diet Special?

The Mediterranean diet is not just a way of eating—it's a **lifestyle** that has captured the attention of health experts and food lovers alike. It stands out among other diets because of its unique blend of **flavor, health benefits**, and **cultural significance**. But what exactly makes it so special?

A Time-Tested Tradition

The Mediterranean diet is rooted in the **ancient civilizations** of Greece, Rome, and Egypt, drawing from centuries of **history, culture**, and **tradition**. Unlike modern fad diets, it has been practiced for thousands of years, making it a **time-tested approach** to eating that promotes both physical and emotional well-being.

Emphasis on Fresh, Natural Ingredients

One of the key features of the Mediterranean diet is its focus on **fresh, whole foods**. It emphasizes:

- **Fruits and vegetables**
- **Whole grains**
- **Legumes**
- **Healthy fats** (primarily from olive oil)
- **Lean proteins**, especially fish

These nutrient-dense ingredients are **minimally processed** and rich in **antioxidants, vitamins, and minerals**, promoting better overall health.

Heart-Healthy Benefits

The Mediterranean diet is world-renowned for its **heart health** benefits. The inclusion of **monounsaturated fats** from olive oil and **omega-3 fatty acids** from fish helps to:

- **Lower bad cholesterol (LDL)**
- **Reduce the risk of heart disease**
- **Regulate blood pressure**

This combination makes it one of the **best diets** for maintaining a healthy cardiovascular system.

A Balanced and Flexible Approach

Unlike restrictive diets that focus on elimination, the Mediterranean diet encourages **balance and variety**. It allows you to enjoy a wide range of foods, making it more **sustainable** and enjoyable in the long term. There's no need for calorie counting or cutting out entire food groups. Instead, it's about making **healthy choices** and savoring **real, flavorful food.**

More Than Just a Diet: A Lifestyle

What truly sets the Mediterranean diet apart is that it's more than just a diet—it's a **way of life**. It encourages **mindful eating**, where meals are celebrated, not rushed. Sharing meals with family and friends is a central part of the culture, promoting **social connections** and **emotional well-being**.

This approach to food reflects a **holistic** view of health, where the joy of eating, community, and personal satisfaction are just as important as physical nourishment.

Proven Health Benefits

Modern scientific research has consistently shown that the Mediterranean diet offers **extensive health benefits**, including:

- **Reduced risk of chronic diseases** like diabetes, cancer, and Alzheimer's
- **Improved weight management**
- **Enhanced longevity**

It's no surprise that regions where the Mediterranean diet is most commonly practiced, like the Greek island of Ikaria, are known for their **high life expectancy** and **low rates of chronic illness.**

Beginner tips for grocery shopping, meal prep, and cooking

Starting a new diet can feel overwhelming, but with the Mediterranean diet, simplicity and enjoyment are key. Here are some beginner-friendly tips for grocery shopping, meal prep, and cooking that will help you ease into this healthy and flavorful way of eating.

Grocery Shopping Tips

1. Focus on Fresh, Whole Foods: The foundation of the Mediterranean diet is fresh, unprocessed ingredients. When shopping, prioritize fresh fruits, vegetables, whole grains, legumes, nuts, seeds, and lean proteins like fish and poultry. Visit your local farmers' market or the produce section of your grocery store to find the best seasonal ingredients.

2. Stock Up on Pantry Staples: Having a well-stocked pantry is essential for quick and easy meal preparation. Keep items like olive oil, canned tomatoes, beans, whole grains (such as quinoa, brown rice, and farro), pasta, nuts, and dried herbs on hand. These staples form the base of many Mediterranean dishes and allow you to whip up a meal in no time.

3. Choose Quality Over Quantity: When it comes to ingredients like olive oil, cheese, and bread, quality matters. Invest in good-quality extra virgin olive oil, artisan whole-grain bread, and fresh cheese. These items may cost a bit more, but their superior flavor and nutritional value make them worth it.

4. Plan Your Meals: Before heading to the store, plan your meals for the week. This will help you create a focused shopping list and reduce the temptation to buy processed or unhealthy foods. Planning ahead also ensures that you have all the ingredients you need, making it easier to stick to the diet.

Meal Prep Tips

1. Prep Ingredients Ahead of Time: To save time during the week, consider prepping ingredients in advance. Wash and chop vegetables, cook a batch of grains, or marinate meat or fish. Store these prepped ingredients in airtight containers in the fridge, so they're ready to use when you need them.

2. Cook in Batches: Cooking larger quantities of food and storing portions for later can be a lifesaver on busy days. Prepare a big batch of soup, stew, or grain salad that you can enjoy throughout the week. This not only saves time but also ensures that you always have a healthy meal on hand.

3. Embrace One-Pot Meals: One-pot meals, such as soups, stews, and casseroles, are a staple of the Mediterranean diet. They're easy to prepare, require minimal cleanup, and are perfect for beginners. Plus, they often taste even better as leftovers, making them ideal for meal prep.

4. Keep It Simple: Mediterranean cooking is all about letting the natural flavors of ingredients shine. You don't need complicated recipes or a long list of ingredients. Focus on simple, flavorful dishes that highlight the quality of your ingredients.

Cooking Tips

1. Use Healthy Fats: Olive oil is a cornerstone of Mediterranean cooking. Use it generously for sautéing, roasting, and dressing salads. Not only does it add flavor, but it's also packed with heart-healthy monounsaturated fats.

2. Incorporate Herbs and Spices: Fresh herbs like basil, parsley, cilantro, and mint, along with spices such as oregano, thyme, and cumin, add depth and complexity to Mediterranean dishes. Don't be afraid to experiment with different combinations to enhance the flavor of your meals.

3. Cook Seasonally: One of the joys of the Mediterranean diet is eating with the seasons. Choose seasonal produce whenever possible; it's fresher, more flavorful, and often more affordable. Seasonal cooking also encourages variety in your diet, helping you to enjoy a wide range of nutrients.

4. Practice Mindful Cooking: Take your time when preparing meals, and enjoy the process. Cooking is not just a task; it's an opportunity to connect with your food, experiment with new flavors, and create something nourishing. Mindful cooking leads to mindful eating, which is an essential part of the Mediterranean lifestyle.

By following these tips, you'll find that grocery shopping, meal prep, and cooking on the Mediterranean diet can be a relaxing and enjoyable experience. The key is to keep things simple, focus on fresh and quality ingredients, and savor the process of creating delicious, wholesome meals.

Chapter 1

Easy Mediterranean Breakfasts

The Mediterranean diet is celebrated not only for its health benefits but also for its simple, fresh, and flavorful approach to meals. When it comes to breakfast, this diet offers a vibrant array of options that are both nourishing and delicious, setting the perfect tone for the day ahead. With a focus on whole grains, fruits, vegetables, and healthy fats like olive oil, Mediterranean breakfasts fuel the body with balanced energy, helping you start your day feeling satisfied and revitalized.

In this section, "Easy Mediterranean Breakfasts," you'll find recipes that capture the essence of this lifestyle — quick to prepare, full of wholesome ingredients, and designed to fit seamlessly into a busy morning routine. Whether you're craving a hearty dish to keep you going until lunch or a light and refreshing option, these recipes offer a variety of flavors and textures that embody the Mediterranean way of living.

Greek Pita Wrap with Egg, Spinach, and Feta

Prep. time: 5 min | Cook time: 10 min | Serves: 2

Ingredients:

- Whole wheat pita bread: 2 small pitas (or gluten-free pita if needed)
- Eggs: 4 large
- Fresh spinach: 2 cups, chopped
- Feta cheese: 1/4 cup, crumbled
- Extra virgin olive oil: 2 teaspoons
- Garlic: 1 clove, minced
- Salt: 1/4 teaspoon (or to taste)
- Black pepper: 1/4 teaspoon
- Dried oregano: 1/2 teaspoon (optional)
- Fresh parsley or dill: 1 tablespoon, chopped (optional for garnish)
- Lemon juice: 1 teaspoon (optional, for extra freshness)

Directions:

Warm the pita bread: Preheat your oven to 350°F (175°C) or use a skillet to gently warm the pita bread for 1-2 minutes on each side. This step makes the pita more pliable and enhances the flavor. **Sauté the spinach:** Heat 1 teaspoon of olive oil in a medium skillet over medium heat. Add the minced garlic and sauté for about 30 seconds until fragrant. Add the spinach and cook for 2-3 minutes until wilted. Season with a pinch of salt and pepper. Remove from heat and set aside.
Scramble the eggs: In a bowl, whisk the eggs with a pinch of salt, pepper, and dried oregano (if using). In the same skillet, heat the remaining 1 teaspoon of olive oil over medium heat. Pour the eggs into the skillet and gently scramble for 2-3 minutes until the eggs are cooked but still soft and fluffy. **Assemble the pita wrap:** Spread a thin layer of sautéed spinach over each pita. Divide the scrambled eggs evenly between the two pitas and top with crumbled feta cheese. If using, drizzle with a teaspoon of lemon juice for brightness and garnish with fresh parsley or dill. **Wrap and serve:** Fold the pita in half or roll it up tightly. Serve immediately while warm.

Nutritional Information (Per Serving): Calories: 320 kcal, Protein: 16g, Carbohydrates: 28g, Total Fat: 17g, Saturated Fat: 5g, Fiber: 5g, Cholesterol: 375mg, Sodium: 560mg, Potassium: 510mg.

Overnight Oats with Dried Fruits and Seeds

Prep. time: 10 min | Cook time: None | Serves: 2

Ingredients:

- 1 cup rolled oats
- 1 1/2 cups unsweetened almond milk (or any other plant-based milk)
- 1/4 cup Greek yogurt (optional for creaminess and added protein)
- 2 tablespoons chia seeds
- 2 tablespoons flaxseeds
- 1/4 cup mixed dried fruits (such as apricots, raisins, cranberries, or figs), chopped
- 1 tablespoon honey or maple syrup (optional for sweetness)
- 1/2 teaspoon vanilla extract (optional)
- 1/4 teaspoon ground cinnamon (optional)
- Fresh fruit and nuts for topping (optional)

Directions:

Prepare the Base: In a medium-sized bowl or a large mason jar, combine the rolled oats, unsweetened almond milk, Greek yogurt (if using), chia seeds, and flaxseeds. Stir well to ensure the seeds are evenly distributed and start to absorb the liquid. Add the
Flavorings: Add the chopped mixed dried fruits to the oat mixture. If desired, stir in honey or maple syrup for added sweetness, vanilla extract for depth of flavor, and ground cinnamon for a hint of warmth. Mix everything until well combined.
Refrigerate Overnight: Cover the bowl or mason jar with a lid or plastic wrap, and place it in the refrigerator. Let the oats soak and absorb the flavors overnight (or for at least 4 hours).
Serve: In the morning, give the oats a good stir. If the mixture is too thick, add a splash of almond milk to reach your desired consistency. Divide the oats into two serving bowls. **Top and Enjoy:** Top each serving with fresh fruit (such as sliced bananas, berries, or apples) and a sprinkle of nuts (such as almonds, walnuts, or pistachios) for added crunch and nutrition. Serve immediately.

Nutritional Information (Per Serving): Calories: 350 kcal, Protein: 10g, Carbohydrates: 55g, Fats: 12g, Fiber: 10g, Cholesterol: 0mg, Sodium: 75mg, Potassium: 600mg.

Mediterranean Veggie Omelet with Feta

Prep. time: 10 min | Cook time: 10 min | Serves: 2

Ingredients:

- Eggs: 4 large eggs
- Feta cheese: 1/3 cup crumbled
- Olive oil: 1 tablespoon (extra virgin, cold-pressed)
- Red bell pepper: 1/2, diced
- Zucchini: 1/2, thinly sliced
- Red onion: 1/4, thinly sliced
- Cherry tomatoes: 1/2 cup, halved
- Spinach: 1 cup fresh leaves
- Garlic: 1 clove, minced
- Fresh herbs: 1 tablespoon chopped parsley or dill (customizable)
- Salt: 1/4 teaspoon (or to taste)
- Black pepper: 1/4 teaspoon (freshly ground)
- Dried oregano: 1/2 teaspoon (optional)

Directions:

Prepare the Vegetables: Wash and chop the vegetables. Dice the bell pepper, slice the zucchini and red onion, halve the cherry tomatoes, and chop the herbs.

Whisk the Eggs: Crack the eggs into a small bowl, whisk lightly with salt, pepper, and oregano. Set aside.

Sauté the Vegetables: Heat 1 tablespoon olive oil in a skillet over medium heat. Add the onion, bell pepper, and zucchini. Sauté for 3-4 minutes until softened.

Add Garlic and Spinach: Add garlic and cook for 1 minute. Stir in spinach and tomatoes. Cook for 1-2 minutes until the spinach wilts and the tomatoes soften.

Cook the Eggs: Lower the heat to medium-low. Pour eggs over the vegetables. Cook undisturbed for 2-3 minutes until the edges set.

Add Feta and Finish Cooking: Sprinkle with feta. Cover and cook for 2-3 minutes until fully set.

Fold and Serve: Fold the omelet, slide onto a plate, and garnish with herbs and olive oil, if desired.

Nutritional Information (Per Serving): Calories: 330 kcal, Protein: 17g, Carbohydrates: 10g, Total Fat: 26g, Saturated Fat: 8g, Fiber: 3g, Cholesterol: 370mg, Sodium: 600mg, Potassium: 500mg.

Greek Yogurt with Honey, Almonds and Berries

Prep. time: 5 min | Cook time: None | Serves: 2

Ingredients:

- Greek yogurt: 1 1/2 cups (plain, full-fat or low-fat)
- Honey: 2 tablespoons (preferably raw, local honey)
- Almonds: 1/4 cup (toasted and roughly chopped)
- Fresh berries: 1/2 cup (a mix of strawberries, blueberries, raspberries, or blackberries)
- Vanilla extract: 1/2 teaspoon (optional for extra flavor)
- Lemon zest: 1/4 teaspoon (optional, for brightness)

Customizable elements: Substitute almonds with walnuts, pistachios, or hazelnuts. Add cinnamon or nutmeg. Chia or flaxseeds . Swap berries for seasonal fruits like figs, pomegranates.

Directions:

Mix the Yogurt: In a medium bowl, stir the Greek yogurt with the optional vanilla extract and lemon zest. This will add extra flavor and enhance the yogurt's taste. Set aside.

Toast the Almonds: In a dry skillet, toast the almonds over medium heat for 2-3 minutes, stirring constantly to ensure even browning and to prevent burning. Once they are golden and fragrant, remove from heat and let them cool slightly before chopping. **Assemble the Yogurt Bowls:** Divide the Greek yogurt evenly into two bowls or serving glasses. Drizzle 1 tablespoon of honey over each portion. You can swirl the honey into the yogurt for an integrated flavor or leave it on top for a decorative touch. **Add the Toppings:** Evenly distribute the fresh berries (strawberries, blueberries, raspberries, or your choice) on top of the yogurt. Sprinkle the chopped, toasted almonds over the berries and yogurt to add a crunchy texture.

Finish and Serve: Optionally, sprinkle a pinch of cinnamon or chia seeds on top for added flavor and nutrients. Serve immediately, or refrigerate for up to 2 hours to enjoy as a chilled snack or breakfast.

Nutritional Information (Per Serving): Calories: 280 kcal, Protein: 12g, Carbohydrates: 27g, Total Fat: 14g, Saturated Fat: 3g, Fiber: 4g, Cholesterol: 10mg, Sodium: 65mg, Potassium: 330mg.

Spinach and Sundried Tomato Frittata

Prep. time: 10 min | Cook time: 20 min | Serves: 4

Ingredients:

- Eggs: 6 large
- Olive oil: 1 tablespoon (extra virgin, cold-pressed)
- Fresh spinach: 2 cups (roughly chopped)
- Sundried tomatoes: 1/3 cup (in oil, drained and chopped)
- Red onion: 1/2 medium, thinly sliced
- Garlic: 1 clove, minced
- Feta cheese: 1/3 cup, crumbled
- Parmesan cheese: 2 tablespoons, grated (optional)
- Fresh herbs: 1 tablespoon chopped basil or parsley (optional)
- Salt: 1/4 teaspoon (or to taste)
- Black pepper: 1/4 teaspoon (freshly ground)
- Dried oregano: 1/2 teaspoon

Directions:

Preheat the Oven: Preheat your oven to 375°F (190°C). If your skillet is not oven-safe, prepare a lightly oiled baking dish. **Sauté the Aromatics:** In an oven-safe skillet, heat olive oil over medium heat. Add the sliced red onion and cook for 2-3 minutes until softened. Stir in the garlic and sundried tomatoes, cooking for another minute. **Cook the Spinach:** Add the chopped spinach to the skillet, stirring frequently for 1-2 minutes until wilted. Remove the skillet from heat. **Prepare the Egg Mixture:** In a medium bowl, whisk together the eggs, crumbled feta, Parmesan (if using), salt, pepper, and dried oregano. Optionally, stir in fresh herbs like basil or parsley for extra flavor. **Combine Eggs and Vegetables:** Pour the egg mixture into the skillet with the sautéed vegetables. Gently stir to distribute the ingredients evenly. **Cook on the Stovetop:** Return the skillet to medium heat. Cook for 2-3 minutes until the edges start to set, while the center remains slightly runny. **Bake the Frittata:** Transfer the skillet to the preheated oven and bake for 8-10 minutes, or until the frittata is fully set and golden on top. If using a baking dish, transfer the mixture to the dish before baking. **Cool and Serve:** Cool for 5 minutes before slicing. Garnish with herbs if desired.

Nutritional Information (Per Serving): Calories: 220 kcal, Protein: 12g, Carbohydrates: 6g, Total Fat: 16g, Saturated Fat: 5g, Fiber: 2g, Cholesterol: 260mg, Sodium: 470mg, Potassium: 480mg.

Avocado Toast with Olive Oil & Cherry Tomatoes

Prep. time: 5 min | Cook time: 5 min | Serves: 2

Ingredients:

- Whole grain bread: 2 slices (toasted)
- Avocado: 1 ripe, peeled and mashed
- Extra virgin olive oil: 2 teaspoons
- Cherry tomatoes: 1/2 cup (halved)
- Lemon juice: 1 teaspoon (freshly squeezed)
- Salt: 1/4 teaspoon (or to taste)
- Black pepper: 1/4 teaspoon (freshly ground)
- Dried oregano: 1/4 teaspoon (optional)
- Fresh basil or parsley: 1 tablespoon (chopped, optional for garnish)

Customizable elements:
Add a pinch of red pepper flakes for heat.
Swap cherry tomatoes for sliced cucumber or radishes for variety.

Directions:

Toast the Bread: Toast whole grain bread to your preferred crispness using a toaster or grill in a skillet over medium heat for 1-2 minutes per side.

Mash the Avocado: In a small bowl, mash the ripe avocado with a fork, leaving some texture. Add lemon juice, salt, and pepper to enhance the flavor. Stir until well combined.

Season the Tomatoes: In a separate bowl, toss halved cherry tomatoes with 1 teaspoon of olive oil, a pinch of salt, and dried oregano (if desired).

Assemble the Toast: Spread the mashed avocado evenly over each slice of toast. Top with seasoned cherry tomatoes, dividing them equally between the slices. Drizzle the remaining teaspoon of olive oil over each slice.

Add Finishing Touches: For extra flavor, sprinkle fresh herbs like basil or parsley on top. Serve immediately while the toast is crisp and the toppings are fresh.

Serving Suggestions: Pair with a small arugula salad dressed with lemon for a light Mediterranean meal. For extra protein, add a poached or fried egg on top. Serve with Greek yogurt drizzled with honey and sprinkled with nuts for a complete meal.

Nutritional Information (Per Serving): Calories: 280 kcal, Protein: 6g, Carbohydrates: 28g, Total Fat: 19g, Saturated Fat: 3g, Fiber: 8g, Cholesterol: 0mg, Sodium: 310mg, Potassium: 670mg.

Whole Grain Pancakes with Pomegranate Syrup

Prep. time: 10 min | Cook time: 15 min | Serves: 4 (makes about 8 pancakes)

Ingredients:

For the Pancakes:

- Whole wheat flour: 1 cup
- Baking powder: 1 1/2 teaspoons
- Salt: 1/4 teaspoon
- Ground cinnamon: 1/2 teaspoon
- Egg: 1 large
- Milk: 1 cup
- Extra virgin olive oil: 1 tablespoon
- Honey: 1 tablespoon (or maple syrup for a vegan option)
- Vanilla extract: 1 teaspoon
- Pomegranate seeds: 1/4 cup (optional, for texture in the pancakes)

For the Pomegranate Syrup:

- Pomegranate juice: 1 cup
- Honey: 2 tablespoons
- Lemon juice: 1 teaspoon

Directions:

Prepare the Syrup: In a small saucepan, combine pomegranate juice, honey, and lemon juice. Bring to a simmer over medium heat, cooking for 10-12 minutes, stirring occasionally, until it thickens and reduces by half. Remove from heat and let it cool while you make the pancakes.

Mix the Dry Ingredients: In a medium bowl, whisk together whole wheat flour, baking powder, salt, and ground cinnamon (if using). **Mix the Wet Ingredients:** In a separate bowl, whisk together the egg, milk, olive oil, honey, and vanilla extract until smooth. **Combine and Fold:** Pour the wet ingredients into the dry ingredients, stirring until just combined. Be careful not to overmix. If using pomegranate seeds, fold them gently into the batter. **Cook the Pancakes:** Heat a non-stick skillet or griddle over medium heat. Lightly grease with olive oil or cooking spray. Pour 1/4 cup of batter onto the skillet for each pancake. Cook for 2-3 minutes until bubbles form on the surface and edges set. Flip and cook for another 1-2 minutes until golden brown.

Serve: Stack pancakes on a plate, drizzle with pomegranate syrup, and sprinkle with extra pomegranate seeds. Serve immediately.

Nutritional Information (Per Serving): Calories: 250 kcal, Protein: 7g, Carbohydrates: 40g, Total Fat: 7g, Saturated Fat: 1g, Fiber: 5g, Cholesterol: 45mg, Sodium: 300mg, Potassium: 320mg.

Smoked Salmon and Cream Cheese Bagel

Prep. time: 10 min | Cook time: None | Serves: 2

Ingredients:

- Whole grain or multigrain bagels: 2, sliced and toasted
- Cream cheese: 1/4 cup (light or regular)
- Smoked salmon: 4 oz (thinly sliced)
- Cucumber: 1/2 medium, thinly sliced
- Red onion: 1/4 small, thinly sliced
- Capers: 1 tablespoon (optional)
- Extra virgin olive oil: 1 teaspoon (for drizzling)
- Lemon juice: 1 teaspoon (freshly squeezed)
- Fresh dill or parsley: 2 teaspoons, chopped (optional)
- Salt: To taste
- Black pepper: To taste

Directions:

Toast the Bagels: Slice the bagels in half and toast them in a toaster or on a skillet over medium heat until golden and crisp.

Prepare the Cream Cheese Mixture: While the bagels are toasting, mix cream cheese, lemon juice, and a pinch of black pepper in a small bowl until smooth.

Assemble the Bagels: Once toasted, spread the cream cheese mixture evenly onto each half of the bagel. Top with slices of smoked salmon, followed by thin slices of cucumber and red onion. Sprinkle with capers (if using) and fresh dill or parsley for added flavor. Lightly drizzle extra virgin olive oil on top, then season with a small pinch of salt and black pepper.

Serve: Serve immediately with a side salad or fresh fruit for a balanced meal.

Nutritional Information (Per Serving): Calories: 390 kcal, Protein: 19g, Carbohydrates: 45g, Total Fat: 15g, Saturated Fat: 6g, Fiber: 7g, Cholesterol: 45mg, Sodium: 840mg, Potassium: 320mg

Breakfast Bowl with Quinoa and Avocado

Prep. time: 10 min | Cook time: 15 min | Serves: 2

Ingredients:

- Quinoa: 1/2 cup (uncooked, or 1 cup cooked)
- Water or vegetable broth: 1 cup
- Extra virgin olive oil: 2 teaspoons
- Avocado: 1 ripe, sliced or diced
- Cherry tomatoes: 1/2 cup, halved
- Cucumber: 1/2 cup, diced
- Kalamata olives: 1/4 cup, pitted and halved
- Feta cheese: 1/4 cup, crumbled
- Eggs: 2 large (optional, soft or hard-boiled)
- Fresh parsley: 2 tablespoons, chopped
- Fresh lemon juice: 2 teaspoons
- Salt: 1/4 teaspoon (or to taste)
- Black pepper: 1/4 teaspoon (ground)
- Dried oregano: 1/2 teaspoon (optional)

Directions:

Cook the Quinoa: Rinse the quinoa under cold water. In a small saucepan, combine 1/2 cup quinoa with 1 cup water or vegetable broth. Bring to a boil over medium heat, then reduce to low, cover, and simmer for 12-15 minutes, until the quinoa is cooked and the liquid is absorbed. Fluff with a fork and set aside.

Prep the Vegetables: While the quinoa cooks, slice the avocado, halve the cherry tomatoes, dice the cucumber, and chop the parsley. Set aside.

Cook the Eggs (Optional): For soft-boiled eggs, bring a small pot of water to a boil. Add the eggs and cook for 6-7 minutes. For hard-boiled eggs, cook for 9-10 minutes. Transfer to ice water, cool, peel, and slice. **Assemble the Bowls:** Divide the cooked quinoa between two bowls. Arrange the sliced avocado, cherry tomatoes, cucumber, olives, and crumbled feta around the quinoa. Add the egg halves (if using).

Dress and Garnish: Drizzle 1 teaspoon of olive oil and 1 teaspoon of lemon juice over each bowl. Sprinkle with salt, black pepper, and dried oregano (if using). Garnish with fresh parsley.

Serve: Serve immediately while the quinoa is warm and the vegetables are fresh.

Nutritional Information (Per Serving): Calories: 390 kcal, Protein: 14g, Carbohydrates: 36g, Total Fat: 22g, Saturated Fat: 5g, Fiber: 9g, Cholesterol: 200mg (with egg), Sodium: 480mg, Potassium: 780mg.

Egg Muffins with Spinach, Feta, and Oregano

Prep. time: 10 min | Cook time: 20 min | Serves: 2 (6 muffins)

Ingredients:

- Eggs: 6 large
- Fresh spinach: 1 cup (roughly chopped)
- Feta cheese: 1/3 cup, crumbled
- Red bell pepper: 1/2, diced (optional for extra color and flavor)
- Red onion: 1/4 cup, finely chopped
- Garlic: 1 clove, minced
- Extra virgin olive oil: 1 teaspoon
- Dried oregano: 1/2 teaspoon
- Salt: 1/4 teaspoon (or to taste)
- Black pepper: 1/4 teaspoon (ground)
- Fresh parsley: 1 tablespoon, chopped (optional for garnish)

Customizable elements:

Swap spinach for kale or Swiss chard.

Incorporate olives, sun-dried tomatoes, or artichokes

Directions:

Preheat the Oven: Preheat your oven to 350°F (175°C). Lightly grease a 6-cup muffin tin with olive oil or use silicone muffin liners for easy removal.

Sauté the Vegetables: In a small skillet, heat 1 teaspoon of olive oil over medium heat. Add the chopped red onion and garlic, sautéing for 2-3 minutes until softened. Add the spinach and cook for 1-2 minutes until wilted. Remove from heat and set aside.

Prepare the Egg Mixture: In a medium bowl, whisk the eggs until fully combined. Stir in dried oregano, salt, and black pepper. Add the crumbled feta cheese, sautéed spinach mixture, and optional diced red bell pepper. Mix well.

Fill the Muffin Cups: Pour the egg mixture evenly into the greased muffin cups, filling each about 3/4 full. Ensure the vegetables and feta are evenly distributed in each cup.

Bake the Egg Muffins: Place the muffin tin in the preheated oven and bake for 18-20 minutes, or until the eggs are set and slightly golden. To check for doneness, insert a toothpick into the center of a muffin—it should come out clean.

Cool and Serve: Once baked, let the muffins cool in the tin for 5 minutes. Gently loosen the edges with a knife and transfer to a plate.

Nutritional Information (Per Serving): Calories: 200 kcal, Protein: 14g, Carbohydrates: 5g, Total Fat: 13g, Saturated Fat: 5g, Fiber: 1g, Cholesterol: 380mg, Sodium: 420mg, Potassium: 290mg.

Zucchini and Olive Oil Breakfast Loaf

Prep. time: 15 min | Cook time: 50 min | Serves: 10

Ingredients:

- Zucchini: 1 1/2 cups, grated
- Whole wheat flour: 1 1/2 cups
- All-purpose flour: 1/2 cup
- Baking powder: 1 teaspoon
- Baking soda: 1/2 teaspoon
- Salt: 1/2 teaspoon
- Ground cinnamon: 1 teaspoon
- Eggs: 2 large
- Extra virgin olive oil: 1/2 cup
- Honey: 1/3 cup (or maple syrup)
- Greek yogurt: 1/4 cup (use almond or coconut yogurt for a dairy-free option)
- Vanilla extract: 1 teaspoon
- Walnuts or almonds: 1/4 cup, chopped (optional)
- Lemon zest: 1 teaspoon (optional, for brightness)

Directions:

Preheat the Oven: Preheat your oven to 350°F (175°C). Grease a 9x5-inch loaf pan with olive oil or line it with parchment paper.

Prep the Zucchini: Grate the zucchini and squeeze out excess moisture using a kitchen towel. Set aside.

Mix the Dry Ingredients: In a medium bowl, whisk together whole wheat flour, all-purpose flour, baking powder, baking soda, salt, and cinnamon.

Mix the Wet Ingredients: In a large bowl, whisk eggs, olive oil, honey (or maple syrup), Greek yogurt, and vanilla until well combined.

Combine and Fold: Gradually stir the dry ingredients into the wet mixture until just combined. Gently fold in the grated zucchini, walnuts (if using), and lemon zest (if using). **Bake the Loaf:** Pour the batter into the prepared pan and spread evenly. Bake for 45-50 minutes, or until a toothpick inserted into the center comes out clean and the top is golden brown.

Cool and Serve: Let the loaf cool in the pan for 10 minutes, then transfer to a wire rack to cool completely. Slice and serve warm or at room temperature.

Nutritional Information (Per Serving): Calories: 190 kcal, Protein: 4g, Carbohydrates: 26g, Total Fat: 8g, Saturated Fat: 1g, Fiber: 3g, Cholesterol: 35mg, Sodium: 160mg, Potassium: 150mg,

Almond & Orange Smoothie with Chia Seeds

Prep. time: 5 min | Cook time: None | Serves: 2

Ingredients:

- Unsweetened almond milk: 1 cup
- Freshly squeezed orange juice: 1/2 cup (about 1 medium orange)
- Almonds: 1/4 cup (raw or lightly toasted)
- Chia seeds: 1 tablespoon
- Greek yogurt: 1/4 cup (or plant-based yogurt for a vegan option)
- Honey: 1 tablespoon (or maple syrup for a vegan option)
- Banana: 1 small (for natural sweetness and creaminess)
- Orange zest: 1/2 teaspoon (optional, for extra citrus flavor)
- Vanilla extract: 1/2 teaspoon
- Ice cubes: 4-5 (optional for a thicker, colder smoothie).

Directions:

Soak the chia seeds (optional): If you prefer a thicker smoothie, you can soak the chia seeds in the almond milk for about 10 minutes before blending. This step helps the chia seeds absorb liquid and creates a more gel-like texture.

Blend the ingredients: In a high-speed blender, add the almond milk, freshly squeezed orange juice, almonds, chia seeds, Greek yogurt, honey, banana, orange zest (if using), and vanilla extract.

Blend until smooth and creamy, about 30-60 seconds. If using ice cubes, add them now and blend until the ice is fully crushed.

Taste and adjust: Taste the smoothie and adjust sweetness by adding more honey or orange juice if desired. If the smoothie is too thick, add a little more almond milk or water to thin it out to your preferred consistency.

Serve: Pour the smoothie into two glasses and enjoy immediately. You can garnish with extra chia seeds or a sprinkle of orange zest for a decorative touch.

Nutritional Information (Per Serving): Calories: 210 kcal, Protein: 6g, Carbohydrates: 28g, Total Fat: 9g, Saturated Fat: 1g, Fiber: 6g, Cholesterol: 0mg, Sodium: 60mg, Potassium: 430mg.

Scrambled Eggs with Roasted Peppers and Olives

Prep. time: 5 min | Cook time: 10 min | Serves: 2

Ingredients:

- Eggs: 4 large
- Roasted red peppers: 1/2 cup, sliced (use jarred or homemade)
- Kalamata olives: 1/4 cup, pitted and halved
- Extra virgin olive oil: 1 tablespoon
- Garlic: 1 clove, minced
- Fresh parsley or basil: 1 tablespoon, chopped (optional for garnish)
- Salt: 1/4 teaspoon (or to taste)
- Black pepper: 1/4 teaspoon (freshly ground)
- Feta cheese: 1/4 cup, crumbled (optional)
- Dried oregano: 1/2 teaspoon (optional)

Directions:

Whisk the Eggs: Crack the eggs into a small bowl and whisk lightly with a fork. Add salt, pepper, and dried oregano (if using). Set aside.

Sauté the Garlic: Heat 1 tablespoon of olive oil in a medium non-stick skillet over medium heat. Add minced garlic and cook for about 1 minute until fragrant, but not browned.

Add Peppers and Olives: Add roasted red peppers and Kalamata olives to the skillet. Sauté for 1-2 minutes to heat through.

Cook the Eggs: Pour the whisked eggs into the skillet. Lower the heat to medium-low and gently stir as they begin to set, cooking slowly and evenly.

Add Feta (Optional): When the eggs are nearly done but still soft, sprinkle crumbled feta over the top. Stir gently to combine.

Finish and Serve: Once fully cooked, remove the eggs from heat. Garnish with fresh parsley or basil if desired. Serve immediately.

Nutritional Information (Per Serving): Calories: 250 kcal, Protein: 14g, Carbohydrates: 5g, Total Fat: 20g, Saturated Fat: 5g, Fiber: 1g, Cholesterol: 375mg, Sodium: 580mg, Potassium: 300mg.

Tahini Banana Smoothie with Sesame Seeds

Prep. time: 5 min | Cook time: None | Serves: 2

Ingredients:

- Banana: 1 large (preferably frozen for creaminess)
- Unsweetened almond milk: 1 cup (or any plant-based milk)
- Tahini (sesame seed paste): 2 tablespoons
- Greek yogurt: 1/4 cup (optional, use plant-based yogurt for a vegan option)
- Honey: 1 tablespoon (or maple syrup for a vegan option)
- Ground cinnamon: 1/2 teaspoon
- Vanilla extract: 1/2 teaspoon
- Sesame seeds: 1 tablespoon (plus extra for garnish)
- Ice cubes: 4-5 (optional for a thicker smoothie)

Directions:

Prepare the ingredients:

If your banana is not already frozen, slice it and freeze for a few hours to achieve a creamy texture. This step is optional, but it makes the smoothie thicker and creamier.

Blend the ingredients:

In a high-speed blender, combine the frozen banana, almond milk, tahini, Greek yogurt (if using), honey, ground cinnamon, vanilla extract, sesame seeds, and ice cubes (if using). Blend on high until smooth and creamy, about 30-60 seconds.

Taste and adjust:

Taste the smoothie and adjust the sweetness by adding more honey or maple syrup if desired. If it's too thick, add more almond milk to reach your preferred consistency.

Serve:

Pour the smoothie into two glasses. Garnish with a sprinkle of sesame seeds or an extra drizzle of tahini for an extra touch of Mediterranean flair.

Pair this smoothie with whole grain toast or a handful of nuts for a more filling meal. Serve as a light breakfast, mid-morning snack, or even a post-workout recovery drink.

Nutritional Information (Per Serving): Calories: 260 kcal, Protein: 8g, Carbohydrates: 33g, Total Fat: 12g, Saturated Fat: 2g, Fiber: 4g, Cholesterol: 5mg, Sodium: 65mg, Potassium: 510mg.

Breakfast Tacos with Hummus and Veggies

Prep. time: 10 min | Cook time: 10 min | Serves: 2 (makes 4 tacos)

Ingredients:

- Whole grain tortillas: 4 small
- Hummus: 1/2 cup
- Eggs: 2 large (optional)
- Cherry tomatoes: 1/2 cup, halved
- Cucumber: 1/2 cup, diced
- Kalamata olives: 1/4 cup, pitted and sliced
- Red onion: 1/4 cup, thinly sliced
- Feta cheese: 1/4 cup, crumbled (optional)
- Fresh spinach: 1 cup, chopped
- Extra virgin olive oil: 1 tablespoon
- Ground cumin: 1/4 teaspoon
- Ground paprika: 1/4 teaspoon
- Salt: 1/4 teaspoon (or to taste)
- Black pepper: 1/4 teaspoon
- Lemon juice: 1 tablespoon
- Fresh parsley: 1 tablespoon, chopped

Directions:

Prepare the Eggs (Optional): In a small bowl, whisk the eggs with salt, pepper, and paprika. Heat 1 teaspoon of olive oil in a small skillet over medium heat. Scramble the eggs for 2-3 minutes until cooked through. Set aside.

Sauté the Vegetables: In another skillet, heat the remaining olive oil over medium heat. Add the chopped spinach, sliced red onion, and a sprinkle of cumin. Sauté for 2-3 minutes until the spinach wilts and onion softens. Remove from heat.

Warm the Tortillas: Warm the tortillas in a dry skillet or microwave for 30 seconds to make them pliable.

Assemble the Tacos: Spread 2 tablespoons of hummus on each tortilla. Layer with the sautéed spinach and onion mixture, scrambled eggs (if using), halved cherry tomatoes, diced cucumber, Kalamata olives, and crumbled feta.

Add Finishing Touches: Drizzle with lemon juice, sprinkle with paprika, black pepper, and chopped parsley. Optionally, drizzle with olive oil.

Serve: Serve the breakfast tacos immediately, garnished with fresh herbs if desired.

Nutritional Information (Per Serving): Calories: 320 kcal, Protein: 12g, Carbohydrates: 35g, Total Fat: 16g, Saturated Fat: 3g, Fiber: 8g, Cholesterol: 95mg (with eggs), Sodium: 520mg, Potassium: 450mg.

Shakshuka with Fresh Herbs and Crumbled Feta

Prep. time: 10 min | Cook time: 25 min | Serves: 4

Ingredients:

- Extra virgin olive oil: 2 tablespoons
- Onion: 1 medium, diced
- Bell pepper: 1 medium, diced
- Garlic: 3 cloves, minced
- Canned diced tomatoes: 1 (14.5 oz) can (or 4 ripe tomatoes, chopped)
- Tomato paste: 1 tablespoon
- Ground cumin: 1 teaspoon
- Ground paprika: 1 teaspoon
- Ground cayenne pepper: 1/4 teaspoon (optional, for heat)
- Salt: 1/2 teaspoon (or to taste)
- Black pepper: 1/4 teaspoon
- Eggs: 4 large
- Feta cheese: 1/4 cup, crumbled
- Fresh parsley: 2 tablespoons, chopped
- Fresh cilantro: 2 tablespoons,
- Fresh basil: 1 tablespoon, chopped
- Fresh lemon juice: 1 teaspoon

Directions:

Sauté the Vegetables: Heat olive oil in a large skillet over medium heat. Add the diced onion and bell pepper, sautéing for 5-7 minutes until softened. Add minced garlic and cook for 1 minute until fragrant.

Add the Spices and Tomatoes: Stir in cumin, paprika, cayenne pepper (if using), salt, and black pepper. Add diced tomatoes and tomato paste, stirring to combine. Reduce heat to low and simmer for 10-15 minutes, allowing the sauce to thicken.

Cook the Eggs: Make four small wells in the tomato mixture. Crack one egg into each well, keeping the yolks intact. Cover the skillet and cook for 5-7 minutes, or until the egg whites are set but the yolks remain runny. For firmer yolks, cook an additional 2 minutes.

Finish with Feta and Garnish: Sprinkle crumbled feta over the shakshuka. Garnish with fresh parsley, cilantro, and basil. Drizzle with lemon juice for added brightness, if desired.

Serve: Serve directly from the skillet with warm pita, crusty whole-grain bread, or a side of quinoa for a complete meal.

Nutritional Information (Per Serving): Calories: 230 kcal, Protein: 11g, Carbohydrates: 14g, Total Fat: 15g, Saturated Fat: 4g, Fiber: 4g, Cholesterol: 185mg, Sodium: 570mg, Potassium: 480mg.

Chapter 2

Snacks and Appetizers

Snacks and appetizers in the Mediterranean diet are more than just a quick bite—they're an opportunity to enjoy flavorful, wholesome ingredients in their simplest form. With a focus on fresh vegetables, creamy dips, nuts, olives, and whole grains, these small dishes capture the essence of Mediterranean cuisine, offering a perfect balance between nutrition and taste. Whether you're hosting a gathering or just looking for a light, satisfying snack, Mediterranean-style appetizers provide both nourishment and delight.

In this section, "Snacks and Appetizers," you'll find easy-to-prepare recipes that are ideal for any occasion. From traditional favorites like hummus and tzatziki to inventive twists on classic Mediterranean bites, these dishes are designed to impress while staying true to the healthy, flavorful principles of the Mediterranean way of eating.

Mediterranean Bruschetta with Tomatoes and Basil

Prep. time: 10 min | Cook time: 5 min | Serves: 4

Ingredients:

- Whole grain baguette or sourdough bread: 1 small loaf, sliced into 8 pieces
- Extra virgin olive oil: 3 tablespoons (divided)
- Garlic cloves: 2, halved
- Cherry tomatoes: 1 cup, chopped
- Fresh basil leaves: 1/4 cup, chopped
- Balsamic vinegar: 1 tablespoon
- Salt: 1/4 teaspoon
- Black pepper: 1/4 teaspoon

Directions:

Prepare the Bread:

Preheat the oven to 400°F (200°C) or use a grill pan.

Brush the bread slices with 1 tablespoon of olive oil on both sides and place them on a baking sheet.

Toast the bread in the oven for 5 minutes or until crispy and golden, or grill for a minute on each side.

Prepare the Topping:

In a medium bowl, combine the chopped cherry tomatoes, fresh basil, 2 tablespoons olive oil, balsamic vinegar, salt, and black pepper. Toss to mix well.

Assemble the Bruschetta:

Rub each toasted bread slice with the halved garlic cloves for extra flavor.

Spoon the tomato-basil mixture over each piece of bread, spreading evenly.

Serve: Serve the bruschetta immediately as a light snack or appetizer, perfect for Mediterranean-style entertaining.

Nutritional Information (Per Serving): Calories: 160 kcal, Protein: 3g, Carbohydrates: 18g, Total Fat: 9g, Saturated Fat: 1g, Fiber: 2g, Cholesterol: 0mg, Sodium: 230mg, Potassium: 200mg.

Hummus with Roasted Red Peppers & Pine Nuts

Prep. time: 10 min | Cook time: 10 min | Serves: 6

Ingredients:

- Chickpeas: 1 (15-ounce) can, drained and rinsed (or 1 1/2 cups cooked chickpeas)
- Roasted red peppers: 1/2 cup, chopped (jarred or homemade)
- Tahini: 1/4 cup
- Fresh lemon juice: 2 tablespoons
- Extra virgin olive oil: 3 tablespoons
- Garlic: 1 clove, minced
- Ground cumin: 1/2 teaspoon
- Salt: 1/2 teaspoon (or to taste)
- Paprika: 1/4 teaspoon (optional for garnish)
- Pine nuts: 2 tablespoons, toasted
- Water: 2-3 tablespoons (to adjust consistency)
- Fresh parsley: 1 tablespoon, chopped (optional for garnish)

Directions:

Toast the pine nuts:

In a small skillet, toast the pine nuts over medium heat for 3-4 minutes, stirring occasionally, until they are golden brown and fragrant. Be careful not to burn them. Remove from heat and set aside.

Prepare the hummus:

In a food processor, combine the chickpeas, roasted red peppers, tahini, lemon juice, 2 tablespoons of olive oil, garlic, cumin, and salt. Process until smooth and creamy.

Adjust the consistency:

If the hummus is too thick, add water, one tablespoon at a time, until you reach your desired consistency. Blend again until smooth.

Serve and garnish:

Transfer the hummus to a serving bowl. Drizzle the remaining 1 tablespoon of olive oil over the top and sprinkle with toasted pine nuts, paprika, and fresh parsley (if using).

Nutritional Information (Per Serving): Calories: 190 kcal, Protein: 5g, Carbohydrates: 15g, Total Fat: 12g, Saturated Fat: 1.5g, Fiber: 4g, Cholesterol: 0mg, Sodium: 270mg, Potassium: 160mg

Olive Tapenade with Whole Wheat Crackers

Prep. time: 10 min | Cook time: None (unless making crackers from scratch) | Serves: 6

Ingredients:

For the Olive Tapenade:
- Kalamata olives: 1 cup, pitted
- Green olives: 1/2 cup, pitted
- Capers: 2 tablespoons, rinsed and drained
- Extra virgin olive oil: 2 tablespoons
- Garlic: 1 clove, minced
- Fresh lemon juice: 1 tablespoon
- Fresh parsley: 2 tablespoons, chopped
- Fresh thyme: 1 teaspoon (or 1/2 teaspoon dried thyme)
- Black pepper: 1/4 teaspoon
- Red pepper flakes: 1/4 teaspoon

For Whole Wheat Crackers:
- Whole wheat flour: 1 cup
- Extra virgin olive oil: 2 tablespoons
- Water: 1/4 cup Salt: 1/4 teaspoon
- Dried oregano: 1/2 teaspoon

Directions:

For the Olive Tapenade: Rinse and pit the olives if needed. Rinse and drain the capers. In a food processor, combine the Kalamata olives, green olives, capers, garlic, lemon juice, olive oil, parsley, thyme, and black pepper. Pulse a few times until the ingredients are finely chopped and form a slightly chunky paste. Be careful not to over-process; the tapenade should have texture, not be too smooth. Taste the tapenade and adjust seasoning if necessary, adding more lemon juice, black pepper, or red pepper flakes if desired. For best flavor, allow the tapenade to rest in the refrigerator for 30 minutes before serving. **For Whole Wheat Crackers:** Preheat your oven to 375°F (190°C). Line a baking sheet with parchment paper. In a medium bowl, combine the whole wheat flour, olive oil, water, salt, and dried oregano (if using). Stir until a dough forms. If the dough is too dry, add a little more water, 1 teaspoon at a time. On a lightly floured surface, roll out the dough until it's about 1/8-inch thick. Use a knife or pizza cutter to cut the dough into small squares or rectangles. Transfer the dough pieces to the prepared baking sheet. Prick each cracker with a fork to prevent puffing. Bake for 12-15 minutes, or until the crackers are golden and crisp. Let them cool on the baking sheet.

Nutritional Information (Per Serving): Calories: 210 kcal, Protein: 3g, Carbohydrates: 15g, Total Fat: 17g, Saturated Fat: 2g, Fiber: 3g, Cholesterol: 0mg, Sodium: 500mg, Potassium: 110mg.

Stuffed Grape Leaves with Lemon and Dill

Prep. time: 30 min | Cook time: 50 min | Serves: 6 (makes about 30 stuffed grape leaves)

Ingredients:

- Grape leaves: 30-35 leaves (jarred or fresh)
- Short-grain rice: 1 cup
- Extra virgin olive oil: 1/4 cup
- Onion: 1 medium, finely chopped
- Garlic: 2 cloves, minced
- Fresh dill: 1/4 cup, chopped
- Fresh parsley: 1/4 cup, chopped
- Fresh mint: 2 tablespoons, chopped (optional)
- Lemon zest: 1 teaspoon
- Lemon juice: 1/4 cup (about 2 lemons, plus extra for serving)
- Water or vegetable broth: 2 cups
- Salt: 1 teaspoon (or to taste)
- Black pepper: 1/2 teaspoon
- Ground cumin: 1/2 teaspoon (optional)

Directions:

Prepare the grape leaves: For jarred leaves, rinse under cold water and soak in warm water to soften, then drain. For fresh leaves, blanch in boiling water for 2 minutes, then drain. **Prepare the rice filling:** Heat 2 tbsp olive oil in a skillet. Sauté onion and garlic for 3-4 minutes. Add rice and cook 2 minutes. Pour in 1 cup water or broth, lemon zest, salt, pepper, and cumin (if using). Simmer 10-12 minutes until rice is partially cooked and liquid absorbed. Remove from heat, stir in dill, parsley, and mint. **Stuff the grape leaves:** Place 1 tbsp rice mixture on each grape leaf (shiny side down), fold sides, and roll tightly into cylinders. Repeat with remaining leaves. **Cook the stuffed leaves:** Line a pot with extra grape leaves or lemon slices. Arrange stuffed leaves seam-side down. Drizzle with olive oil, lemon juice, and pour 1 cup water or broth to cover.
Simmer: Place a heatproof plate on top, cover, and simmer on low heat for 40-50 minutes until rice is cooked and leaves are tender. Add water if needed.
Cool and serve:
Let cool slightly, serve warm or at room temperature with lemon wedges and olive oil.

Nutritional Information (Per Serving): Calories: 190 kcal, Protein: 3g, Carbohydrates: 20g, Total Fat: 10g, Saturated Fat: 1.5g, Fiber: 3g, Cholesterol: 0mg, Sodium: 250mg, Potassium: 150mg.

Greek Yogurt Dip with Cucumber and Dill (Tzatziki)

Prep. time: 10 min | Cook time: None | Serves: 6

Ingredients:

- Greek yogurt: 1 1/2 cups (plain, full-fat or low-fat)
- Cucumber: 1/2 medium, grated and excess water squeezed out
- Fresh dill: 2 tablespoons, chopped
- Garlic: 2 cloves, minced
- Extra virgin olive oil: 1 tablespoon
- Fresh lemon juice: 1 tablespoon
- Salt: 1/2 teaspoon (or to taste)
- Black pepper: 1/4 teaspoon (freshly ground)
- Red wine vinegar: 1 teaspoon (optional, for extra tang)

Directions:

Prepare the cucumber: Grate the cucumber using a box grater. Place the grated cucumber in a clean kitchen towel or paper towel, and squeeze out as much excess water as possible. This prevents the dip from becoming too watery.

Mix the ingredients: In a medium bowl, combine the Greek yogurt, grated cucumber, chopped dill, minced garlic, olive oil, lemon juice, salt, and black pepper. If using, add red wine vinegar for extra tang.

Taste and adjust: Taste the dip and adjust the seasoning as needed, adding more lemon juice or salt to suit your preference.

Chill (optional): For the best flavor, refrigerate the dip for at least 30 minutes before serving to allow the flavors to meld together.

Serve: Transfer the tzatziki to a serving dish and drizzle with a little extra olive oil for garnish. You can also sprinkle additional chopped dill or fresh herbs on top for extra freshness.

Nutritional Information (Per Serving): Calories: 80 kcal, Protein: 5g, Carbohydrates: 3g, Total Fat: 5g, Saturated Fat: 2g, Fiber: 0g, Cholesterol: 10mg, Sodium: 210mg, Potassium: 120mg.

Mediterranean Chickpea Fritters (Falafel)

Prep. time: 20 min | Cook time: 15 min (plus 30 minutes chilling time) | Serves: 4 (makes about 12 fritters)

Ingredients:

- Chickpeas: 1 (15 oz) can, drained and rinsed (or 1 1/2 cups cooked)
- Fresh parsley: 1/2 cup, chopped
- Fresh cilantro: 1/2 cup, chopped
- Garlic: 2 cloves, minced
- Red onion: 1/2 small, finely chopped
- Ground cumin: 1 teaspoon
- Ground coriander: 1 teaspoon
- Baking powder: 1 teaspoon
- Flour: 1/4 cup (whole wheat or chickpea flour for a gluten-free option)
- Fresh lemon juice: 1 tablespoon
- Salt: 1/2 teaspoon
- Black pepper: 1/4 teaspoon
- Extra virgin olive oil: 2 tablespoons (for pan-frying)

Directions:

Prepare the chickpea mixture: In a food processor, combine the chickpeas, parsley, cilantro, garlic, red onion, cumin, coriander, lemon juice, salt, and pepper. Pulse the mixture until it becomes coarse and holds together when pressed. Be careful not to over-process; the mixture should be slightly chunky, not smooth. **Add flour and baking powder:** Transfer the mixture to a bowl and stir in the flour and baking powder until well combined. If the mixture is too wet, add more flour, 1 tablespoon at a time, until you can form small patties or balls. **Chill the mixture:** Cover the bowl and refrigerate the mixture for 30 minutes. This helps the fritters hold together during cooking.

Form the fritters: Once chilled, use your hands or a spoon to shape the mixture into small patties or balls, about 2 inches in diameter. **Pan-fry the fritters:** Heat the olive oil in a large skillet over medium heat. Add the chickpea fritters in batches, making sure not to overcrowd the pan. Cook for 3-4 minutes on each side, or until golden brown and crispy. Transfer to a plate lined with paper towels to drain any excess oil. **Serve:** Serve the fritters warm with your choice of dipping sauces, pita bread, or over a salad.

Nutritional Information (Per Serving): Calories: 210 kcal, Protein: 6g, Carbohydrates: 24g, Total Fat: 10g, Saturated Fat: 1.5g, Fiber: 5g, Cholesterol: 0mg, Sodium: 300mg, Potassium: 240mg.

Tzatziki with Fresh Veggie Sticks

Prep. time: 10 min | Cook time: None | Serves: 6

Ingredients:

For the Tzatziki:

- Greek yogurt: 1 1/2 cups (plain, full-fat or low-fat)
- Cucumber: 1/2 medium, grated and excess water squeezed out
- Garlic: 2 cloves, minced
- Fresh dill: 2 tablespoons, chopped
- Fresh lemon juice: 1 tablespoon
- Extra virgin olive oil: 1 tablespoon
- Salt: 1/2 teaspoon (or to taste)
- Black pepper: 1/4 teaspoon
- Red wine vinegar: 1 teaspoon

For the Veggie Sticks:

- Carrots: 2 medium, cut into sticks
- Cucumbers: 1 large, sliced into sticks
- Red bell pepper: 1, sliced into strips
- Celery: 2 stalks, cut into sticks
- Cherry tomatoes: 1 cup, halved

Directions:

Prepare the Tzatziki:
Grate the cucumber using a box grater. Place the grated cucumber in a clean kitchen towel or paper towel and squeeze out as much excess water as possible. This step helps prevent the tzatziki from becoming watery.

In a medium-sized bowl, combine the Greek yogurt, grated cucumber, minced garlic, chopped dill, lemon juice, olive oil, salt, and black pepper. Stir until well blended. If using, add the red wine vinegar for extra tang.

Taste the tzatziki and adjust the seasoning by adding more salt, lemon juice, or garlic to your liking.

For best flavor, refrigerate the tzatziki for at least 30 minutes before serving to allow the flavors to meld together.

Prepare the Veggie Sticks:
While the tzatziki chills, prepare the vegetables by cutting the carrots, cucumbers, bell peppers, and celery into sticks. Arrange the veggie sticks on a serving platter along with the halved cherry tomatoes.

Nutritional Information (Per Serving): Calories: 90 kcal, Protein: 5g, Carbohydrates: 10g, Total Fat: 4g, Saturated Fat: 1.5g, Fiber: 2g, Cholesterol: 5mg, Sodium: 260mg, Potassium: 280mg.

Baked Feta with Olives and Herbs

Prep. time: 5 min | Cook time: 20 min | Serves: 4

Ingredients:

- Feta cheese: 8 ounces (one block)
- Kalamata olives: 1/3 cup, pitted and halved
- Extra virgin olive oil: 3 tablespoons
- Fresh thyme: 2 teaspoons, chopped (or 1 teaspoon dried thyme)
- Fresh oregano: 1 teaspoon, chopped (or 1/2 teaspoon dried oregano)
- Fresh rosemary: 1 teaspoon, chopped (optional)
- Garlic: 2 cloves, thinly sliced
- Cherry tomatoes: 1/2 cup, halved
- Red pepper flakes: 1/4 teaspoon (optional, for heat)
- Black pepper: 1/4 teaspoon
- Fresh lemon zest: 1 teaspoon (optional, for garnish)

Directions:

Preheat the oven: Preheat your oven to 375°F (190°C). Lightly grease a small baking dish with olive oil.

Prepare the feta and ingredients: Place the block of feta cheese in the center of the baking dish. Scatter the halved Kalamata olives, cherry tomatoes, and garlic slices around the feta. Sprinkle the fresh thyme, oregano, and rosemary (if using) over the top.

Drizzle with olive oil: Drizzle the olive oil evenly over the feta and the surrounding olives and tomatoes. Sprinkle with black pepper and red pepper flakes (if using) for a little heat.

Bake the feta: Bake in the preheated oven for 20 minutes, or until the feta is soft and golden on the edges, and the olives and tomatoes are tender.

Finish and serve: Once baked, remove the dish from the oven. If desired, sprinkle with lemon zest for a bright finish. Serve warm, drizzling any remaining olive oil and juices from the baking dish over the top.

Nutritional Information (Per Serving): Calories: 210 kcal, Protein: 7g, Carbohydrates: 4g, Total Fat: 19g, Saturated Fat: 7g, Fiber: 1g, Cholesterol: 30mg, Sodium: 650mg, Potassium: 140mg.

Garlic and Lemon Shrimp Skewers

Prep. time: 15 min | Cook time: 10 min | Marinating Time: 15-30 minutes | Serves: 4

Ingredients:

- Large shrimp: 1 pound (peeled and deveined, tails on or off)
- Extra virgin olive oil: 3 tablespoons
- Fresh lemon juice: 2 tablespoons (about 1 lemon)
- Lemon zest: 1 teaspoon
- Garlic: 3 cloves, minced
- Fresh parsley: 2 tablespoons, chopped
- Dried oregano: 1 teaspoon
- Red pepper flakes: 1/4 teaspoon (optional, for a little heat)
- Salt: 1/2 teaspoon (or to taste)
- Black pepper: 1/4 teaspoon
- Wooden or metal skewers: 8-10 skewers

Directions:

Prepare the marinade: In a medium bowl, whisk together the olive oil, fresh lemon juice, lemon zest, minced garlic, chopped parsley, oregano, red pepper flakes (if using), salt, and black pepper. **Marinate the shrimp:** Add the shrimp to the bowl with the marinade and toss to coat evenly. Cover the bowl and let the shrimp marinate in the refrigerator for 15-30 minutes (but not longer, as the lemon juice can start to "cook" the shrimp).

Preheat the grill: Preheat an outdoor grill or stovetop grill pan over medium-high heat. If using wooden skewers, soak them in water for 10-15 minutes to prevent them from burning. **Assemble the skewers**: Thread the marinated shrimp onto the skewers, about 4-5 shrimp per skewer. If using vegetables, alternate between shrimp and vegetables.

Grill the shrimp: Place the shrimp skewers on the preheated grill. Cook for 2-3 minutes per side, or until the shrimp are opaque and pink, and the edges are slightly charred. Be careful not to overcook the shrimp, as they can become tough.

Serve: Remove the skewers from the grill and transfer to a serving platter. Garnish with additional fresh parsley and lemon wedges for squeezing over the top.

Nutritional Information (Per Serving): Calories: 180 kcal, Protein: 22g, Carbohydrates: 2g, Total Fat: 9g, Satur ated Fat: 1.5g, Fiber: 0g, Cholesterol: 170mg, Sodium: 470mg, Potassium: 200mg.

Roasted Eggplant Dip with Pita Chips (Baba Ganoush)

Prep. time: 10 min | Cook time: 40 min | Serves: 6

Ingredients:

For the Roasted Eggplant Dip:
- Eggplant: 1 large (1 1/2 pounds)
- Tahini: 1/4 cup
- Garlic: 2 cloves, minced
- Fresh lemon juice: 2 tablespoons
- Extra virgin olive oil: 2 tablespoons
- Ground cumin: 1/2 teaspoon
- Smoked paprika: 1/4 teaspoon
- Salt: 1/2 teaspoon (or to taste)
- Black pepper: 1/4 teaspoon
- Pomegranate seeds: 2 tablespoons, Fresh parsley: 2 tablespoons, chopped (optional, for garnish)

For the Pita Chips:
- Whole wheat pita bread: 3 large pitas
- Extra virgin olive oil: 2 tablespoons
- Dried oregano: 1/2 teaspoon
- Salt: 1/4 teaspoon
- Black pepper: 1/4 teaspoon

Directions:

For the Roasted Eggplant Dip:

Preheat the oven: Heat oven to 400°F (200°C). Line a baking sheet with parchment paper. **Roast the eggplant:** Prick eggplant with a fork, place on the sheet, and roast for 30-35 minutes, turning halfway. The skin should wrinkle, and the flesh should be soft. Let cool. Prepare the flesh: Cut the eggplant in half, scoop out the flesh, and drain in a sieve for 10 minutes. **Blend the dip:** In a food processor, blend eggplant, tahini, garlic, lemon juice, olive oil, cumin, smoked paprika (optional), salt, and pepper until smooth but slightly chunky. Adjust seasoning as needed.

Garnish and serve: Transfer to a bowl, drizzle with olive oil, and garnish with parsley and pomegranate seeds (optional).

For the Pita Chips:

Prepare the pita: Cut pita into triangles and arrange on a baking sheet. Season the pita chips: Mix olive oil, oregano, salt, and pepper. Brush on the pita. Bake the pita chips: Bake at 400°F (200°C) for 8-10 minutes until golden and crispy. Watch closely.

Nutritional Information (Per Serving): Calories: 180 kcal, Protein: 4g, Carbohydrates: 16g, Total Fat: 11g, Saturated Fat: 2g, Fiber: 4g, Cholesterol: 0mg, Sodium: 300mg, Potassium: 340mg.

Caprese Skewers with Balsamic Drizzle

Prep. time: 10 min | Cook time: 10 min | Serves: 4 (makes about 12 skewers)

Ingredients:

- Cherry tomatoes: 1 pint (about 20-24)
- Fresh mozzarella balls: 12 small (bocconcini or ciliegine)
- Fresh basil leaves: 12 medium to large leaves
- Balsamic vinegar: 1/2 cup
- Extra virgin olive oil: 1 tablespoon (optional for drizzle)
- Salt: 1/4 teaspoon
- Black pepper: 1/4 teaspoon
- Wooden or metal skewers: 12 small skewers (about 4 inches long)

Customizable Elements:

- Substitute cherry tomatoes with grape tomatoes or sun-dried tomatoes for a different flavor.

Directions:

Prepare the balsamic reduction:

In a small saucepan, pour the 1/2 cup of balsamic vinegar and bring it to a boil over medium heat. Once it boils, reduce the heat to low and simmer for 5-7 minutes, stirring occasionally, until the vinegar thickens into a syrupy consistency. Remove from heat and allow to cool slightly.

Assemble the skewers:

Take one skewer and thread a cherry tomato, followed by a basil leaf, then a mozzarella ball. Repeat this process for all 12 skewers.

Season the skewers:

Arrange the skewers on a serving platter. Lightly drizzle with olive oil (optional), and season with salt and black pepper to taste.

Drizzle with balsamic reduction:

Once the balsamic reduction has cooled slightly, drizzle it over the assembled skewers for a tangy finish. You can also serve additional balsamic reduction on the side for dipping.

Nutritional Information (Per Serving): Calories: 120 kcal, Protein: 6g, Carbohydrates: 6g, Total Fat: 8g, Saturated Fat: 3g, Fiber: 1g, Cholesterol: 15mg, Sodium: 200mg, Potassium: 160mg.

Marinated Artichokes with Lemon and Herbs

Prep. time: 15 min | Cook time: 20 min (if cooking fresh artichokes) | Serves: 4

Ingredients:

- For the Artichokes:
- Artichoke hearts: 1 (14-ounce) can or jar, drained (or 4 fresh artichokes, cooked and trimmed)
- Extra virgin olive oil: 1/4 cup
- Fresh lemon juice: 2 tablespoons (about 1 lemon)
- Lemon zest: 1 teaspoon
- Garlic: 2 cloves, minced
- Fresh parsley: 2 tablespoons, chopped
- Fresh oregano: 1 tablespoon, chopped (or 1/2 teaspoon dried oregano)
- Red pepper flakes: 1/4 teaspoon (optional, for a little heat)
- Salt: 1/2 teaspoon (or to taste)
- Black pepper: 1/4 teaspoon
- Capers: 1 tablespoon (optional)

Directions:

For Canned or Jarred Artichokes: In a medium bowl, whisk together the olive oil, fresh lemon juice, lemon zest, minced garlic, chopped parsley, oregano, red pepper flakes (if using), salt, and black pepper. Stir in capers if desired. Add the drained artichoke hearts to the bowl and gently toss to coat them in the marinade. Cover the bowl and refrigerate for at least 30 minutes, or up to 2 hours, to allow the flavors to meld. Once marinated, remove the artichokes from the fridge, toss them again, and serve. You can drizzle extra olive oil and garnish with additional fresh herbs before serving if desired.

For Fresh Artichokes (Optional Cooking Instructions): Trim the artichokes by removing the tough outer leaves, cutting off the tops, and trimming the stems. Cut each artichoke in half and remove the fuzzy choke with a spoon. Bring a large pot of salted water to a boil. Add the artichoke halves and cook for 15-20 minutes, or until tender. Drain and let cool slightly before cutting into quarters or smaller pieces. Once the artichokes are cooked, follow the steps above for marinating with the lemon and herb mixture.

Nutritional Information (Per Serving): Calories: 140 kcal, Protein: 2g, Carbohydrates: 10g, Total Fat: 10g, Saturated Fat: 1.5g, Fiber: 4g, Cholesterol: 0mg, Sodium: 400mg, Potassium: 180mg.

Spicy Roasted Chickpeas with Paprika

Prep. time: 5 min | Cook time: 30 min | Serves: 4

Ingredients:

- Chickpeas: 1 (15-ounce) can, drained, rinsed, and dried (or 1 1/2 cups cooked chickpeas)
- Extra virgin olive oil: 1 tablespoon
- Paprika: 1 teaspoon (smoked paprika for extra flavor)
- Ground cumin: 1/2 teaspoon
- Garlic powder: 1/2 teaspoon
- Cayenne pepper: 1/4 teaspoon (optional for added spice)
- Salt: 1/2 teaspoon (or to taste)
- Black pepper: 1/4 teaspoon

Customizable Elements:

- Add ground turmeric or ground coriander for a different flavor profile.
- Use fresh herbs like rosemary or thyme for an herbal twist.

Directions:

Preheat the oven: Preheat your oven to 400°F (200°C). Line a baking sheet with parchment paper for easy cleanup.

Dry the chickpeas: After rinsing and draining the chickpeas, spread them on a clean kitchen towel or paper towel to dry thoroughly. Removing excess moisture ensures they become crispy when roasted.

Season the chickpeas:

In a medium bowl, toss the chickpeas with olive oil, paprika, cumin, garlic powder, cayenne pepper (if using), salt, and black pepper. Mix well to coat the chickpeas evenly.

Roast the chickpeas:

Spread the seasoned chickpeas in a single layer on the prepared baking sheet. Roast in the preheated oven for 30-35 minutes, stirring halfway through, until the chickpeas are golden and crispy.

Cool and serve:

Once roasted, remove the chickpeas from the oven and let them cool on the baking sheet. They will become even crispier as they cool.

Nutritional Information (Per Serving): Calories: 130 kcal, Protein: 5g, Carbohydrates: 18g, Total Fat: 4g, Saturated Fat: 0.5g, Fiber: 5g, Cholesterol: 0mg, Sodium: 350mg, Potassium: 230mg.

Stuffed Mini Peppers with Feta and Spinach

Prep. time: 15 min | Cook time: 20 min | Serves: 4 (about 16 stuffed peppers)

Ingredients:

- Mini sweet bell peppers: 16 (about 1 pound)
- Fresh spinach: 2 cups (chopped)
- Feta cheese: 1/2 cup, crumbled
- Garlic: 2 cloves, minced
- Extra virgin olive oil: 2 tablespoons (divided)
- Fresh dill: 1 tablespoon, chopped (or 1 teaspoon dried dill)
- Fresh parsley: 1 tablespoon, chopped
- Ground black pepper: 1/4 teaspoon
- Red pepper flakes: 1/4 teaspoon (optional, for heat)
- Lemon zest: 1 teaspoon (optional, for brightness)
- Salt: 1/4 teaspoon (or to taste)

Directions:

Preheat the Oven: Preheat your oven to 375°F (190°C) and line a baking sheet with parchment paper. **Prepare the Peppers:** Slice the mini peppers in half lengthwise and remove the seeds and membranes. Set aside. **Sauté the Spinach:** Heat 1 tablespoon of olive oil in a skillet over medium heat. Add minced garlic and sauté for 1 minute until fragrant. Add the spinach and cook for 2-3 minutes until wilted. Remove from heat and let cool slightly. **Make the Filling:** In a medium bowl, combine the sautéed spinach, crumbled feta, dill, parsley, black pepper, red pepper flakes (if using), and lemon zest. Mix well. Adjust seasoning with salt if needed. **Stuff the Peppers:** Use a small spoon to fill each pepper half with the spinach and feta mixture. Place the stuffed peppers on the prepared baking sheet. Drizzle with the remaining olive oil.

Bake: Bake for 15-20 minutes, or until the peppers are tender and the filling is lightly golden on top.

Serve: Let the stuffed peppers cool slightly before serving. Optionally, garnish with fresh herbs or a sprinkle of lemon zest for added brightness.

Nutritional Information (Per Serving): Calories: 150 kcal, Protein: 5g, Carbohydrates: 10g, Total Fat: 10g, Saturated Fat: 3g, Fiber: 3g, Cholesterol: 15mg, Sodium: 330mg, Potassium: 250mg.

Herb-Crusted Goat Cheese Balls with Crackers

Prep. time: 15 min | Cook time: None | Serves: 6 (about 12 goat cheese balls)

Ingredients:

For the Goat Cheese Balls:
- Goat cheese: 8 ounces (soft, room temperature)
- Fresh parsley: 2 tablespoons, chopped
- Fresh chives: 2 tablespoons, chopped
- Fresh thyme: 1 tablespoon, chopped
- Walnuts or almonds: 1/4 cup, finely chopped
- Lemon zest: 1 teaspoon
- Cracked black pepper: 1/4 teaspoon
- Extra virgin olive oil: 1 tablespoon (optional for drizzling)

For Serving:
- Whole grain crackers: 20-24 (or gluten-free crackers if needed)

Directions:

Prepare the herbs and nuts: In a shallow bowl or on a plate, combine the chopped parsley, chives, thyme, walnuts (or almonds), and lemon zest. Mix well to create the herb and nut coating for the goat cheese balls.

Form the goat cheese balls: Using a spoon or a small cookie scoop, portion out about 1 tablespoon of goat cheese at a time. Roll the goat cheese into small balls using your hands.

Coat the goat cheese balls: Gently roll each goat cheese ball in the herb and nut mixture, pressing lightly to ensure the coating adheres well. Repeat with the remaining goat cheese balls.

Chill the cheese balls (optional): For best texture, refrigerate the goat cheese balls for about 15 minutes before serving to allow them to firm up slightly. If you're short on time, they can be served immediately.

Serve: Arrange the herb-crusted goat cheese balls on a serving platter. Drizzle with extra virgin olive oil if desired for added richness. Serve alongside whole grain crackers.

Nutritional Information (Per Serving): Calories: 180 kcal, Protein: 6g, Carbohydrates: 12g, Total Fat: 13g, Saturated Fat: 5g, Fiber: 2g, Cholesterol: 15mg, Sodium: 220mg, Potassium: 120mg.

Stuffed Mini Peppers with Quinoa and Feta

Prep. time: 15 min | Cook time: 20 min | Serves: 6

Ingredients:

- Mini bell peppers: 12, tops removed and seeded
- Quinoa: 1/2 cup, uncooked
- Water or vegetable broth: 1 cup
- Feta cheese: 1/2 cup, crumbled
- Fresh parsley: 1/4 cup, chopped
- Olive oil: 2 tablespoons, divided
- Garlic: 1 clove, minced
- Lemon juice: 1 tablespoon
- Dried oregano: 1 teaspoon
- Sea salt: 1/4 teaspoon
- Black pepper: 1/4 teaspoon
- Red pepper flakes, chopped mint, or pine nuts (optional): for topping

Directions:

Prepare the Quinoa: Rinse quinoa under cold water. In a small saucepan, combine quinoa and water (or broth). Bring to a boil, reduce heat, cover, and simmer for 15 minutes or until liquid is absorbed and quinoa is cooked. Fluff with a fork and let cool slightly.

Prepare the Peppers: Preheat oven to 375°F (190°C). Brush the inside of mini bell peppers with 1 tablespoon of olive oil and arrange in a baking dish.

Prepare the Filling: In a bowl, mix cooked quinoa, feta, parsley, garlic, lemon juice, oregano, salt, and black pepper.

Stuff the Peppers: Spoon the quinoa mixture into each pepper. Drizzle with remaining 1 tablespoon of olive oil.

Bake the Peppers: Bake for 15-20 minutes, until peppers are tender and slightly browned.

Serving Suggestions: Garnish with red pepper flakes, mint, or pine nuts. Serve warm or at room temperature.

Nutritional Information (Per Serving): Calories: 130 kcal, Protein: 4 g, Carbohydrates: 10 g, Total Fat: 8 g, Fiber: 2 g, Cholesterol: 10 mg, Sodium: 180 mg, Potassium: 220 mg.

Chapter

3

Salad Recipes

Salads are a cornerstone of the Mediterranean diet, celebrated for their ability to combine fresh, nutrient-dense ingredients into dishes that are both light and satisfying. With a focus on seasonal vegetables, hearty grains, lean proteins, and a drizzle of extra virgin olive oil, Mediterranean salads offer a vibrant and nourishing approach to everyday meals. Each bite is a harmonious blend of flavors and textures, reflecting the region's rich culinary heritage.

In this section, "Salad Recipes," you'll discover a variety of salad ideas that go beyond the ordinary. From classic Greek and Caprese salads to innovative combinations of grains, legumes, and greens, these recipes are designed to be both versatile and easy to prepare. Whether served as a side dish or the main event, these salads are a celebration of fresh ingredients and balanced nutrition, perfect for any time of day.

Avocado and Tomato Salad with Lemon Dressing

Prep. time: 10 min | Cook time: None | Serves: 4

Ingredients:

- Avocados: 2 ripe, diced
- Cherry tomatoes: 1 cup, halved
- Red onion: 1/4 small, thinly sliced
- Fresh parsley: 1/4 cup, chopped
- Extra virgin olive oil: 2 tablespoons
- Fresh lemon juice: 2 tablespoons
- Salt: 1/4 teaspoon
- Black pepper: 1/4 teaspoon

Directions:

Prepare the Salad:

In a large bowl, combine the diced avocados, halved cherry tomatoes, sliced red onion, and fresh parsley.

Make the Dressing:

In a small bowl, whisk together the olive oil, lemon juice, salt, and black pepper.

Toss the Salad:

Pour the dressing over the salad and gently toss to combine all ingredients without mashing the avocado.

Serve:

Serve immediately as a light and refreshing salad. This salad pairs well with grilled fish or as a healthy appetizer.

Nutritional Information (Per Serving): Calories: 200 kcal, Protein: 2g, Carbohydrates: 10g, Total Fat: 18g, Saturated Fat: 3g, Fiber: 7g, Cholesterol: 0mg, Sodium: 150mg, Potassium: 550mg.

Classic Greek Salad with Feta and Olives

Prep. time: 10 min | Cook time: None | Serves: 4

Ingredients:

- Cucumber: 1 large, sliced or diced
- Tomatoes: 2 large (or 1 pint cherry tomatoes), cut into wedges or halved
- Red onion: 1/2 medium, thinly sliced
- Green bell pepper: 1 medium, sliced into rings or strips
- Kalamata olives: 1/2 cup, pitted
- Feta cheese: 1/2 cup, crumbled or cut into small cubes
- Extra virgin olive oil: 3 tablespoons
- Fresh lemon juice: 2 tablespoons (about 1 lemon)
- Dried oregano: 1 teaspoon
- Salt: 1/4 teaspoon (or to taste)
- Black pepper: 1/4 teaspoon
- Fresh parsley: 1 tablespoon, chopped (optional for garnish)

Directions:

Prepare the vegetables: Slice the cucumber, tomatoes, red onion, and bell pepper. Place them in a large mixing bowl.

Add the olives and feta:

Toss in the Kalamata olives and crumbled (or cubed) feta cheese, distributing them evenly throughout the salad.

Make the dressing:

In a small bowl, whisk together the olive oil, fresh lemon juice, dried oregano, salt, and black pepper until well combined.

Toss the salad:

Drizzle the dressing over the vegetables, olives, and feta. Gently toss to coat all the ingredients in the dressing, being careful not to crumble the feta too much.

Serve:

Transfer the salad to a serving bowl or platter. Garnish with chopped fresh parsley if desired. Serve immediately.

Nutritional Information (Per Serving): Calories: 180 kcal, Protein: 6g, Carbohydrates: 10g, Total Fat: 14g, Saturated Fat: 4g, Fiber: 3g, Cholesterol: 15mg, Sodium: 400mg, Potassium: 400mg.

Quinoa Salad with Lemon Vinaigrette

Prep. time: 15 min | Cook time: 15 min | Serves: 4

Ingredients:

For the Salad:
- Quinoa: 1 cup (uncooked)
- Water or vegetable broth: 2 cups
- Cherry tomatoes: 1 cup, halved
- Cucumber: 1 medium, diced
- Red bell pepper: 1 medium, diced
- Kalamata olives: 1/2 cup, halved
- Red onion: 1/4 cup, finely chopped
- Feta cheese: 1/3 cup, crumbled
- Fresh parsley: 1/4 cup, chopped
- Fresh mint: 2 tablespoons (optional)

For the Lemon Vinaigrette:
- Extra virgin olive oil: 1/4 cup
- Fresh lemon juice: 3 tablespoons
- Dijon mustard: 1 teaspoon
- Garlic: 1 clove, minced
- Dried oregano: 1/2 teaspoon
- Salt: 1/2 teaspoon (or to taste)
- Black pepper: 1/4 teaspoon

Directions:

Cook the quinoa: Rinse the quinoa under cold water to remove its natural bitterness. In a medium saucepan, combine the rinsed quinoa with 2 cups of water or vegetable broth. Bring to a boil, reduce heat to low, cover, and simmer for about 15 minutes, or until the quinoa is tender and all the liquid is absorbed. Remove from heat and fluff with a fork. Let it cool slightly. **Prepare the vegetables:** While the quinoa is cooking, prepare the vegetables. Halve the cherry tomatoes, dice the cucumber and red bell pepper, and finely chop the red onion and herbs. Set aside. **Make the lemon vinaigrette:** In a small bowl, whisk together the olive oil, fresh lemon juice, Dijon mustard, minced garlic, dried oregano, salt, and black pepper until well combined. **Assemble the salad:** In a large mixing bowl, combine the cooked quinoa, cherry tomatoes, cucumber, red bell pepper, red onion, Kalamata olives, and crumbled feta cheese. Pour the lemon vinaigrette over the salad and toss gently to combine. **Add fresh herbs:** Stir in the chopped parsley and mint (if using) for a burst of freshness. **Serve:** Transfer the salad to a serving dish. It can be served immediately at room temperature or chilled for 30 minutes for a colder, more refreshing option.

Nutritional Information (Per Serving): Calories: 320 kcal, Protein: 9g, Carbohydrates: 32g, Total Fat: 18g, Saturated Fat: 4g, Fiber: 5g, Cholesterol: 15mg, Sodium: 520mg, Potassium: 500mg.

Cucumber, Tomato, and Red Onion Salad

Prep. time: 10 min | Cook time: None | Serves: 4

Ingredients:

- Cucumber: 1 large (about 1 1/2 cups), sliced or diced
- Tomatoes: 2 large, diced (or 1 cup cherry tomatoes, halved)
- Red onion: 1/2 small, thinly sliced
- Extra virgin olive oil: 2 tablespoons
- Red wine vinegar: 1 tablespoon (or apple cider vinegar)
- Fresh lemon juice: 1 tablespoon (optional for extra brightness)
- Dried oregano: 1 teaspoon
- Salt: 1/2 teaspoon (or to taste)
- Black pepper: 1/4 teaspoon
- Fresh parsley: 2 tablespoons, chopped (optional)
- Kalamata olives: 1/4 cup, halved (optional)

Directions:

Prepare the vegetables:
Slice or dice the cucumber, dice the tomatoes (or halve the cherry tomatoes), and thinly slice the red onion. Place the vegetables in a large mixing bowl.

Make the dressing:
In a small bowl, whisk together the olive oil, red wine vinegar, lemon juice (if using), dried oregano, salt, and black pepper until well combined.

Combine and toss:
Pour the dressing over the vegetables in the bowl. Gently toss the salad until the vegetables are evenly coated with the dressing.

Add optional ingredients: Stir in the chopped parsley and Kalamata olives if using, for extra flavor and Mediterranean flair.

Serve:
Transfer the salad to a serving dish. Serve immediately, or refrigerate for about 15 minutes to allow the flavors to meld together.

Nutritional Information (Per Serving): Calories: 100 kcal, Protein: 1.5g, Carbohydrates: 8g, Total Fat: 7g, Saturated Fat: 1g, Fiber: 2g, Cholesterol: 0mg, Sodium: 320mg, Potassium: 280mg.

Roasted Beet Salad with Goat Cheese and Walnuts

Prep. time: 10 min | Cook time: 45-60 minutes (for roasting the beets) | Serves: 4

Ingredients:

- Beets: 4 medium, scrubbed and trimmed
- Goat cheese: 1/4 cup, crumbled
- Walnuts: 1/4 cup, toasted and chopped
- Mixed salad greens: 4 cups (arugula, spinach, or spring mix)
- Fresh parsley: 2 tablespoons, chopped (optional)
- For the Dressing:
- Extra virgin olive oil: 3 tablespoons
- Fresh lemon juice: 2 tablespoons (or balsamic vinegar)
- Dijon mustard: 1 teaspoon
- Honey: 1 teaspoon (optional for a touch of sweetness)
- Salt: 1/2 teaspoon (or to taste)
- Black pepper: 1/4 teaspoon

Directions:

Roast the beets: Preheat your oven to 400°F (200°C). Wrap each beet in aluminum foil and place them on a baking sheet. Roast for 45-60 minutes, or until the beets are tender when pierced with a fork. Remove from the oven, let cool, then peel and cut into wedges or slices.

While the beets are roasting, toast the walnuts in a dry skillet over medium heat for 3-5 minutes, stirring frequently until fragrant and lightly browned. Set aside to cool.

In a small bowl, whisk together the olive oil, lemon juice (or balsamic vinegar), Dijon mustard, honey (if using), salt, and black pepper until well combined.

Assemble the salad: In a large salad bowl, combine the mixed greens, roasted beet wedges, and toasted walnuts. Drizzle the dressing over the salad and toss gently to coat all ingredients.

Add goat cheese: Sprinkle the crumbled goat cheese over the top of the salad. Garnish with fresh parsley if desired.

Serve: Serve immediately as a side dish or light main course. For extra texture, you can add an additional drizzle of olive oil or a sprinkle of more toasted nuts.

Nutritional Information (Per Serving): Calories: 220 kcal, Protein: 6g, Carbohydrates: 20g, Total Fat: 14g, Saturated Fat: 4g, Fiber: 4g, Cholesterol: 10mg, Sodium: 330mg, Potassium: 450mg.

Lentil Salad with Fresh Herbs and Olive Oil

Prep. time: 10 min | Cook time: 25 min | Serves: 4

Ingredients:

- Green or brown lentils: 1 cup (uncooked)
- Water or vegetable broth: 3 cups
- Cucumber: 1 medium, diced
- Cherry tomatoes: 1 cup, halved
- Red onion: 1/4 cup, finely chopped
- Fresh parsley: 1/4 cup, chopped
- Fresh mint: 2 tablespoons, chopped
- Kalamata olives: 1/4 cup, pitted and halved (optional), Feta cheese: 1/4 cup, crumbled (optional)

For the Dressing:
- Extra virgin olive oil: 3 tablespoons
- Fresh lemon juice: 2 tablespoons
- Garlic: 1 clove, minced
- Dijon mustard: 1 teaspoon
- Dried oregano: 1/2 teaspoon
- Salt: 1/2 teaspoon (or to taste)
- Black pepper: 1/4 teaspoon

Directions:

Cook the lentils: Rinse the lentils under cold water. In a medium saucepan, combine the lentils with 3 cups of water or vegetable broth. Bring to a boil, then reduce the heat and simmer for 20-25 minutes, or until the lentils are tender but not mushy. Drain and allow to cool slightly. **Prepare the vegetables:** While the lentils are cooking, dice the cucumber, halve the cherry tomatoes, and finely chop the red onion. Set aside.

Make the dressing: In a small bowl, whisk together the olive oil, fresh lemon juice, minced garlic, Dijon mustard, dried oregano, salt, and black pepper until well combined.

Assemble the salad: In a large mixing bowl, combine the cooked lentils, cucumber, cherry tomatoes, red onion, fresh parsley, mint, and Kalamata olives (if using). Drizzle the dressing over the salad and toss gently to combine.

Optional: Add feta cheese: For an added touch of creaminess, sprinkle crumbled feta cheese over the salad before serving.

Serve: Serve the salad immediately at room temperature, or refrigerate for 15-20 minutes to let the flavors meld together.

Nutritional Information (Per Serving): Calories: 260 kcal, Protein: 10g, Carbohydrates: 30g, Total Fat: 12g, Saturated Fat: 1.5g, Fiber: 10g, Cholesterol: 0mg, Sodium: 320mg, Potassium: 600mg.

Chickpea and Avocado Salad with Lemon Dressing

Prep. time: 10 min | Cook time: None | Serves: 4

Ingredients:

For the Salad:
- Chickpeas: 1 (15-ounce) can, drained and rinsed (or 1 1/2 cups cooked chickpeas)
- Avocado: 2 medium, diced
- Cucumber: 1 medium, diced
- Cherry tomatoes: 1 cup, halved
- Red onion: 1/4 cup, finely chopped
- Fresh parsley: 1/4 cup, chopped
- Fresh cilantro or mint: 2 tablespoons, chopped (optional)

For the Lemon Dressing:
- Extra virgin olive oil: 2 tablespoons
- Fresh lemon juice: 2 tablespoons
- Garlic: 1 clove, minced
- Dijon mustard: 1 teaspoon
- Honey: 1 teaspoon (optional)
- Salt: 1/2 teaspoon (or to taste)
- Black pepper: 1/4 teaspoon

Directions:

Prepare the salad ingredients:

In a large mixing bowl, combine the drained and rinsed chickpeas, diced avocado, cucumber, cherry tomatoes, red onion, and fresh parsley (and cilantro or mint if using).

Make the lemon dressing:

In a small bowl, whisk together the olive oil, fresh lemon juice, minced garlic, Dijon mustard, honey (if using), salt, and black pepper until well combined.

Toss the salad:

Drizzle the lemon dressing over the chickpea and avocado mixture. Gently toss the salad to ensure all the ingredients are evenly coated with the dressing.

Serve:

Transfer the salad to a serving dish and garnish with additional fresh herbs if desired. Serve immediately for the freshest flavor.

Nutritional Information (Per Serving): Calories: 290 kcal, Protein: 7g, Carbohydrates: 24g, Total Fat: 19g, Saturated Fat: 3g, Fiber: 10g, Cholesterol: 0mg, Sodium: 320mg, Potassium: 700mg.

Orzo Salad with Olives and Cherry Tomatoes

Prep. time: 10 min | Cook time: 10 min | Serves: 4

Ingredients:

- Orzo pasta: 1 cup (uncooked)
- Kalamata olives: 1/2 cup, pitted and halved
- Cherry tomatoes: 1 cup, halved
- Cucumber: 1 medium, diced
- Red onion: 1/4 cup, finely chopped
- Feta cheese: 1/3 cup, crumbled
- Fresh parsley: 1/4 cup, chopped
- Fresh basil: 2 tablespoons, chopped (optional)

For the Lemon Vinaigrette:
- Extra virgin olive oil: 1/4 cup
- Fresh lemon juice: 3 tablespoons
- Garlic: 1 clove, minced
- Dijon mustard: 1 teaspoon
- Honey: 1 teaspoon (optional)
- Salt: 1/2 teaspoon (or to taste)
- Black pepper: 1/4 teaspoon
- Dried oregano: 1/2 teaspoon

Directions:

Cook the orzo: Bring a medium pot of salted water to a boil. Add the orzo pasta and cook according to the package instructions (about 8-10 minutes), until al dente. Drain the orzo and rinse with cold water to stop the cooking process. Set aside to cool.

Prepare the vegetables: While the orzo is cooking, halve the cherry tomatoes, dice the cucumber, chop the red onion, and pit and halve the Kalamata olives. Set aside.

Make the lemon vinaigrette:

In a small bowl, whisk together the olive oil, fresh lemon juice, minced garlic, Dijon mustard, honey (if using), salt, black pepper, and dried oregano until well combined.

Assemble the salad:

In a large mixing bowl, combine the cooked and cooled orzo, cherry tomatoes, cucumber, red onion, Kalamata olives, crumbled feta cheese, and fresh parsley (and basil if using). Pour the lemon vinaigrette over the salad and toss gently to combine.

Chill and serve:

Refrigerate the salad for 15-20 minutes to let the flavors meld together. Serve chilled or at room temperature.

Nutritional Information (Per Serving): Calories: 330 kcal, Protein: 8g, Carbohydrates: 36g, Total Fat: 18g, Saturated Fat: 5g, Fiber: 4g, Cholesterol: 20mg, Sodium: 500mg, Potassium: 400mg.

Grilled Vegetable Salad with Balsamic Glaze

Prep. time: 10 min | Cook time: 20 min | Serves: 4

Ingredients:

For the Grilled Vegetables:
- Zucchini: 2 medium, sliced into rounds or lengthwise; Eggplant: 1 medium, sliced into rounds
- Red bell pepper: 1, Yellow bell pepper: 1 (sliced into quarters)
- Red onion: 1 large, sliced into rounds
- Cherry tomatoes: 1 cup (optional)
- Extra virgin olive oil: 2 tablespoons
- Salt: 1/2 teaspoon (or to taste)
- Black pepper: 1/4 teaspoon
- Fresh thyme: 1 tablespoon, chopped (or 1 teaspoon dried thyme)

For the Balsamic Glaze:
- Balsamic vinegar: 1/2 cup
- Honey or maple syrup: 1 tablespoon

For Garnish: Fresh basil: 1/4 cup, chopped; Feta cheese: 1/4 cup, crumbled (optional)

Directions:

Prepare the Balsamic Glaze: Make the glaze: In a small saucepan, combine the balsamic vinegar and honey (if using). Bring to a simmer over medium heat, then reduce the heat to low. Simmer for 10-12 minutes, stirring occasionally, until the balsamic has reduced by half and thickened into a glaze. Remove from heat and set aside to cool slightly.

Grill the Vegetables: Preheat your grill or grill pan over medium-high heat. Lightly oil the grill grates if necessary. In a large bowl, toss the sliced zucchini, eggplant, bell peppers, red onion, and cherry tomatoes (if using) with the olive oil, salt, black pepper, and thyme. Place the vegetables on the grill, turning occasionally, until they are tender and have nice grill marks, about 5-7 minutes per side. Grill the cherry tomatoes on skewers to prevent them from falling through the grates. **Assemble the Salad:** Once the vegetables are grilled, transfer them to a large serving platter. Drizzle the balsamic glaze over the grilled vegetables. Garnish with fresh basil and crumbled feta cheese (if using). **Serve:** Serve the grilled vegetable salad warm or at room temperature. Optionally, drizzle with a little extra virgin olive oil before serving.

Nutritional Information (Per Serving): Calories: 180 kcal, Protein: 4g, Carbohydrates: 20g, Total Fat: 9g, Saturated Fat: 1.5g, Fiber: 6g, Cholesterol: 0mg, Sodium: 300mg, Potassium: 600mg.

Spinach Salad with Pomegranate and Feta

Prep. time: 10 min | Cook time: None | Serves: 4

Ingredients:

For the Salad:
- Fresh spinach: 6 cups (about 6 oz)
- Pomegranate seeds: 1/2 cup (from 1 pomegranate)
- Feta cheese: 1/3 cup, crumbled
- Red onion: 1/4 small, thinly sliced
- Walnuts: 1/4 cup, toasted and chopped (optional)

For the Lemon Vinaigrette:
- Extra virgin olive oil: 3 tablespoons
- Fresh lemon juice: 2 tablespoons (about 1 lemon)
- Honey: 1 teaspoon (optional for sweetness)
- Dijon mustard: 1 teaspoon
- Garlic: 1 clove, minced
- Salt: 1/4 teaspoon (or to taste)
- Black pepper: 1/4 teaspoon

Directions:

Prepare the vinaigrette:
In a small bowl, whisk together the olive oil, fresh lemon juice, honey (if using), Dijon mustard, minced garlic, salt, and black pepper until emulsified. Set aside.

Toast the walnuts (optional):
If using walnuts, toast them in a dry skillet over medium heat for 3-4 minutes, stirring occasionally, until they are fragrant and lightly browned. Remove from heat and let cool.

Assemble the salad:
In a large mixing bowl, add the fresh spinach, pomegranate seeds, crumbled feta, red onion slices, and toasted walnuts (if using).

Dress the salad: Drizzle the lemon vinaigrette over the salad and gently toss to coat the ingredients evenly.

Serve: Transfer the salad to a serving platter or individual plates. Serve immediately for the freshest flavor.

Nutritional Information (Per Serving): Calories: 210 kcal, Protein: 6g, Carbohydrates: 12g, Total Fat: 17g, Saturated Fat: 4g, Fiber: 4g, Cholesterol: 15mg, Sodium: 280mg, Potassium: 500mg.

Couscous Salad with Sun-Dried Tomatoes and Parsley

Prep. time: 10 min | Cook time: 5 min | Serves: 4

Ingredients:

For the Couscous Salad:
- Couscous: 1 cup (uncooked)
- Water or vegetable broth: 1 cup (for cooking couscous)
- Sun-dried tomatoes: 1/3 cup, finely chopped (packed in oil, drained)
- Fresh parsley: 1/4 cup, chopped
- Cucumber: 1 medium, diced
- Red onion: 1/4 cup, finely chopped
- Feta cheese: 1/4 cup, crumbled (optional); Kalamata olives: 1/4 cup, pitted and halved (optional)

For the Lemon Dressing:
- Extra virgin olive oil: 3 tablespoons
- Fresh lemon juice: 2 tablespoons
- Garlic: 1 clove, minced
- Dijon mustard: 1 teaspoon
- Salt: 1/2 teaspoon (or to taste)
- Black pepper: 1/4 teaspoon

Directions:

Cook the couscous:

In a medium saucepan, bring 1 cup of water or vegetable broth to a boil. Remove from heat, add the couscous, cover, and let it sit for 5 minutes until the liquid is absorbed. Fluff the couscous with a fork and set aside to cool slightly.

Prepare the vegetables: While the couscous is cooling, finely chop the sun-dried tomatoes, parsley, cucumber, and red onion. Set aside.

Make the lemon dressing:

In a small bowl, whisk together the olive oil, fresh lemon juice, minced garlic, Dijon mustard, salt, and black pepper until well combined.

Assemble the salad: In a large mixing bowl, combine the cooked couscous, sun-dried tomatoes, parsley, cucumber, red onion, and crumbled feta (if using). Drizzle the lemon dressing over the salad and toss gently to coat all the ingredients evenly.

Chill and serve:

For the best flavor, refrigerate the salad for 15-20 minutes before serving. Garnish with Kalamata olives or additional parsley if desired.

Nutritional Information (Per Serving): Calories: 280 kcal, Protein: 6g, Carbohydrates: 34g, Total Fat: 14g, Saturated Fat: 3g, Fiber: 4g, Cholesterol: 10mg, Sodium: 350mg, Potassium: 400mg.

White Bean and Arugula Salad with Lemon Zest

Prep. time: 10 min | Cook time: None | Serves: 4

Ingredients:

For the Salad:
- Arugula: 4 cups (about 4 ounces)
- White beans: 1 (15-ounce) can, drained and rinsed (or 1 1/2 cups cooked)
- Cherry tomatoes: 1 cup, halved
- Cucumber: 1 medium, diced
- Red onion: 1/4 cup, thinly sliced
- Lemon zest: 1 teaspoon
- Parmesan cheese: 1/4 cup, shaved or grated (optional)

For the Lemon Vinaigrette:
- Extra virgin olive oil: 3 tablespoons
- Fresh lemon juice: 2 tablespoons
- Garlic: 1 clove, minced
- Dijon mustard: 1 teaspoon
- Honey: 1 teaspoon (optional)
- Salt: 1/2 teaspoon (or to taste)
- Black pepper: 1/4 teaspoon

Directions:

Prepare the vinaigrette:

In a small bowl, whisk together the olive oil, fresh lemon juice, minced garlic, Dijon mustard, honey (if using), salt, and black pepper until well combined. Set aside.

Assemble the salad:

In a large salad bowl, combine the arugula, white beans, cherry tomatoes, cucumber, red onion, and lemon zest. Toss gently to combine all ingredients.

Dress the salad:

Drizzle the lemon vinaigrette over the salad and toss to coat the ingredients evenly. Taste and adjust seasoning if needed.

Optional: Add Parmesan:

If using, sprinkle the shaved or grated Parmesan cheese over the salad before serving.

Serve:

Serve the salad immediately as a light lunch or side dish. Optionally, you can refrigerate it for 10-15 minutes before serving for a chilled version.

Nutritional Information (Per Serving): Calories: 210 kcal, Protein: 7g, Carbohydrates: 20g, Total Fat: 12g, Saturated Fat: 2g, Fiber: 6g, Cholesterol: 0mg, Sodium: 320mg, Potassium: 420mg.

Farro Salad with Grilled Zucchini and Feta

Prep. time: 10 min | Cook time: 40 min | Serves: 4

Ingredients:

For the Salad:
- Farro: 1 cup (uncooked)
- Water or vegetable broth: 3 cups (for cooking farro); Zucchini: 2 medium, sliced into rounds or lengthwise
- Feta cheese: 1/3 cup, crumbled
- Fresh parsley: 1/4 cup, chopped
- Fresh mint: 2 tablespoons, chopped (optional); Kalamata olives: 1/4 cup, pitted and halved (optional)
- Cherry tomatoes: 1 cup, halved
- Red onion: 1/4 cup, finely chopped

For the Lemon-Olive Oil Dressing:
Extra virgin olive oil: 3 tablespoons;
Fresh lemon juice: 2 tablespoons;
Garlic: 1 clove, minced; Dijon mustard:
1 teaspoon; Salt: 1/2 teaspoon (or to taste); Black pepper: 1/4 teaspoon
Dried oregano: 1/2 teaspoon

Directions:

Cook the farro: Rinse the farro under cold water. In a medium saucepan, bring 3 cups of water or vegetable broth to a boil. Add the farro, reduce heat, and simmer uncovered for about 25-30 minutes, or until the farro is tender but still slightly chewy. Drain any excess water and let the farro cool. **Prepare the zucchini:** While the farro is cooking, preheat a grill or grill pan over medium-high heat. Lightly brush the zucchini slices with olive oil and season with salt and pepper. Grill the zucchini for about 3-4 minutes per side, or until tender and charred. Remove from the grill and set aside to cool slightly.
Prepare the dressing: In a small bowl, whisk together the olive oil, fresh lemon juice, minced garlic, Dijon mustard, salt, black pepper, and dried oregano until well combined.
Assemble the salad: In a large mixing bowl, combine the cooked farro, grilled zucchini, cherry tomatoes, red onion, crumbled feta, parsley, and mint (if using). Drizzle the lemon-olive oil dressing over the salad and toss gently to coat all the ingredients evenly.
Chill and serve: For the best flavor, refrigerate the salad for 15-20 minutes before serving. Garnish with Kalamata olives or additional fresh herbs if desired.

Nutritional Information (Per Serving): Calories: 320 kcal, Protein: 9g, Carbohydrates: 40g, Total Fat: 14g, Saturated Fat: 4g, Fiber: 6g, Cholesterol: 15mg, Sodium: 350mg, Potassium: 500mg.

Bulgur Wheat Salad with Cucumber and Mint

Prep. time: 10 min | Cook time: 10 min | Serves: 4

Ingredients:

For the Salad:
- Bulgur wheat: 1 cup (medium or fine grain)
- Water: 2 cups (for cooking bulgur)
- Cucumber: 1 medium, diced
- Cherry tomatoes: 1 cup, halved
- Red onion: 1/4 cup, finely chopped
- Fresh mint: 1/4 cup, chopped
- Fresh parsley: 1/4 cup, chopped
- Feta cheese: 1/4 cup, crumbled (optional)

For the Lemon-Olive Oil Dressing:
- Extra virgin olive oil: 3 tablespoons
- Fresh lemon juice: 3 tablespoons
- Garlic: 1 clove, minced
- Salt: 1/2 teaspoon (or to taste)
- Black pepper: 1/4 teaspoon
- Ground cumin: 1/2 teaspoon (optional)

Directions:

Cook the bulgur wheat: In a medium saucepan, bring 2 cups of water to a boil. Add the bulgur wheat, reduce heat to low, cover, and simmer for 10-12 minutes, or until the bulgur is tender and the water is absorbed. Remove from heat, fluff with a fork, and allow it to cool slightly.
Prepare the vegetables: While the bulgur is cooking, dice the cucumber, halve the cherry tomatoes, and finely chop the red onion, mint, and parsley.
Make the lemon-olive oil dressing: In a small bowl, whisk together the olive oil, fresh lemon juice, minced garlic, salt, black pepper, and cumin (if using) until well combined.
Assemble the salad: In a large mixing bowl, combine the cooked bulgur wheat, cucumber, cherry tomatoes, red onion, chopped mint, and parsley. Drizzle the lemon-olive oil dressing over the salad and toss gently to coat all the ingredients evenly.
Optional: If using feta, sprinkle it over the salad before serving for a creamy and tangy flavor.
Chill and serve: Refrigerate the salad for 15-20 minutes to let the flavors meld, or serve immediately at room temperature.

Nutritional Information (Per Serving): Calories: 250 kcal, Protein: 6g, Carbohydrates: 35g, Total Fat: 10g, Saturated Fat: 2g, Fiber: 8g, Cholesterol: 10mg, Sodium: 320mg, Potassium: 400mg.

Warm Potato Salad with Capers and Olive Oil

Prep. time: 10 min | Cook time: 25 min | Serves: 4

Ingredients:

For the Salad:
- Small potatoes (baby or new potatoes): 1 1/2 pounds, halved or quartered if large
- Capers: 2 tablespoons, drained and rinsed
- Red onion: 1/4 cup, finely chopped
- Fresh parsley: 1/4 cup, chopped
- Fresh dill or mint: 2 tablespoons, chopped (optional)

For the Dressing:
- Extra virgin olive oil: 1/4 cup
- Fresh lemon juice: 2 tablespoons
- Dijon mustard: 1 teaspoon
- Garlic: 1 clove, minced
- Salt: 1/2 teaspoon (or to taste)
- Black pepper: 1/4 teaspoon
- Red pepper flakes: 1/4 teaspoon (optional, for a bit of heat)

Directions:

Cook the potatoes:
Place the halved or quartered potatoes in a large pot and cover with cold water. Add a pinch of salt and bring to a boil over medium-high heat. Reduce heat and simmer for 15-20 minutes, or until the potatoes are fork-tender. Drain and set aside to cool slightly.

Prepare the dressing:
While the potatoes are cooking, whisk together the olive oil, lemon juice, Dijon mustard, minced garlic, salt, black pepper, and red pepper flakes (if using) in a small bowl. Set aside.

Assemble the salad:
In a large mixing bowl, combine the warm potatoes, capers, red onion, chopped parsley, and dill (if using). Drizzle the dressing over the potatoes and gently toss to coat all the ingredients evenly.

Serve warm:
Transfer the warm potato salad to a serving dish. Optionally, garnish with extra fresh herbs or a sprinkle of lemon zest for added brightness.

Nutritional Information (Per Serving): Calories: 230 kcal, Protein: 4g, Carbohydrates: 30g, Total Fat: 10g, Saturated Fat: 1.5g, Fiber: 4g, Cholesterol: 0mg, Sodium: 360mg, Potassium: 750mg.

Watermelon, Feta, and Mint Salad

Prep. time: 10 min | Cook time: None | Serves: 4

Ingredients:

- Watermelon: 4 cups, cubed (about 1/4 of a medium watermelon)
- Feta cheese: 1/3 cup, crumbled
- Fresh mint leaves: 1/4 cup, roughly chopped
- Red onion: 1/4 small, thinly sliced (optional)
- Extra virgin olive oil: 1 tablespoon
- Fresh lime juice: 1 tablespoon (about 1 lime)
- Salt: A pinch
- Black pepper: A pinch (optional)

Customizable Elements:
- Add arugula or spinach for extra greens.
- Substitute lime juice with lemon juice for a slightly different citrus flavor.
- Include cucumber slices.

Directions:

Prepare the watermelon:
Cut the watermelon into bite-sized cubes and place them in a large mixing bowl.

Add the remaining ingredients:
Add the crumbled feta cheese, chopped mint leaves, and sliced red onion (if using) to the bowl with the watermelon.

Make the dressing:
In a small bowl, whisk together the olive oil and fresh lime juice. Add a pinch of salt and black pepper (if using), and stir to combine.

Toss the salad:
Drizzle the dressing over the watermelon mixture and gently toss to coat all the ingredients evenly.

Serve immediately:
Transfer the salad to a serving dish and enjoy right away for the freshest flavor.

Nutritional Information (Per Serving): Calories: 120 kcal, Protein: 3g, Carbohydrates: 12g, Total Fat: 7g, Saturated Fat: 3g, Fiber: 1g, Cholesterol: 15mg, Sodium: 220mg, Potassium: 270mg.

Chapter

4

Soups & Stews

Soups and stews are at the heart of Mediterranean cuisine, known for their comforting warmth and rich, layered flavors. Made with fresh vegetables, lean proteins, legumes, and aromatic herbs, these dishes offer a delicious way to enjoy the essence of the Mediterranean diet in every spoonful. They are not only satisfying and nourishing but also an ideal way to bring together the season's best ingredients in a simple, flavorful form.

In this section, "Soups & Stews," you'll find a variety of recipes that range from light broths to hearty, slow-cooked stews. Each dish is designed to be both easy to prepare and full of the deep, complex flavors that make Mediterranean cooking so beloved. Whether you're looking for a quick, warming bowl on a chilly day or a robust stew to serve as a main course, these recipes will bring the taste of the Mediterranean right to your table.

Creamy Tomato Basil Soup

Prep. time: 10 min | Cook time: 20 min | Serves: 4

Ingredients:

- Olive oil: 1 tablespoon
- Yellow onion: 1 medium, finely chopped
- Garlic: 2 cloves, minced
- Canned diced tomatoes: 2 cans (28 oz total, no salt added)
- Low-sodium vegetable broth: 1 cup
- Tomato paste: 1 tablespoon
- Fresh basil: 1/4 cup, chopped (or 1 teaspoon dried basil)
- Dried oregano: 1/2 teaspoon
- Coconut milk (unsweetened, or almond milk): 1/2 cup (optional for creaminess)
- Salt and black pepper: to taste
- Red pepper flakes (optional): 1/4 teaspoon for heat
- Balsamic vinegar: 1 teaspoon (optional for added sweetness)

Directions:

Sauté the Aromatics:
In a large pot, heat the olive oil over medium heat. Add the onion and garlic and sauté for 5-7 minutes until softened and fragrant.

Add the Tomatoes and Broth: Stir in the canned diced tomatoes, vegetable broth, and tomato paste. Bring to a gentle boil, then reduce heat and simmer for 10-12 minutes.

Blend the Soup: Use an immersion blender to puree the soup until smooth (or transfer the soup to a blender and puree in batches, being careful with hot liquids).

Add Herbs and Creaminess: Stir in the fresh basil, oregano, and coconut milk (if using). Let the soup simmer for another 5 minutes, stirring occasionally. Season with salt, black pepper, and optional red pepper flakes for a slight kick.

Finish with a Flavor Boost:
Stir in balsamic vinegar for a touch of sweetness and tang (optional). Taste and adjust seasonings if needed.

Serve: Ladle the soup into bowls and garnish with additional basil leaves or a drizzle of olive oil.

Nutritional Information (Per Serving): Calories: 230 kcal, Protein: 4g, Carbohydrates: 30g, Total Fat: 10g, Saturated Fat: 1.5g, Fiber: 4g, Cholesterol: 0mg, Sodium: 360mg, Potassium: 750mg.

Classic Greek Lemon Chicken Soup (Avgolemono)

Prep. time: 10 min | Cook time: 25 min | Serves: 4

Ingredients:

- Olive oil: 1 tablespoon
- Boneless, skinless chicken breasts or thighs: 1 lb (about 2 breasts)
- Low-sodium chicken broth: 6 cups
- Carrot: 1 large, peeled and diced
- Celery: 2 stalks, diced
- Garlic: 2 cloves, minced
- Orzo pasta: 1/3 cup (or substitute rice for gluten-free)
- Eggs: 2 large; Lemon juice: 1/4 cup (about 2 lemons)
- Salt: 1/2 teaspoon (or to taste)
- Black pepper: 1/4 teaspoon (or to taste)
- Fresh parsley (optional for garnish): 2 tablespoons, chopped
- Fresh dill (optional for garnish): 1 tablespoon, chopped

Directions:

Cook the Chicken:
Heat olive oil in a large pot over medium heat. Sear the chicken for 2-3 minutes per side until browned.

Add Broth and Vegetables:
Pour in the chicken broth, add the carrot, celery, and garlic. Simmer for 15 minutes until chicken is cooked through.

Shred Chicken and Cook Orzo:
Remove the chicken, shred it, and set aside. Add orzo to the pot and cook for 8-10 minutes until tender.

Prepare Avgolemono: Whisk eggs and lemon juice together. Gradually add 1 cup of hot soup broth while whisking to temper the eggs.

Combine and Serve:
Stir the egg-lemon mixture back into the soup. Add the shredded chicken and simmer for 1-2 minutes without boiling. Season with salt and pepper, garnish with parsley or dill, and serve.

Nutritional Information (Per Serving): Calories: 270 kcal, Protein: 25g, Carbohydrates: 18g, Total Fat: 10g, Saturated Fat: 2g, Fiber: 2g, Cholesterol: 150mg, Sodium: 400mg, Potassium: 500mg.

Hearty Lentil and Vegetable Soup

Prep. time: 10 min | Cook time: 30 min | Serves: 6

Ingredients:

- Olive oil: 1 tablespoon
- Yellow onion: 1 medium, chopped
- Carrots: 2 large, diced
- Garlic: 2 cloves, minced
- Green or brown lentils: 1 1/2 cups, rinsed
- Low-sodium vegetable broth: 6 cups
- Canned diced tomatoes: 1 can (14.5 oz, no salt added)
- Ground cumin: 1 teaspoon
- Dried oregano: 1 teaspoon
- Salt and black pepper: to taste
- Fresh lemon juice: 2 tablespoons
- Fresh parsley (optional for garnish): 2 tablespoons, chopped

Directions:

Sauté the Vegetables:
Heat olive oil in a large pot over medium heat. Add the onion, carrots, and garlic, and sauté for 5 minutes until softened.

Add Lentils and Broth:
Stir in the lentils, vegetable broth, diced tomatoes, cumin, and oregano. Bring to a boil, then reduce the heat and simmer for 25 minutes, or until the lentils are tender.

Season and Finish:
Add lemon juice, salt, and pepper to taste. Stir well and adjust seasoning if necessary.

Serve:
Ladle the soup into bowls and garnish with fresh parsley if desired.

Serving Suggestions:
Serve with whole wheat bread or pita.
Pair with a light salad for a balanced Mediterranean meal.

Nutritional Information (Per Serving): Calories: 200 kcal, Protein: 9g, Carbohydrates: 30g, Total Fat: 4g, Saturated Fat: 0.6g, Fiber: 10g, Cholesterol: 0mg, Sodium: 300mg, Potassium: 650mg.

Spiced Moroccan Chickpea and Carrot Stew

Prep. time: 10 min | Cook time: 25 min | Serves: 4

Ingredients:

- Olive oil: 2 tablespoons
- Yellow onion: 1 medium, chopped
- Garlic: 3 cloves, minced
- Carrots: 3 large, peeled and sliced
- Canned chickpeas: 1 can (15 oz), drained and rinsed
- Canned diced tomatoes: 1 can (14.5 oz, no salt added)
- Low-sodium vegetable broth: 2 cups
- Ground cumin: 1 teaspoon
- Ground coriander: 1/2 teaspoon
- Ground cinnamon: 1/2 teaspoon
- Salt: 1/2 teaspoon (or to taste)
- Black pepper: 1/4 teaspoon (or to taste); Paprika: 1/2 teaspoon
- Fresh cilantro or parsley (optional for garnish): 2 tablespoons, chopped
- Fresh lemon juice: 1 tablespoon

Directions:

Sauté the Aromatics: Heat the olive oil in a large pot or skillet over medium heat. Add the chopped onion and garlic, sautéing for 3-4 minutes until softened and fragrant.

Add the Carrots and Spices: Stir in the sliced carrots, cumin, coriander, cinnamon, and paprika. Cook for another 2-3 minutes to let the spices release their aroma.

Combine with Chickpeas and Tomatoes:
Add the chickpeas and diced tomatoes to the pot, stirring well to combine. Pour in the vegetable broth and bring the mixture to a boil.

Simmer the Stew:
Reduce the heat to low and let the stew simmer for 15-20 minutes, or until the carrots are tender and the flavors are well combined. Stir occasionally to prevent sticking.

Finish with Lemon Juice and Seasoning:
Stir in the fresh lemon juice and season with salt and black pepper to taste. Adjust any spices as needed.

Serve: Ladle the stew into bowls and garnish with fresh cilantro or parsley if desired.

Nutritional Information (Per Serving): Calories: 260 kcal, Protein: 7g, Carbohydrates: 36g, Total Fat: 10g, Saturated Fat: 1.5g, Fiber: 8g, Cholesterol: 0mg, Sodium: 360mg, Potassium: 720mg.

Tuscan White Bean Soup with Kale

Prep. time: 10 min | Cook time: 25 min | Serves: 4

Ingredients:

- Olive oil: 2 tablespoons; Garlic: 3 cloves, minced; Carrots: 2 medium, diced; Dried thyme: 1 teaspoon
- Yellow onion: 1 medium, chopped
- Canned white beans (cannellini or great northern beans): 2 cans (15 oz each), drained and rinsed
- Low-sodium vegetable broth: 4 cups
- Kale: 3 cups, chopped (stems removed); Dried thyme: 1 teaspoon
- Canned diced tomatoes or 4 fresh tomatoes: 1 can (14.5 oz, no salt added) or equivalent fresh, diced
- Dried rosemary: 1/2 teaspoon
- Salt: 1/2 teaspoon; Black pepper: 1/4 teaspoon (or to taste)
- Fresh lemon juice: 1 tablespoon
- Fresh parsley (optional for garnish): 2 tablespoons, chopped

Directions:

Sauté the Aromatics: Heat the olive oil in a large pot over medium heat. Add the onion, garlic, and carrots. Sauté for about 5-7 minutes, stirring occasionally, until the vegetables are softened and the onions are translucent.

Add Beans, Broth, and Tomatoes: Stir in the white beans, vegetable broth, and diced tomatoes (or fresh tomatoes if using). Add the dried thyme and rosemary. Bring the mixture to a boil.

Simmer with Kale: Once boiling, reduce the heat to low and add the chopped kale. Let the soup simmer for 10-15 minutes until the kale is tender and the flavors are well combined.

Finish with Lemon Juice and Seasoning: Stir in the lemon juice for a fresh burst of flavor (if using) and season with salt and black pepper to taste. Adjust the seasoning as needed.

Serve: Remove from heat, ladle the soup into bowls, and garnish with fresh parsley if desired. Drizzle a little extra olive oil on top for added richness.

Nutritional Information (Per Serving): Calories: 260 kcal, Protein: 12g, Carbohydrates: 38g, Total Fat: 8g, Saturated Fat: 1g, Fiber: 11g, Cholesterol: 0mg, Sodium: 310mg, Potassium: 900mg.

Zesty Mediterranean Tomato and Orzo Soup

Prep. time: 10 min | Cook time: 20 min | Serves: 4

Ingredients:

- Olive oil: 2 tablespoons
- Yellow onion: 1 medium, finely chopped; Garlic: 3 cloves, minced
- Carrots: 1 medium, diced
- Canned diced tomatoes or 4 fresh tomatoes: 1 can (14.5 oz, no salt added) or equivalent fresh, diced
- Low-sodium vegetable broth: 4 cups
- Orzo pasta: 1/2 cup (uncooked)
- Dried oregano: 1 teaspoon
- Dried basil: 1 teaspoon
- Salt: 1/2 teaspoon (or to taste)
- Black pepper: 1/4 teaspoon (or to taste); Fresh lemon juice: 1 tablespoon (for added zest)
- Fresh parsley or basil (optional for garnish): 2 tablespoons, chopped
- Red pepper flakes (optional): a pinch for some heat

Directions:

Sauté the Aromatics: Heat the olive oil in a large pot over medium heat. Add the chopped onion, garlic, and carrot. Sauté for about 5 minutes until the vegetables are softened and the onion is translucent.

Add Tomatoes and Broth: Stir in the diced tomatoes (or fresh tomatoes), vegetable broth, oregano, and basil. Bring the mixture to a gentle boil.

Cook the Orzo: Once the broth is boiling, add the orzo pasta to the pot. Cook for about 8-10 minutes, or until the orzo is tender, stirring occasionally to prevent sticking.

Season and Finish: Stir in the lemon juice for a zesty flavor boost, and season with salt, black pepper, and red pepper flakes (if using). Adjust seasoning to taste.

Serve: Ladle the soup into bowls and garnish with fresh parsley or basil. Drizzle with a little extra olive oil if desired.

Serving Suggestions:

Serve with whole grain bread or crusty garlic toast for dipping. Pair with a Greek salad or a side of grilled vegetables. Top with a dollop of Greek yogurt or a sprinkle of feta cheese for a creamy texture.

Nutritional Information (Per Serving): Calories: 210 kcal, Protein: 6g, Carbohydrates: 32g, Total Fat: 7g, Saturated Fat: 1g, Fiber: 5g, Cholesterol: 0mg, Sodium: 320mg, Potassium: 600mg.

Greek-Style Meatball and Spinach Soup

Prep. time: 15 min | Cook time: 25 min | Serves: 4

Ingredients:

For the Meatballs:
- Ground turkey or chicken: 1 lb (lean)
- Garlic: 2 cloves, minced
- Fresh parsley: 2 tablespoons, chopped
- Dried oregano: 1 teaspoon
- Breadcrumbs: 1/4 cup (whole wheat, if possible); Egg: 1 large; Salt: 1/2 teaspoon; Black pepper: 1/4 teaspoon

For the Soup: Olive oil: 1 tablespoon
- Yellow onion: 1 medium, finely chopped; Garlic: 2 cloves, minced
- Carrots: 2 medium, diced
- Low-sodium chicken broth: 6 cups
- Fresh spinach: 3 cups, chopped
- Fresh lemon juice: 2 tablespoons
- Dried thyme: 1/2 teaspoon
- Salt: to taste; Black pepper: to taste
- Fresh dill or parsley (optional for garnish): 2 tablespoons, chopped

Directions:

Make the Meatballs:
Mix ground turkey, garlic, parsley, oregano, breadcrumbs, egg, salt, and pepper in a bowl. Form into 1-inch meatballs.

Cook the Meatballs:
Heat olive oil in a pot. Brown the meatballs on all sides for 4-5 minutes. Remove and set aside.

Sauté Vegetables:
In the same pot, sauté onion, garlic, and carrots for 5 minutes until softened.

Simmer the Soup:
Add chicken broth, thyme, and meatballs. Simmer for 10-12 minutes until meatballs are fully cooked.

Add Spinach and Season:
Stir in spinach and cook until wilted. Add lemon juice, salt, and pepper to taste.

Serve:
Ladle into bowls and garnish with fresh dill or parsley if desired.

Nutritional Information (Per Serving): Calories: 310 kcal, Protein: 28g, Carbohydrates: 15g, Total Fat: 15g, Saturated Fat: 3g, Fiber: 3g, Cholesterol: 95mg, Sodium: 500mg, Potassium: 800mg.

Sunshine Roasted Red Pepper Soup with Herbs

Prep. time: 10 min | Cook time: 25 min | Serves: 4

Ingredients:

- Red bell peppers: 4 large, halved and seeds removed
- Olive oil: 2 tablespoons (divided)
- Yellow onion: 1 medium, chopped
- Garlic: 3 cloves, minced
- Carrots: 1 medium, diced
- Canned diced tomatoes: 1 can (14.5 oz, no salt added)
- Low-sodium vegetable broth: 3 cups
- Dried oregano: 1 teaspoon
- Dried basil: 1 teaspoon
- Fresh lemon juice: 1 tablespoon
- Salt: 1/2 teaspoon (or to taste)
- Black pepper: 1/4 teaspoon (or to taste)
- Fresh parsley or basil (optional for garnish): 2 tablespoons, chopped

Directions:

Roast the Red Peppers: Preheat your oven to 425°F (220°C). Place the red pepper halves on a baking sheet, skin side up. Drizzle with 1 tablespoon of olive oil and roast for 15-20 minutes, until the skins are blistered and slightly charred.

Once roasted, remove from the oven and let the peppers cool slightly. Peel off the skins and set the peppers aside.

Sauté the Vegetables: In a large pot, heat the remaining 1 tablespoon of olive oil over medium heat. Add the chopped onion, garlic, and diced carrot. Sauté for about 5-7 minutes, until the vegetables are softened.

Combine Ingredients:
Stir in the roasted red peppers, canned tomatoes, vegetable broth, oregano, and basil. Bring the mixture to a boil, then reduce the heat and simmer for 10 minutes.

Blend the Soup: Use an immersion blender to puree the soup until smooth. Alternatively, carefully transfer the soup to a blender and blend in batches until creamy.

Season and Finish: Stir in the lemon juice, salt, and black pepper. Adjust seasonings to taste.

Nutritional Information (Per Serving): Calories: 180 kcal, Protein: 3g, Carbohydrates: 24g, Total Fat: 8g, Saturated Fat: 1g, Fiber: 6g, Cholesterol: 0mg, Sodium: 280mg, Potassium: 700mg.

Quick & Easy Mediterranean Fish Soup

Prep. time: 10 min | Cook time: 20 min | Serves: 4

Ingredients:

- Olive oil: 2 tablespoons
- Yellow onion: 1 medium, finely chopped; Garlic: 3 cloves, minced
- Carrots: 1 medium, diced
- Canned diced tomatoes: 1 can (14.5 oz, no salt added);
- Low-sodium vegetable or fish broth: 4 cups
- White fish fillets (such as cod or tilapia): 1 lb, cut into bite-sized pieces
- Dried oregano: 1 teaspoon
- Dried thyme: 1/2 teaspoon
- Paprika: 1/2 teaspoon
- Fresh lemon juice: 2 tablespoons
- Salt: 1/2 teaspoon (or to taste)
- Black pepper: 1/4 teaspoon (or to taste)
- Fresh parsley or cilantro (optional for garnish): 2 tablespoons, chopped

Directions:

Sauté the Vegetables:

In a large pot, heat the olive oil over medium heat. Add the chopped onion, garlic, and diced carrot. Sauté for about 5-7 minutes until the vegetables are softened and fragrant.

Add Tomatoes and Broth:

Stir in the canned diced tomatoes and the vegetable or fish broth. Add the dried oregano, thyme, and paprika. Bring the mixture to a boil.

Cook the Fish:

Once the soup is boiling, reduce the heat to a simmer. Add the fish pieces and let them cook for about 8-10 minutes, or until the fish is opaque and flakes easily with a fork.

Season and Finish:

Stir in the lemon juice, salt, and black pepper. Adjust the seasoning to taste.

Serve:

Ladle the soup into bowls and garnish with fresh parsley or cilantro if desired. Drizzle a bit of olive oil on top for extra richness.

Nutritional Information (Per Serving): Calories: 220 kcal, Protein: 23g, Carbohydrates: 12g, Total Fat: 9g, Saturated Fat: 1.5g, Fiber: 3g, Cholesterol: 50mg, Sodium: 360mg, Potassium: 800mg.

Saffron-Infused Mediterranean Seafood Stew

Prep. time: 10 min | Cook time: 20 min | Serves: 4

Ingredients:

- Olive oil: 2 tablespoons
- Yellow onion: 1 medium, chopped
- Garlic: 3 cloves, minced
- Tomatoes: 4-5 medium, chopped (or 1 can, 14.5 oz, diced tomatoes, no salt added)
- Low-sodium vegetable broth: 4 cups
- Saffron threads: a pinch (optional but adds great flavor)
- White fish fillets (such as cod or tilapia): 1 lb, cut into bite-sized pieces
- Shrimp: 1/2 lb, peeled and deveined
- Dried oregano: 1 teaspoon
- Salt: 1/2 teaspoon (or to taste)
- Black pepper: 1/4 teaspoon (or to taste)
- Fresh lemon juice: 2 tablespoons
- Fresh parsley (optional for garnish): 2 tablespoons, chopped

Directions:

Sauté the Onion and Garlic:

Heat the olive oil in a large pot over medium heat. Add the chopped onion and garlic, and sauté for about 3-4 minutes until softened.

Add Tomatoes and Broth:

Stir in the chopped fresh tomatoes (or canned tomatoes), vegetable broth, saffron (if using), oregano, salt, and black pepper. Bring the mixture to a boil.

Cook the Seafood:

Add the fish pieces and shrimp to the pot. Reduce the heat to a simmer and cook for about 8-10 minutes until the fish is cooked through and the shrimp are pink and opaque.

Finish and Serve:

Stir in the lemon juice and taste for seasoning, adjusting if needed. Garnish with fresh parsley if desired.

Serving Suggestions: Serve with whole grain bread or garlic toast for dipping. Pair with a simple salad for a light, balanced Mediterranean meal.

Nutritional Information (Per Serving): Calories: 270 kcal, Protein: 30g, Carbohydrates: 14g, Total Fat: 10g, Saturated Fat: 1.5g, Fiber: 3g, Cholesterol: 150mg, Sodium: 420mg, Potassium: 700mg.

Savory Mushroom and Garlic Soup

Prep. time: 10 min | Cook time: 20 min | Serves: 4

Ingredients:

- Olive oil: 2 tablespoons
- Yellow onion: 1 medium, finely chopped
- Garlic: 4 cloves, minced
- Mushrooms: 12 oz (such as cremini, button, or a mix), sliced
- Low-sodium vegetable broth: 4 cups
- Dried thyme: 1 teaspoon
- Dried oregano: 1/2 teaspoon
- Fresh parsley (optional for garnish): 2 tablespoons, chopped
- Fresh lemon juice: 1 tablespoon
- Salt: 1/2 teaspoon (or to taste)
- Black pepper: 1/4 teaspoon (or to taste)

Directions:

Sauté the Onion and Garlic:

Heat the olive oil in a large pot over medium heat. Add the chopped onion and garlic, and sauté for about 5 minutes until softened and fragrant.

Cook the Mushrooms:

Add the sliced mushrooms to the pot and cook for 5-7 minutes, stirring occasionally, until the mushrooms are soft and browned.

Add Broth and Herbs:

Stir in the vegetable broth, dried thyme, and oregano. Bring the mixture to a gentle boil, then reduce the heat and let it simmer for 10 minutes to allow the flavors to blend.

Finish with Lemon and Seasoning:

Stir in the lemon juice, salt, and black pepper. Taste and adjust the seasoning as needed.

Serve:

Ladle the soup into bowls and garnish with fresh parsley if desired. Drizzle with a bit of olive oil for added richness.

Nutritional Information (Per Serving): Calories: 160 kcal, Protein: 5g, Carbohydrates: 12g, Total Fat: 10g, Saturated Fat: 1.5g, Fiber: 3g, Cholesterol: 0mg, Sodium: 360mg, Potassium: 700mg.

Greek Green Bean Stew with Potatoes and Olive Oil

Prep. time: 10 min | Cook time: 35 min | Serves: 4

Ingredients:

- Olive oil: 1/4 cup (key Mediterranean ingredient)
- Yellow onion: 1 medium, finely chopped; Garlic: 3 cloves, minced
- Potatoes: 2 medium, peeled and cut into chunks
- Green beans: 1 lb, trimmed
- Tomatoes: 4-5 medium, chopped (or 1 can, 14.5 oz, diced tomatoes)
- Low-sodium vegetable broth: 2 cups
- Dried oregano: 1 teaspoon
- Dried dill: 1/2 teaspoon (or fresh dill for garnish)
- Salt: 1/2 teaspoon (or to taste)
- Black pepper: 1/4 teaspoon (or to taste)
- Fresh parsley (optional for garnish): 2 tablespoons, chopped

Directions:

Sauté the Onion and Garlic:

Heat the olive oil in a large pot or Dutch oven over medium heat. Add the chopped onion and garlic, and sauté for about 5 minutes until softened and fragrant.

Add Potatoes and Green Beans:

Stir in the potatoes and green beans, cooking for another 3-4 minutes to coat them in the olive oil and enhance their flavors.

Combine Tomatoes and Broth:

Add the chopped tomatoes (or canned tomatoes) and vegetable broth to the pot. Stir in the dried oregano, dill, salt, and black pepper. Bring the mixture to a boil.

Simmer the Stew:

Reduce the heat to low, cover the pot, and let it simmer for about 25-30 minutes, or until the potatoes and green beans are tender and the flavors are well combined.

Finish and Serve: Taste and adjust the seasoning if needed. Garnish with fresh parsley or dill, if desired, before serving.

Nutritional Information (Per Serving): Calories: 250 kcal, Protein: 5g, Carbohydrates: 32g, Total Fat: 12g, Saturated Fat: 1.5g, Fiber: 7g, Cholesterol: 0mg, Sodium: 380mg, Potassium: 800mg.

Cumin-Spiced Butternut Squash and Lentil Soup

Prep. time: 10 min | Cook time: 30 min | Serves: 4

Ingredients:

- Olive oil: 2 tablespoons
- Yellow onion: 1 medium, chopped
- Garlic: 3 cloves, minced
- Butternut squash: 3 cups, peeled and cubed
- Carrots: 2 medium, diced
- Red lentils: 1 cup, rinsed
- Low-sodium vegetable broth: 4 cups
- Cumin: 2 teaspoons
- Ground coriander: 1 teaspoon
- Turmeric: 1/2 teaspoon
- Salt: 1/2 teaspoon (or to taste)
- Black pepper: 1/4 teaspoon (or to taste)
- Fresh lemon juice: 1 tablespoon
- Fresh cilantro or parsley (optional for garnish): 2 tablespoons, chopped

Directions:

Sauté the Onion and Garlic:
Heat the olive oil in a large pot over medium heat. Add the chopped onion and garlic, and sauté for about 5 minutes until softened and fragrant.

Add the Butternut Squash and Carrots:
Stir in the cubed butternut squash and diced carrots. Cook for another 5 minutes, stirring occasionally to coat the vegetables in the oil and enhance their flavors.
Add Lentils, Spices, and Broth: Add the red lentils, cumin, coriander, turmeric, salt, and black pepper. Pour in the vegetable broth and stir well to combine.

Simmer the Soup: Bring the soup to a boil, then reduce the heat to low. Cover and simmer for about 20 minutes, or until the lentils and vegetables are tender.

Blend the Soup (Optional):
For a smoother **texture**, use an immersion blender to blend the soup partially or fully, depending on your preference. If you prefer a chunkier soup, leave it as is.

Finish and Serve: Stir in the fresh lemon juice to brighten the flavors. Taste and adjust seasoning if needed. Garnish with fresh cilantro or parsley if desired.

Nutritional Information (Per Serving): Calories: 280 kcal, Protein: 12g, Carbohydrates: 42g, Total Fat: 7g, Saturated Fat: 1g, Fiber: 12g, Cholesterol: 0mg, Sodium: 350mg, Potassium: 850mg.

Quinoa Soup with Fresh Vegetables

Prep. time: 10 min | Cook time: 25 min | Serves: 4

Ingredients:

- Olive oil: 2 tablespoons
- Yellow onion: 1 medium, chopped
- Garlic: 3 cloves, minced
- Carrots: 2 medium, diced
- Celery: 2 stalks, diced
- Zucchini: 1 medium, diced
- Red bell pepper: 1 medium, chopped
- Tomatoes: 4-5 medium, chopped (or 1 can, 14.5 oz, diced tomatoes, no salt added); Quinoa: 1/2 cup, rinsed
- Low-sodium vegetable broth: 4 cups
- Dried oregano: 1 teaspoon
- Dried basil: 1 teaspoon
- Salt: 1/2 teaspoon; Black pepper: 1/4 teaspoon (or to taste);
- Fresh lemon juice: 1 tablespoon
- Fresh parsley or cilantro (optional for garnish): 2 tablespoons, chopped

Directions:

Sauté the Aromatics:
Heat the olive oil in a large pot over medium heat. Add the chopped onion and garlic, and sauté for about 5 minutes until softened and fragrant.

Cook the Vegetables:
Add the diced carrots, celery, zucchini, and red bell pepper to the pot. Cook for another 5-7 minutes, stirring occasionally, until the vegetables start to soften.

Add Quinoa, Tomatoes, and Broth:
Stir in the rinsed quinoa, fresh tomatoes (or canned tomatoes), vegetable broth, oregano, basil, salt, and black pepper. Bring the mixture to a boil.

Simmer the Soup:
Reduce the heat to low and let the soup simmer for about 15-20 minutes, or until the quinoa is cooked and the vegetables are tender.

Finish with Lemon and Seasoning: Stir in the fresh lemon juice to brighten the flavors. Taste and adjust seasoning if needed.

Nutritional Information (Per Serving): Calories: 210 kcal, Protein: 7g, Carbohydrates: 28g, Total Fat: 8g, Saturated Fat: 1g, Fiber: 6g, Cholesterol: 0mg, Sodium: 320mg, Potassium: 750mg.

Chapter 5

Grains, Pasta, and Rice Recipes

Grains, pasta, and rice are essential elements of the Mediterranean diet, providing a nourishing foundation for a wide range of dishes. With ingredients like whole grains, fiber-rich pasta, and aromatic rice varieties, these recipes offer both sustenance and flavor in every bite. The Mediterranean approach to grains emphasizes balance, combining them with fresh vegetables, herbs, and healthy fats to create meals that are satisfying, wholesome, and packed with nutrition.

In this section, "Grains, Pasta, and Rice Recipes," you'll explore diverse and flavorful ways to prepare these staple ingredients. From hearty grain salads to comforting pasta dishes and fragrant rice creations, these recipes are designed to bring the best of Mediterranean cuisine to your table. Whether you're looking for a quick weekday meal or something more elaborate, these dishes offer endless versatility and a delicious celebration of simple, high-quality ingredients.

Creamy Lemon Basil Rice Risotto

Prep. time: 10 min | Cook time: 25 min | Serves: 4

Ingredients:

- Arborio rice: 1 cup
- Olive oil: 2 tablespoons
- Garlic: 2 cloves, minced
- Onion: 1 small, finely chopped
- Vegetable or chicken broth: 4 cups (warmed)
- White wine (optional): 1/4 cup
- Fresh lemon juice: 2 tablespoons
- Lemon zest: 1 teaspoon
- Fresh basil: 1/4 cup, chopped
- Parmesan cheese: 1/4 cup, grated
- Salt: 1/2 teaspoon
- Black pepper: 1/4 teaspoon

Directions:

Sauté the Aromatics:

In a large skillet or saucepan, heat the olive oil over medium heat. Add the chopped onion and garlic, and cook until softened and fragrant, about 3-4 minutes.

Toast the Rice: Add the Arborio rice to the pan and stir, toasting it for 1-2 minutes until the rice is lightly golden.

Add Wine (Optional):

Pour in the white wine (if using) and cook until the liquid has mostly evaporated.

Add Broth Gradually: Begin adding the warm broth, 1/2 cup at a time, stirring continuously. Allow the rice to absorb the broth before adding more. Continue this process for 20-25 minutes until the rice is tender and creamy.

Finish the Risotto: Stir in the lemon juice, lemon zest, grated Parmesan cheese, salt, and black pepper. Mix well and cook for another 1-2 minutes.

Add Basil: Remove the risotto from heat and gently fold in the fresh basil.

Serve: Serve immediately, garnished with extra Parmesan and fresh basil if desired.

Nutritional Information (Per Serving): Calories: 330 kcal, Protein: 8g, Carbohydrates: 50g, Total Fat: 10g, Saturated Fat: 3g, Fiber: 2g, Cholesterol: 10mg, Sodium: 700mg, Potassium: 150mg.

Mediterranean Brown Rice with Roasted Garlic

Prep. time: 10 min | Cook time: 45 min | Serves: 4

Ingredients:

For the Brown Rice:
- Brown rice: 1 cup (uncooked)
- Water or vegetable broth: 2 1/2 cups (for cooking rice)
- Extra virgin olive oil: 2 tablespoons
- Roasted garlic: 1 whole head of garlic
- Fresh parsley: 1/4 cup, chopped
- Fresh thyme or oregano: 2 tablespoons, chopped (optional)
- Lemon zest: 1 teaspoon
- Lemon juice: 1 tablespoon (about 1/2 lemon)
- Salt: 1/2 teaspoon (or to taste)
- Black pepper: 1/4 teaspoon

For Roasting Garlic:
- Garlic head: 1, whole and unpeeled
- Olive oil: 1 teaspoon
- Salt: A pinch

Directions:

Roast the Garlic: Preheat your oven to 400°F (200°C). Slice the top off the garlic head to expose the cloves. Drizzle with 1 teaspoon of olive oil and sprinkle with a pinch of salt. Wrap the garlic head in foil and place it in the oven. Roast for about 35-40 minutes, or until the garlic cloves are soft and golden. Let it cool slightly, then squeeze the roasted garlic cloves out of their skins and mash them with a fork.

Cook the Brown Rice: In a medium saucepan, bring 2 1/2 cups of water or vegetable broth to a boil. Add the brown rice, reduce the heat to low, cover, and simmer for 40-45 minutes, or until the rice is tender and has absorbed all the liquid. Remove from heat and let it sit, covered, for 5 minutes. Fluff the rice with a fork and set aside.

Assemble the Dish: In a large mixing bowl, combine the cooked brown rice with the mashed roasted garlic. Drizzle 2 tablespoons of olive oil over the rice and add the chopped parsley, thyme (if using), lemon zest, and lemon juice. Season with salt and black pepper to taste. Gently toss the rice to ensure the roasted garlic and herbs are evenly distributed. Transfer the rice to a serving platter and garnish with additional fresh herbs if desired. Serve warm.

Nutritional Information (Per Serving): Calories: 260 kcal, Protein: 4g, Carbohydrates: 40g, Total Fat: 10g, Saturated Fat: 1.5g, Fiber: 4g, Cholesterol: 0mg, Sodium: 300mg, Potassium: 200mg.

Quinoa with Roasted Red Peppers and Feta

Prep. time: 10 min | Cook time: 30 min | Serves: 4

Ingredients:

- Quinoa: 1 cup (uncooked)
- Water or vegetable broth: 2 cups (for cooking quinoa)
- Roasted red peppers: 2 large, chopped (you can use store-bought jarred roasted red peppers or roast them at home)
- Feta cheese: 1/3 cup, crumbled
- Fresh parsley: 1/4 cup, chopped
- Fresh basil: 2 tablespoons, chopped (optional)
- Extra virgin olive oil: 2 tablespoons
- Lemon juice: 1 tablespoon (about 1/2 lemon)
- Garlic: 1 clove, minced
- Salt: 1/2 teaspoon (or to taste)
- Black pepper: 1/4 teaspoon

Directions:

Cook the Quinoa:
Rinse quinoa under cold water.
In a saucepan, bring 2 cups of water (or broth) to a boil. Add quinoa, reduce heat, cover, and simmer for 15 minutes until liquid is absorbed. Let sit covered for 5 minutes, then fluff with a fork.

Prepare the Roasted Red Peppers:
Using jarred: Drain and chop.
Roasting at home: Roast whole peppers at 450°F (230°C) for 20-25 minutes until charred. Steam in a covered bowl for 10 minutes, peel, seed, and chop.

Make the Dressing:
Whisk together olive oil, lemon juice, garlic, salt, and pepper.

Assemble the Dish:
Mix cooked quinoa, roasted peppers, feta, parsley, and basil.
Drizzle with dressing and toss gently. Adjust seasoning as needed.
Serve warm or at room temperature.

Nutritional Information (Per Serving): Calories: 280 kcal, Protein: 9g, Carbohydrates: 30g, Total Fat: 14g, Saturated Fat: 3g, Fiber: 5g, Cholesterol: 15mg, Sodium: 360mg, Potassium: 400mg.

Farro with Sun-Dried Tomatoes and Basil

Prep. time: 5 min | Cook time: 20 min | Serves: 4

Ingredients:

- Farro: 1 cup (uncooked)
- Water or vegetable broth: 3 cups (for cooking farro)
- Sun-dried tomatoes: 1/3 cup, chopped (packed in oil, drained)
- Fresh basil: 1/4 cup, chopped
- Garlic: 2 cloves, minced
- Extra virgin olive oil: 3 tablespoons
- Fresh lemon juice: 1 tablespoon
- Parmesan cheese: 1/4 cup, grated (optional)
- Salt: 1/2 teaspoon (or to taste)
- Black pepper: 1/4 teaspoon
- Red pepper flakes: 1/4 teaspoon (optional, for a bit of heat)

Directions:

Cook the Farro:
Rinse farro under cold water.
In a saucepan, bring 3 cups of water (or broth) to a boil. Add farro, reduce heat, cover, and simmer for 25-30 minutes until tender. Drain any excess liquid.

Prepare Sun-Dried Tomatoes and Garlic:
Heat 3 tablespoons of olive oil in a skillet.
Sauté minced garlic for 1 minute until fragrant, then add chopped sun-dried tomatoes and cook for 1-2 more minutes.

Assemble the Dish:
Stir cooked farro into the skillet, coating it with the garlic and tomato mixture.
Remove from heat and mix in fresh basil, lemon juice, Parmesan (optional), salt, pepper, and red pepper flakes (optional).
Serve warm, garnishing with more basil or Parmesan if desired.

Nutritional Information (Per Serving): Calories: 320 kcal, Protein: 8g, Carbohydrates: 45g, Total Fat: 12g, Saturated Fat: 2g, Fiber: 8g, Cholesterol: 5mg (if using Parmesan), Sodium: 300mg, Potassium: 450mg.

Orzo with Spinach and Pine Nuts

Prep. time: 10 min | Cook time: None | Serves: 6

Ingredients:

- Orzo pasta: 1 cup (uncooked)
- Fresh spinach: 4 cups (about 4 ounces), roughly chopped
- Pine nuts: 1/4 cup, toasted
- Garlic: 2 cloves, minced
- Extra virgin olive oil: 2 tablespoons
- Lemon juice: 2 tablespoons (about 1 lemon)
- Lemon zest: 1 teaspoon
- Salt: 1/2 teaspoon (or to taste)
- Black pepper: 1/4 teaspoon
- Fresh parsley: 1/4 cup, chopped (optional)
- Grated Parmesan cheese: 1/4 cup (optional)

Directions:

Cook the Orzo:

Boil orzo in salted water for 8-10 minutes until al dente. Drain and set aside.

Toast the Pine Nuts:

Toast pine nuts in a dry skillet over medium heat for 3-4 minutes until golden. Set aside.

Sauté the Spinach and Garlic:

Sauté minced garlic in 2 tablespoons of olive oil for 1 minute. Add spinach and cook for 2-3 minutes until wilted.

Assemble the Dish:

Add cooked orzo to the skillet with spinach, then stir in pine nuts, lemon juice, zest, salt, pepper, and parsley. Toss to combine.

Optional:

Add grated Parmesan if desired.

Serve warm and garnish with extra parsley or pine nuts if desired.

Nutritional Information (Per Serving): Calories: 320 kcal, Protein: 8g, Carbohydrates: 38g, Total Fat: 14g, Saturated Fat: 2g, Fiber: 4g, Cholesterol: 5mg (if using Parmesan), Sodium: 350mg, Potassium: 450mg.

Mediterranean Barley with Lemon and Olive Oil

Prep. time: 10 min | Cook time: 30 min | Serves: 4

Ingredients:

- Pearl barley: 1 cup (uncooked)
- Water or vegetable broth: 3 cups (for cooking barley)
- Extra virgin olive oil: 3 tablespoons
- Fresh lemon juice: 2 tablespoons (about 1 lemon)
- Lemon zest: 1 teaspoon
- Garlic: 2 cloves, minced
- Fresh parsley: 1/4 cup, chopped
- Fresh basil or mint: 2 tablespoons, chopped (optional)
- Salt: 1/2 teaspoon (or to taste)
- Black pepper: 1/4 teaspoon
- Red pepper flakes: 1/4 teaspoon (optional, for a bit of heat)
- Feta cheese: 1/4 cup, crumbled (optional)

Directions:

Cook the Barley: Rinse the barley under cold water to remove excess starch.

In a medium saucepan, bring 3 cups of water or vegetable broth to a boil. Stir in the barley, reduce heat to low, cover, and simmer for 30-35 minutes, or until the barley is tender but still slightly chewy. Drain any excess liquid and set aside.

Prepare the Lemon-Olive Oil Dressing: In a small bowl, whisk together the olive oil, fresh lemon juice, lemon zest, minced garlic, salt, black pepper, and red pepper flakes (if using).

Assemble the Dish: In a large mixing bowl, combine the cooked barley with the lemon-olive oil dressing. Toss to coat the barley evenly.

Add herbs and cheese: Stir in the chopped parsley, basil or mint (if using), and crumbled feta (if using). Taste and adjust seasoning with more salt or lemon juice if needed.

Serve warm or at room temperature: Transfer the barley mixture to a serving dish and garnish with additional herbs or feta if desired.

Nutritional Information (Per Serving): Calories: 280 kcal, Protein: 6g, Carbohydrates: 42g, Total Fat: 11g, Saturated Fat: 2g, Fiber: 8g, Cholesterol: 5mg (if using feta), Sodium: 320mg, Potassium: 400mg.

Bulgur Pilaf with Fresh Herbs and Chickpeas

Prep. time: 10 min | Cook time: 20 min | Serves: 4

Ingredients:

- Bulgur wheat: 1 cup (uncooked)
- Water or vegetable broth: 2 cups (for cooking bulgur)
- Chickpeas: 1 (15-ounce) can, drained and rinsed (or 1 1/2 cups cooked chickpeas)
- Extra virgin olive oil: 3 tablespoons
- Fresh lemon juice: 2 tablespoons (about 1 lemon)
- Garlic: 2 cloves, minced
- Fresh parsley: 1/4 cup, chopped
- Fresh mint: 2 tablespoons, chopped (optional)
- Green onions: 1/4 cup, finely chopped
- Salt: 1/2 teaspoon (or to taste)
- Black pepper: 1/4 teaspoon
- Red pepper flakes: 1/4 teaspoon (optional, for a bit of heat)

Directions:

Cook the Bulgur:
In a medium saucepan, bring 2 cups of water or vegetable broth to a boil. Stir in the bulgur, reduce the heat to low, cover, and simmer for 12-15 minutes, or until the bulgur is tender and has absorbed the liquid. Remove from heat and let it sit, covered, for 5 minutes. Fluff with a fork.

Prepare the Dressing: In a small bowl, whisk together the olive oil, lemon juice, minced garlic, salt, black pepper, and red pepper flakes (if using).

Assemble the Dish: In a large mixing bowl, combine the cooked bulgur with the drained chickpeas, chopped parsley, mint (if using), and green onions. Pour the lemon-olive oil dressing over the mixture and toss to combine.

Taste and adjust: Taste the pilaf and adjust the seasoning with more salt, lemon juice, or pepper if desired.

Serve warm or at room temperature: Transfer the bulgur pilaf to a serving dish and garnish with additional fresh herbs if desired. Serve immediately or store in the fridge for up to 2 days for a chilled version.

Nutritional Information (Per Serving): Calories: 290 kcal, Protein: 9g, Carbohydrates: 42g, Total Fat: 10g, Saturated Fat: 1.5g, Fiber: 10g, Cholesterol: 0mg, Sodium: 360mg, Potassium: 420mg.

Lemon Saffron Rice with Olives

Prep. time: 10 min | Cook time: 20 min | Serves: 4

Ingredients:

- Basmati or long-grain white rice: 1 cup (uncooked)
- Water or vegetable broth: 2 cups (for cooking rice)
- Saffron threads: 1/4 teaspoon
- Extra virgin olive oil: 2 tablespoons
- Fresh lemon juice: 2 tablespoons (about 1 lemon)
- Lemon zest: 1 teaspoon
- Kalamata olives: 1/4 cup, pitted and halved
- Garlic: 2 cloves, minced
- Onion: 1 small, finely chopped
- Salt: 1/2 teaspoon (or to taste)
- Black pepper: 1/4 teaspoon
- Fresh parsley: 1/4 cup, chopped (optional for garnish)

Directions:

Infuse the Saffron: In a small bowl, soak the saffron threads in 2 tablespoons of warm water for 5 minutes to release their flavor and color.

Cook the Rice: In a medium saucepan, heat 1 tablespoon of olive oil over medium heat. Add the chopped onion and sauté for 3-4 minutes until softened and translucent. Stir in the minced garlic and cook for another 1 minute until fragrant. Add the uncooked rice to the saucepan and stir to coat the rice in the oil, allowing it to toast slightly for about 1-2 minutes. Pour the saffron mixture (including the water) into the saucepan, followed by 2 cups of water or vegetable broth, lemon zest, salt, and black pepper. Bring to a boil, then reduce the heat to low, cover, and simmer for 15-20 minutes, or until the rice is tender and has absorbed all the liquid. Once the rice is cooked, remove the saucepan from heat and let it sit, covered, for 5 minutes. Fluff the rice with a fork.

Assemble the Dish: Stir in the fresh lemon juice, Kalamata olives, and the remaining 1 tablespoon of olive oil. Toss gently to combine. Transfer the rice to a serving dish and garnish with fresh parsley if desired. Serve warm.

Nutritional Information (Per Serving): Calories: 220 kcal, Protein: 4g, Carbohydrates: 34g, Total Fat: 8g, Saturated Fat: 1g, Fiber: 2g, Cholesterol: 0mg, Sodium: 360mg, Potassium: 200mg.

Pasta with Pesto and Sundried Tomatoes

Prep. time: 10 min | Cook time: 12 min | Serves: 4

Ingredients:

For the Pasta:
- Pasta (whole wheat or regular): 8 oz (about 2 cups, uncooked)
- Sundried tomatoes: 1/3 cup, chopped (packed in oil, drained)
- Cherry tomatoes: 1 cup, halved ; Parmesan cheese: 1/4 cup, grated (optional)
- Fresh basil: 1/4 cup, chopped (for garnish)

For the Pesto:
- Fresh basil: 2 cups, loosely packed
- Pine nuts, walnuts or almonds: 1/4 cup ; Garlic: 2 cloves
- Extra virgin olive oil: 1/4 cup
- Parmesan cheese: 1/4 cup, grated
- Lemon juice: 1 tablespoon
- Salt: 1/2 teaspoon (or to taste)
- Black pepper: 1/4 teaspoon

Directions:

Prepare the Pesto: In a food processor or blender, combine the fresh basil, pine nuts, garlic, and Parmesan cheese (if using). Pulse until the ingredients are coarsely chopped. With the machine running, slowly add the olive oil and lemon juice until the pesto reaches a smooth, creamy consistency. Season with salt and black pepper to taste.

Cook the Pasta: Bring a large pot of salted water to a boil. Add the pasta and cook according to the package instructions (about 8-10 minutes) until al dente. Drain the pasta, reserving 1/4 cup of the cooking water.

Prepare the Sundried Tomatoes: In a large skillet, heat 1 tablespoon of the reserved sun-dried tomato oil over medium heat. Add the chopped sun-dried tomatoes and cherry tomatoes (if using) and sauté for 2-3 minutes until they are softened.

Combine the Pasta and Pesto: Add the cooked pasta to the skillet with the sun-dried tomatoes. Toss gently to combine. Stir in the prepared pesto and mix until the pasta is evenly coated. If the pasta seems too dry, add a little of the reserved pasta water to loosen the sauce. **Garnish and serve:** Remove the skillet from heat and garnish with fresh basil and grated Parmesan cheese (if desired).

Nutritional Information (Per Serving): Calories: 390 kcal, Protein: 12g, Carbohydrates: 50g, Total Fat: 16g, Saturated Fat: 3g, Fiber: 7g, Cholesterol: 5mg (if using Parmesan), Sodium: 350mg, Potassium: 450mg.

Greek-Style Brown Rice with Feta and Spinach

Prep. time: 10 min | Cook time: 35 min | Serves: 4

Ingredients:

- Brown rice: 1 cup (uncooked)
- Water or vegetable broth: 2 1/2 cups (for cooking rice)
- Extra virgin olive oil: 2 tablespoons
- Garlic: 2 cloves, minced
- Fresh spinach: 4 cups (about 4 oz), roughly chopped
- Feta cheese: 1/3 cup, crumbled
- Lemon juice: 2 tablespoons (about 1/2 lemon)
- Lemon zest: 1 teaspoon
- Fresh dill or parsley: 2 tablespoons, chopped
- Green onions: 1/4 cup, finely chopped
- Salt: 1/2 teaspoon (or to taste)
- Black pepper: 1/4 teaspoon
- Red pepper flakes: 1/4 teaspoon (optional)

Directions:

Cook the Brown Rice: In a medium saucepan, bring 2 1/2 cups of water or vegetable broth to a boil. Add the brown rice, reduce the heat to low, cover, and simmer for 35-40 minutes, or until the rice is tender and has absorbed all the liquid. Remove from heat and let it sit, covered, for 5 minutes. Fluff with a fork.

Sauté the Spinach and Garlic:

In a large skillet, heat 2 tablespoons of olive oil over medium heat. Add the minced garlic and sauté for about 1 minute until fragrant but not browned.

Add the chopped spinach to the skillet and cook for 2-3 minutes, stirring occasionally, until wilted.

Assemble the Dish: Add the cooked brown rice to the skillet with the sautéed spinach. Stir to combine. Stir in the lemon juice, lemon zest, crumbled feta, fresh dill or parsley, green onions, salt, black pepper, and red pepper flakes (if using). Toss gently until everything is well combined.

Serve warm: Transfer the Greek-style brown rice to a serving dish and garnish with additional herbs or feta if desired. Serve warm or at room temperature.

Nutritional Information (Per Serving): Calories: 280 kcal, Protein: 7g, Carbohydrates: 40g, Total Fat: 10g, Saturated Fat: 3g, Fiber: 5g, Cholesterol: 15mg, Sodium: 350mg, Potassium: 400mg.

Roasted Red Pepper Quinoa with Basil and Garlic

Prep. time: 10 min | Cook time: 30 min | Serves: 4

Ingredients:

- Quinoa: 1 cup (uncooked)
- Water or vegetable broth: 2 cups (for cooking quinoa)
- Roasted red peppers: 2 large, chopped (you can use jarred or roast your own)
- Garlic: 2 cloves, minced
- Extra virgin olive oil: 2 tablespoons
- Fresh basil: 1/4 cup, chopped
- Lemon juice: 2 tablespoons (about 1 lemon)
- Lemon zest: 1 teaspoon (optional)
- Salt: 1/2 teaspoon (or to taste)
- Black pepper: 1/4 teaspoon
- Red pepper flakes: 1/4 teaspoon (optional, for a bit of heat)
- Pine nuts: 2 tablespoons, toasted (optional, for garnish)

Directions:

Cook the Quinoa: Rinse quinoa. Boil 2 cups of water or broth, add quinoa, reduce heat, cover, and simmer for 15-20 minutes. Let sit for 5 minutes, then fluff.

Prepare the Roasted Red Peppers: Preheat the oven to 450°F (230°C). Place whole red peppers on a baking sheet and roast for about 20-25 minutes, turning occasionally, until the skin is charred. Remove the peppers and place them in a covered bowl or plastic bag to steam for 10 minutes. Peel off the skin, remove the seeds, and chop the peppers.

Sauté the Garlic: In a large skillet, heat the olive oil over medium heat. Add the minced garlic and sauté for 1 minute, or until fragrant but not browned.

Assemble the Dish: Combine cooked quinoa, chopped peppers, basil, lemon juice, zest, salt, pepper, and red pepper flakes in the skillet with garlic. Toss to combine.

Optional: Toast pine nuts: In a small dry skillet, toast the pine nuts over medium heat for 2-3 minutes, stirring frequently, until golden brown. Remove from heat and set aside for garnish. Transfer the quinoa mixture to a serving dish and garnish with toasted pine nuts and additional fresh basil if desired. Serve warm or at room temperature.

Nutritional Information (Per Serving): Calories: 250 kcal, Protein: 7g, Carbohydrates: 35g, Total Fat: 9g, Saturated Fat: 1g, Fiber: 5g, Cholesterol: 0mg, Sodium: 320mg, Potassium: 450mg.

Whole Wheat Spaghetti with Olive Oil and Garlic

Prep. time: 5 min | Cook time: 15 min | Serves: 4

Ingredients:

- Whole wheat spaghetti: 8 oz (about 2 cups, uncooked)
- Extra virgin olive oil: 1/4 cup
- Garlic: 4 cloves, thinly sliced or minced
- Red pepper flakes: 1/4 teaspoon (optional for a bit of heat)
- Fresh parsley: 1/4 cup, chopped
- Fresh basil: 2 tablespoons, chopped (optional)
- Lemon zest: 1 teaspoon (optional, for brightness)
- Salt: 1/2 teaspoon (or to taste)
- Black pepper: 1/4 teaspoon
- Grated Parmesan cheese: 1/4 cup (optional)

Directions:

Cook the Spaghetti: Bring a large pot of salted water to a boil. Add the whole wheat spaghetti and cook according to the package instructions (about 10-12 minutes) until al dente. Drain the pasta, reserving 1/4 cup of the pasta cooking water, and set aside.

Prepare the Olive Oil and Garlic: While the pasta is cooking, heat the extra virgin olive oil in a large skillet over medium heat. Add the sliced or minced garlic and red pepper flakes (if using) to the skillet. Sauté for 1-2 minutes, or until the garlic is golden and fragrant, but not browned. Be careful not to burn the garlic.

Combine the Pasta and Olive Oil: Add the cooked spaghetti to the skillet with the garlic and olive oil. Toss to coat the pasta evenly in the oil and garlic. If the pasta seems dry, add a few tablespoons of the reserved pasta water to loosen the sauce.

Stir in the chopped parsley, basil (if using), lemon zest (if using), salt, and black pepper. Toss until everything is well combined.

Garnish and serve: Transfer the pasta to a serving dish and garnish with additional parsley or basil. Optionally, sprinkle with grated Parmesan cheese before serving.

Nutritional Information (Per Serving): Calories: 320 kcal, Protein: 10g, Carbohydrates: 46g, Total Fat: 12g, Saturated Fat: 2g, Fiber: 6g, Cholesterol: 5mg (if using Parmesan), Sodium: 180mg, Potassium: 220mg.

Chickpea Pasta with Roasted Eggplant and Tomatoes

Prep. time: 15 min | Cook time: 30 min | Serves: 4

Ingredients:

- Chickpea pasta: 8 oz (about 2 cups, uncooked)
- Eggplant: 1 medium, diced into 1-inch cubes
- Cherry tomatoes: 1 pint (about 2 cups), halved
- Garlic: 4 cloves, minced
- Extra virgin olive oil: 1/4 cup
- Fresh basil: 1/4 cup, chopped
- Fresh parsley: 2 tablespoons, chopped
- Red pepper flakes: 1/4 teaspoon (optional)
- Salt: 1/2 teaspoon (or to taste)
- Black pepper: 1/4 teaspoon
- Lemon juice: 1 tablespoon (optional, for brightness)
- Grated Parmesan or vegan cheese: 1/4 cup (optional)

Directions:

Roast the Eggplant and Tomatoes: Preheat your oven to 400°F (200°C). On a large baking sheet, toss the diced eggplant and cherry tomatoes with 2 tablespoons of olive oil, minced garlic, salt, black pepper, and red pepper flakes (if using). Spread the vegetables in a single layer and roast for 20-25 minutes, stirring halfway through, until the eggplant is tender and golden brown, and the tomatoes are soft and blistered.

Cook the Chickpea Pasta: While the vegetables are roasting, bring a large pot of salted water to a boil. Add the chickpea pasta and cook according to the package instructions (usually 8-10 minutes) until al dente. Drain the pasta, reserving 1/4 cup of the cooking water, and set aside. In a large skillet, heat the remaining 2 tablespoons of olive oil over medium heat. Add the roasted eggplant and tomatoes to the skillet, along with the cooked pasta. Toss to combine, adding a little of the reserved pasta water if needed to loosen the sauce. Stir in the chopped basil, parsley, and lemon juice (if using). Toss until everything is well combined. Taste and adjust seasoning with more salt and pepper if needed. **Serve warm:** Transfer the pasta to a serving dish and optionally top with grated Parmesan or vegan cheese. Garnish with extra fresh herbs if desired.

Nutritional Information (Per Serving): Calories: 360 kcal, Protein: 15g, Carbohydrates: 45g, Total Fat: 14g, Saturated Fat: 2g, Fiber: 10g, Cholesterol: 0mg (unless using Parmesan), Sodium: 340mg, Potassium: 800mg.

Lemon and Parsley Couscous Salad with Zucchini

Prep. time: 10 min | Cook time: 10 min | Serves: 4

Ingredients:

- Couscous: 1 cup (uncooked)
- Water or vegetable broth: 1 1/4 cups (for cooking couscous)
- Zucchini: 2 medium, diced
- Extra virgin olive oil: 3 tablespoons
- Fresh lemon juice: 2 tablespoons (about 1 lemon)
- Lemon zest: 1 teaspoon
- Garlic: 2 cloves, minced
- Fresh parsley: 1/4 cup, chopped
- Fresh mint: 2 tablespoons, chopped (optional)
- Salt: 1/2 teaspoon (or to taste)
- Black pepper: 1/4 teaspoon
- Feta cheese: 1/4 cup, crumbled (optional)
- Red pepper flakes: 1/4 teaspoon (optional for heat)

Directions:

Prepare the Couscous: In a medium saucepan, bring 1 1/4 cups of water or vegetable broth to a boil. Remove from heat, stir in the couscous, cover, and let it sit for 5 minutes until the liquid is absorbed. Fluff with a fork and set aside.

Sauté the Zucchini: In a large skillet, heat 1 tablespoon of olive oil over medium heat. Add the diced zucchini to the skillet and sauté for 5-6 minutes, stirring occasionally, until tender and lightly golden. Add the minced garlic in the last 1-2 minutes of cooking and sauté until fragrant. Remove from heat.

Prepare the Dressing: In a small bowl, whisk together the remaining 2 tablespoons of olive oil, fresh lemon juice, lemon zest, salt, and black pepper.

Assemble the Salad: In a large mixing bowl, combine the cooked couscous, sautéed zucchini, fresh parsley, mint (if using), and crumbled feta (if using).

Drizzle the lemon dressing over the couscous mixture and toss gently to coat all the ingredients evenly. Transfer the couscous salad to a serving dish, garnish with extra parsley or feta if desired, and serve warm or at room temperature.

Nutritional Information (Per Serving): Calories: 260 kcal, Protein: 7g, Carbohydrates: 37g, Total Fat: 10g, Saturated Fat: 2g, Fiber: 4g, Cholesterol: 10mg (if using feta), Sodium: 320mg, Potassium: 350mg.

Chapter 6

Fish and Seafood

Fish and seafood are central to the Mediterranean diet, celebrated for their rich flavors and abundant health benefits. Packed with lean protein, omega-3 fatty acids, and essential nutrients, dishes featuring fish and seafood are both nourishing and flavorful. Mediterranean cuisine makes the most of the bounty from the sea, combining fresh, high-quality seafood with simple yet vibrant ingredients like olive oil, garlic, lemon, and herbs to create delicious and wholesome meals.

In this section, "Fish and Seafood," you'll discover a variety of recipes that showcase the diversity of Mediterranean seafood cuisine. From light and refreshing grilled fish to hearty stews and flavorful shellfish dishes, these recipes highlight the region's dedication to fresh, clean flavors. Whether you're cooking a quick weekday dinner or a special meal for guests, these fish and seafood dishes will bring the essence of the Mediterranean to your table.

Baked Tilapia with Garlic and Herbs

Prep. time: 10 min | Cook time: 15 min | Serves: 4

Ingredients:

- Tilapia fillets: 4 (about 5-6 oz each)
- Extra virgin olive oil: 2 tablespoons
- Garlic: 3 cloves, minced
- Fresh lemon juice: 2 tablespoons
- Dried oregano: 1 teaspoon
- Paprika: 1/2 teaspoon
- Salt: 1/2 teaspoon
- Black pepper: 1/4 teaspoon
- Fresh parsley: 2 tablespoons, chopped (for garnish)
- Lemon wedges: for serving

Directions:

Preheat the Oven:
Preheat your oven to 400°F (200°C).

Prepare the Tilapia:
Place the tilapia fillets in a baking dish. Drizzle with olive oil and lemon juice.
In a small bowl, mix the minced garlic, oregano, paprika, salt, and black pepper. Sprinkle this mixture evenly over the fillets.

Bake the Tilapia:
Bake the fillets in the preheated oven for 12-15 minutes, or until the fish flakes easily with a fork and is fully cooked through.

Garnish and Serve:
Once baked, remove from the oven and garnish with fresh parsley. Serve with lemon wedges on the side for extra flavor.
This dish pairs well with steamed rice, roasted vegetables, or a light salad.

Nutritional Information (Per Serving): Calories: 220 kcal, Protein: 30g, Carbohydrates: 2g, Total Fat: 10g, Saturated Fat: 2g, Fiber: 1g, Cholesterol: 70mg, Sodium: 500mg, Potassium: 450mg.

Grilled Salmon with Lemon and Capers

Prep. time: 10 min | Cook time: 12 min | Serves: 4

Ingredients:

- Salmon fillets: 4 (4-6 oz each), skin-on or skinless
- Extra virgin olive oil: 3 tablespoons
- Lemon juice: 2 tablespoons (about 1 lemon)
- Lemon zest: 1 teaspoon
- Capers: 2 tablespoons, drained
- Garlic: 2 cloves, minced
- Fresh parsley: 1/4 cup, chopped
- Salt: 1/2 teaspoon (or to taste)
- Black pepper: 1/4 teaspoon
- Red pepper flakes: 1/4 teaspoon (optional for heat)
- Lemon slices: For garnish (optional)

Directions:

Prepare the Marinade: In a small bowl, whisk together 2 tablespoons of olive oil, lemon juice, lemon zest, minced garlic, salt, black pepper, and red pepper flakes (if using). **Marinate the salmon:** Brush the salmon fillets with the marinade and let them sit for 10-15 minutes to absorb the flavors. **Grill the Salmon:** Preheat your grill to medium-high heat (about 400°F). If you don't have a grill, you can use a grill pan or cast-iron skillet on the stovetop. Lightly oil the grill grates or grill pan. Place the salmon fillets skin-side down (if using skin-on fillets) and grill for about 4-5 minutes per side, depending on the thickness of the fillets. The salmon should be opaque and flake easily with a fork when done. **Make the Lemon Caper Sauce:** In a small skillet, heat the remaining 1 tablespoon of olive oil over medium heat. Add the capers and sauté for 1 minute until fragrant. Stir in the chopped parsley and cook for another 30 seconds. Remove from heat and stir in the fresh lemon juice. Place the grilled salmon fillets on a serving dish and spoon the lemon caper sauce over the top. Garnish with lemon slices and additional parsley, if desired. Serve the grilled salmon immediately, with your choice of sides like roasted vegetables, quinoa, couscous, or a fresh salad.

Nutritional Information (Per Serving): Calories: 320 kcal, Protein: 30g, Carbohydrates: 2g, Total Fat: 22g, Saturated Fat: 3g, Fiber: 1g, Cholesterol: 80mg, Sodium: 350mg, Potassium: 850mg.

Shrimp Scampi with Garlic and Olive Oil

Prep. time: 10 min | Cook time: 10 min | Serves: 4

Ingredients:

- Large shrimp: 1 lb (peeled and deveined, tail on or off)
- Extra virgin olive oil: 1/4 cup
- Garlic: 4 cloves, minced
- Lemon juice: 2 tablespoons (about 1 lemon)
- Lemon zest: 1 teaspoon
- White wine (optional): 1/4 cup
- Fresh parsley: 1/4 cup, chopped
- Red pepper flakes: 1/4 teaspoon (optional for heat)
- Salt: 1/2 teaspoon (or to taste)
- Black pepper: 1/4 teaspoon
- Butter: 1 tablespoon (optional for richness)
- Lemon wedges: For garnish

Directions:

Prepare the Shrimp:
Pat the shrimp dry and season them lightly with salt and pepper.
In a large skillet, heat the olive oil over medium heat. Add the minced garlic and red pepper flakes (if using), and sauté for about 1-2 minutes, until fragrant but not browned.
Add the shrimp to the skillet in a single layer. Cook for 2-3 minutes on each side until the shrimp are pink and opaque. Be careful not to overcook them.
Add the white wine (if using), lemon juice, and lemon zest to the skillet. Let it simmer for 1-2 minutes until the sauce slightly reduces.
If using, add the butter for extra richness and stir to combine.
Stir in the chopped parsley and toss the shrimp to coat evenly in the sauce.

Garnish and serve:
Transfer the shrimp scampi to a serving dish. Garnish with lemon wedges and additional parsley if desired. Serve immediately.

Nutritional Information (Per Serving): Calories: 250 kcal, Protein: 28g, Carbohydrates: 4g, Total Fat: 14g, Saturated Fat: 2g, Fiber: 0.5g, Cholesterol: 170mg, Sodium: 600mg, Potassium: 350mg.

Baked Cod with Tomatoes and Olives

Prep. time: 10 min | Cook time: 20 min | Serves: 4

Ingredients:

- Cod fillets: 4 (4-6 oz each)
- Cherry tomatoes: 1 1/2 cups, halved (or use diced Roma tomatoes)
- Kalamata olives: 1/4 cup, pitted and halved
- Garlic: 3 cloves, minced
- Extra virgin olive oil: 2 tablespoons
- Fresh lemon juice: 2 tablespoons (about 1 lemon)
- Fresh parsley: 1/4 cup, chopped
- Dried oregano: 1 teaspoon
- Salt: 1/2 teaspoon (or to taste)
- Black pepper: 1/4 teaspoon
- Red pepper flakes: 1/4 teaspoon (optional, for heat)
- Lemon slices: For garnish (optional)

Directions:

Preheat the Oven: Preheat your oven to 400°F (200°C).
Prepare the Vegetables and Seasoning:
In a medium bowl, combine the halved cherry tomatoes, olives, minced garlic, oregano, salt, black pepper, and red pepper flakes (if using). Drizzle with 1 tablespoon of olive oil and toss to coat evenly.
Assemble the Dish: Lightly season the cod fillets with salt and pepper. Place them in a baking dish large enough to hold the fillets in a single layer. Spoon the tomato and olive mixture evenly over the cod fillets. Drizzle the remaining tablespoon of olive oil and the lemon juice over the fish and vegetables.
Bake the Cod: Place the dish in the preheated oven and bake for 20-25 minutes, or until the cod is opaque and flakes easily with a fork. The cooking time will depend on the thickness of the fillets.
Garnish and serve: Remove the baked cod from the oven and sprinkle with fresh parsley. Garnish with lemon slices if desired. Serve warm.

Nutritional Information (Per Serving): Calories: 280 kcal, Protein: 32g, Carbohydrates: 6g, Total Fat: 12g, Saturated Fat: 2g, Fiber: 2g, Cholesterol: 75mg, Sodium: 480mg, Potassium: 750mg.

Tuna Salad with Olive Oil and Herbs

Prep. time: 10 min | Cook time: None | Serves: 4

Ingredients:

- Canned tuna in olive oil: 2 (5-oz) cans, drained
- Cherry tomatoes: 1 cup, halved
- Cucumber: 1 medium, diced
- Red onion: 1/4 cup, finely sliced
- Kalamata olives: 1/4 cup, pitted and halved
- Fresh parsley: 1/4 cup, chopped
- Fresh basil: 2 tablespoons, chopped (optional)
- Capers: 1 tablespoon (optional)
- Extra virgin olive oil: 3 tablespoons
- Fresh lemon juice: 2 tablespoons (about 1 lemon)
- Garlic: 1 clove, minced
- Dijon mustard: 1 teaspoon (optional)
- Salt: 1/2 teaspoon (or to taste)
- Black pepper: 1/4 teaspoon

Directions:

Prepare the Ingredients:

Drain the canned tuna and break it into large chunks with a fork. Set aside.
In a large mixing bowl, combine halved cherry tomatoes, diced cucumber, sliced red onion, and Kalamata olives. Toss lightly.

Make the Dressing:

In a small bowl, whisk together olive oil, fresh lemon juice, minced garlic, Dijon mustard (optional), salt, and black pepper.

Assemble the Salad:

Add the tuna to the vegetables. Pour the dressing over the salad and gently toss to coat all the ingredients. Stir in chopped parsley, basil (optional), and capers (optional).

Serve:

Transfer to a serving dish and serve immediately, or refrigerate for up to an hour to allow the flavors to meld.

Nutritional Information (Per Serving): Calories: 90 kcal, Protein: 5g, Carbohydrates: 10g, Total Fat: 4g, Saturated Fat: 1.5g, Fiber: 2g, Cholesterol: 5mg, Sodium: 260mg, Potassium: 280mg.

Seared Scallops with Lemon and Garlic

Prep. time: 10 min | Cook time: 8 min | Serves: 4

Ingredients:

- Scallops: 1 lb (about 16 large sea scallops)
- Extra virgin olive oil: 3 tablespoons
- Garlic: 3 cloves, minced
- Fresh lemon juice: 2 tablespoons (about 1 lemon)
- Lemon zest: 1 teaspoon
- Salt: 1/2 teaspoon
- Black pepper: 1/4 teaspoon
- Fresh parsley: 1/4 cup, chopped
- Red pepper flakes: 1/4 teaspoon (optional, for a bit of heat)
- Butter: 1 tablespoon (optional for added richness)

Directions:

Prepare the Scallops: Pat the scallops dry with a paper towel to remove excess moisture. Season both sides with salt and black pepper.

Sear the Scallops:

In a large skillet, heat 2 tablespoons of olive oil over medium-high heat until shimmering. Add the scallops, ensuring they are not overcrowded, and sear for 2-3 minutes per side until golden-brown. Remove scallops from the skillet and set aside.

Make the Lemon Garlic Sauce:

Lower the heat to medium, add 1 tablespoon olive oil and minced garlic. Sauté for 1 minute. Stir in lemon juice, zest, and red pepper flakes (optional). Add 1 tablespoon of butter for extra richness (optional) and simmer for 1-2 minutes.

Assemble the Dish:

Return the scallops to the skillet, tossing gently in the sauce. Sprinkle with fresh parsley and cook for 1 minute to warm through. Serve immediately, spooning the sauce over the scallops.

Nutritional Information (Per Serving): Calories: 200 kcal, Protein: 22g, Carbohydrates: 3g, Total Fat: 10g, Saturated Fat: 2g, Fiber: 1g, Cholesterol: 50mg, Sodium: 380mg, Potassium: 350mg.

Baked Trout with Lemon and Fresh Herbs

Prep. time: 10 min | Cook time: 20 min | Serves: 4

Ingredients:

- Whole trout or trout fillets: 4 fillets (about 6 oz each)
- Extra virgin olive oil: 3 tablespoons
- Fresh lemon juice: 2 tablespoons (about 1 lemon)
- Lemon slices: 1 lemon, thinly sliced
- Garlic: 2 cloves, minced
- Fresh parsley: 1/4 cup, chopped
- Fresh thyme or rosemary: 1 tablespoon, chopped
- Salt: 1/2 teaspoon (or to taste)
- Black pepper: 1/4 teaspoon
- Red pepper flakes: 1/4 teaspoon (optional, for a bit of heat)

Directions:

Preheat the Oven:
Preheat your oven to 400°F (200°C) and line a baking sheet with parchment paper or lightly grease it with olive oil.

Prepare the Trout:
Pat the trout fillets dry. Drizzle both sides with 2 tablespoons of olive oil and lemon juice. Season with salt, black pepper, and red pepper flakes (optional).
Sprinkle minced garlic, parsley, and thyme (or rosemary) over the fillets. Lay lemon slices on top.

Bake the Trout:
Place the trout fillets skin-side down on the prepared baking sheet. Bake for 15-20 minutes until the trout is opaque and flakes easily with a fork.

Serve:
Remove from the oven, drizzle with the remaining olive oil, and garnish with parsley if desired. Serve immediately.

Nutritional Information (Per Serving): Calories: 280 kcal, Protein: 29g, Carbohydrates: 3g, Total Fat: 18g, Saturated Fat: 2.5g, Fiber: 1g, Cholesterol: 80mg, Sodium: 330mg, Potassium: 500mg.

Grilled Sardines with Olive Oil and Parsley

Prep. time: 10 min | Cook time: 8 min | Serves: 4

Ingredients:

- Fresh sardines: 8 whole sardines (cleaned and scaled)
- Extra virgin olive oil: 4 tablespoons
- Fresh lemon juice: 2 tablespoons (about 1 lemon)
- Lemon zest: 1 teaspoon
- Garlic: 2 cloves, minced
- Fresh parsley: 1/4 cup, chopped
- Salt: 1/2 teaspoon
- Black pepper: 1/4 teaspoon
- Red pepper flakes: 1/4 teaspoon (optional, for a bit of heat)
- Lemon wedges: For garnish (optional)

Directions:

Prepare the Sardines: If needed, clean the sardines by removing the scales and guts, then rinse them under cold water and pat dry with paper towels. Drizzle the sardines with 2 tablespoons of olive oil and fresh lemon juice. Season both sides with salt, black pepper, and red pepper flakes (optional).

Prepare the Grill: Preheat the grill to medium-high heat (about 400°F). Ensure the grill grates are clean and lightly oiled to prevent sticking. If using a grill pan, preheat it over medium-high heat. **Grill the Sardines:** Place the sardines directly on the grill grates or in the grill pan. Cook for about 3-4 minutes per side until the skin is crispy and the fish is cooked through. The flesh should be opaque and easily flake with a fork.

Prepare the Dressing: In a small bowl, mix 2 tablespoons of olive oil, lemon zest, minced garlic, and chopped parsley. Once the sardines are off the grill, drizzle them with the olive oil, garlic, and parsley dressing.

Serve: Transfer the grilled sardines to a serving platter. Garnish with lemon wedges for an extra squeeze of fresh lemon juice before serving.

Nutritional Information (Per Serving): Calories: 320 kcal, Protein: 25g, Carbohydrates: 2g, Total Fat: 24g, Saturated Fat: 4g, Fiber: 1g, Cholesterol: 80mg, Sodium: 350mg, Potassium: 500mg.

Shrimp and Couscous with Fresh Vegetables

Prep. time: 15 min | Cook time: 15 min | Serves: 4

Ingredients:

- Shrimp: 1 lb (large shrimp, peeled)
- Couscous: 1 cup (uncooked)
- Water or vegetable broth: 1 1/4 cups
- Cherry tomatoes: 1 cup, halved
- Cucumber: 1 medium, diced
- Bell pepper: 1 medium (red, yellow, or orange), diced
- Red onion: 1/4 cup, finely chopped
- Olive oil: 4 tablespoons
- Lemon juice: 2 tablespoons
- Garlic: 2 cloves, minced
- Fresh parsley: 1/4 cup, chopped
- Fresh mint: 2 tablespoons, chopped (optional); Paprika: 1/2 teaspoon
- Ground cumin: 1/2 teaspoon
- Salt: 1/2 teaspoon (or to taste)
- Black pepper: 1/4 teaspoon
- Red pepper flakes: 1/4 teaspoon; Feta cheese: 1/4 cup, crumbled (optional)

Directions:

Prepare the Couscous: In a medium saucepan, bring 1 1/4 cups of water or vegetable broth to a boil. Stir in the couscous, cover, and remove from heat. Let it sit for 5 minutes until the liquid is absorbed, then fluff with a fork. Set aside.

Cook the Shrimp: Toss the shrimp with 1 tablespoon of olive oil, minced garlic, cumin, paprika, salt, and black pepper. Heat 1 tablespoon of olive oil in a skillet over medium-high heat. Sauté the shrimp for 2-3 minutes per side until pink and cooked through. Remove and set aside.

Prepare the Vegetables: While the couscous is resting and the shrimp is cooking, chop the cherry tomatoes, cucumber, bell pepper, and red onion.

Assemble the Dish: In a large bowl, combine the cooked couscous, shrimp, and chopped vegetables. Add parsley, mint (optional), and feta (optional).

Make the Dressing: Whisk together 2 tablespoons olive oil, lemon juice, salt, black pepper, and red pepper flakes (optional). Drizzle over the salad and toss to combine.

Serve: Transfer the shrimp and couscous salad to a serving dish. Garnish with fresh herbs or more feta if desired, and serve immediately.

Nutritional Information (Per Serving): Calories: 380 kcal, Protein: 25g, Carbohydrates: 35g, Total Fat: 16g, Saturated Fat: 3g, Fiber: 4g, Cholesterol: 190mg, Sodium: 500mg, Potassium: 500mg.

Roasted Sea Bass with Tomatoes and Olives

Prep. time: 10 min | Cook time: 20 min | Serves: 4

Ingredients:

- Sea bass fillets: 4 (6-8 oz each)
- Cherry tomatoes: 1 1/2 cups, halved
- Kalamata olives: 1/2 cup, pitted and halved
- Garlic: 3 cloves, minced
- Extra virgin olive oil: 4 tablespoons
- Fresh lemon juice: 2 tablespoons (about 1 lemon)
- Fresh parsley: 1/4 cup, chopped
- Fresh thyme: 1 tablespoon, chopped (or use rosemary for variation)
- Salt: 1/2 teaspoon (or to taste)
- Black pepper: 1/4 teaspoon
- Red pepper flakes: 1/4 teaspoon (optional for heat)
- Lemon slices: For garnish (optional)

Directions:

Preheat the Oven: Preheat the oven to 400°F (200°C). Lightly grease a baking dish or line with parchment paper.

Prepare the Sea Bass and Vegetables:

Pat the sea bass fillets dry and drizzle with 2 tablespoons of olive oil and lemon juice. Season with salt, black pepper, and red pepper flakes (optional).

In a bowl, mix halved cherry tomatoes, Kalamata olives, garlic, parsley, thyme, and the remaining 2 tablespoons of olive oil. Toss to coat.

Assemble the Dish:

Place the sea bass fillets skin-side down in the baking dish. Spoon the tomato and olive mixture evenly over and around the fillets.

Roast the Fish: Roast in the preheated oven for 20-25 minutes until the sea bass is opaque and flakes easily with a fork.

Serve:

Remove from the oven, garnish with lemon slices and parsley if desired, and serve warm.

Nutritional Information (Per Serving): Calories: 320 kcal, Protein: 35g, Carbohydrates: 6g, Total Fat: 18g, Saturated Fat: 3g, Fiber: 2g, Cholesterol: 85mg, Sodium: 450mg, Potassium: 800mg.

Tuna Steaks with Lemon Garlic Dressing

Prep. time: 10 min | Cook time: 10 min | Serves: 4

Ingredients:

For the Tuna Steaks:
- Tuna steaks: 4 (about 6 oz each)
- Olive oil: 2 tablespoons (for searing)
- Salt: 1/2 teaspoon (or to taste)
- Black pepper: 1/4 teaspoon
- Red pepper flakes: 1/4 teaspoon (optional, for heat)

For the Lemon Garlic Dressing:
- Extra virgin olive oil: 3 tablespoons
- Fresh lemon juice: 2 tablespoons (about 1 lemon)
- Lemon zest: 1 teaspoon
- Garlic: 2 cloves, minced
- Fresh parsley: 1/4 cup, chopped
- Dijon mustard: 1 teaspoon (optional for extra tang)
- Salt: 1/4 teaspoon
- Black pepper: 1/4 teaspoon

Directions:

Prepare the Tuna Steaks:
Pat the tuna steaks dry and drizzle with 2 tablespoons of olive oil. Season both sides with salt, black pepper, and red pepper flakes (optional).

Make the Lemon Garlic Dressing:
In a small bowl, whisk together 3 tablespoons olive oil, lemon juice, lemon zest, minced garlic, Dijon mustard (optional), parsley, salt, and black pepper. Set aside.

Sear the Tuna Steaks:
Heat a skillet or grill pan over medium-high heat. Sear the tuna steaks for 2-3 minutes on each side for medium-rare, or cook longer for desired doneness. The exterior should be browned and the interior slightly pink. Remove and set aside.

Assemble the Dish:
Place the seared tuna on a platter and drizzle with the lemon garlic dressing.

Garnish and serve:
Garnish with additional fresh parsley and serve immediately.

Nutritional Information (Per Serving): Calories: 340 kcal, Protein: 40g, Carbohydrates: 2g, Total Fat: 20g, Saturated Fat: 3g, Fiber: 0.5g, Cholesterol: 70mg, Sodium: 400mg, Potassium: 650mg.

Seafood Paella with Saffron

Prep. time: 20 min | Cook time: 45 min | Serves: 6

Ingredients:

- Olive oil: 3 tablespoons
- Onion: 1 medium, finely chopped; Garlic: 4 cloves, minced; Red bell pepper: 1, diced; Tomatoes: 2 medium, grated or finely chopped
- Saffron threads: 1/2 teaspoon (soaked in 1 tablespoon warm water)
- Smoked paprika: 1 teaspoon
- Arborio or Bomba rice: 1 1/2 cups (Bomba rice is preferred); Vegetable or fish stock: 4 cups, warmed
- White wine: 1/2 cup (optional)
- Sea salt: 1 teaspoon (or to taste)
- Black pepper: 1/4 teaspoon

For the Seafood: Shrimp: 1/2 lb (peeled and deveined); Mussels: 1/2 lb, Clams: 1/2 lb (cleaned); Squid: 1/2 lb, cleaned and sliced into rings; Fresh parsley: 1/4 cup, chopped; Lemon wedges

Directions:

Prepare the Base:
Heat 3 tablespoons of olive oil in a large paella pan or skillet over medium heat. Sauté the chopped onion and red bell pepper for 5-6 minutes until softened. Add garlic and cook for 1 minute. Stir in grated tomatoes, smoked paprika, and saffron with its soaking liquid. Cook for 3-4 minutes until fragrant.

Cook the Rice: Add Arborio or Bomba rice and stir to coat in the tomato mixture. Toast the rice for 2 minutes. Pour in warm vegetable or fish stock and white wine (optional), season with salt and pepper, and bring to a boil. Reduce heat to low and simmer uncovered for 15 minutes, stirring occasionally.

Cook the Seafood:
After 15 minutes, arrange shrimp, mussels, clams, and squid on top of the rice. Cover with a lid or foil and cook for 10-15 minutes until the seafood is cooked through (shrimp pink, mussels and clams open).

Serve: Remove from heat, sprinkle with fresh parsley, and let rest for 5 minutes. Serve with lemon wedges for added freshness.

Nutritional Information (Per Serving): Calories: 420 kcal, Protein: 26g, Carbohydrates: 42g, Total Fat: 12g, Saturated Fat: 2g, Fiber: 3g, Cholesterol: 170mg, Sodium: 750mg, Potassium: 550mg.

Mussels with White Wine and Garlic

Prep. time: 10 min | Cook time: 12 min | Serves: 4

Ingredients:

- Fresh mussels: 2 lbs (cleaned and debearded)
- Olive oil: 2 tablespoons
- Garlic: 4 cloves, minced
- Shallots: 1 small, finely chopped (optional)
- White wine: 1 cup (dry white wine, such as Sauvignon Blanc)
- Fresh lemon juice: 2 tablespoons (about 1 lemon)
- Fresh parsley: 1/4 cup, chopped
- Red pepper flakes: 1/4 teaspoon (optional for a bit of heat)
- Salt: 1/4 teaspoon (or to taste)
- Black pepper: 1/4 teaspoon
- Lemon wedges: For serving (optional)

Directions:

Prepare the Mussels:
Scrub the mussels under cold water and remove the "beards." Discard any that remain open after tapping.

Sauté the Aromatics:
Heat olive oil in a large pot over medium heat. Sauté minced garlic and shallots for 1-2 minutes until fragrant. Add red pepper flakes for heat, if desired.

Steam the Mussels:
Pour in white wine and lemon juice, and bring to a simmer. Add the mussels, cover, and cook for 5-7 minutes until they open, stirring occasionally.

Finish with Fresh Herbs:
Stir in fresh parsley, season with salt and pepper, and discard any unopened mussels.

Serve:
Transfer mussels to bowls, pouring the broth over. Garnish with lemon wedges and serve immediately.

Nutritional Information (Per Serving): Calories: 250 kcal, Protein: 25g, Carbohydrates: 6g, Total Fat: 10g, Saturated Fat: 1.5g, Fiber: 1g, Cholesterol: 80mg, Sodium: 450mg, Potassium: 350mg.

Grilled Octopus with Lemon and Oregano

Prep. time: 20 min (plus 1 hour for cooking and cooling the octopus) | Cook time: 10 min(for grilling) | Serves: 4

Ingredients:

- Fresh octopus: 2-3 lbs (cleaned)
- Olive oil: 1/4 cup (divided)
- Lemon juice: 3 tablespoons (about 1 lemon)
- Lemon zest: 1 teaspoon
- Garlic: 3 cloves, minced
- Fresh oregano: 2 tablespoons, chopped (or 1 teaspoon dried oregano)
- Red pepper flakes: 1/4 teaspoon (optional, for heat)
- Bay leaves: 2
- Salt: 1/2 teaspoon (or to taste)
- Black pepper: 1/4 teaspoon
- Lemon wedges: For serving
- Fresh parsley: 1/4 cup, chopped (for garnish, optional)

Directions:

Prepare and Tenderize the Octopus:
Boil water in a large pot, add bay leaves and a pinch of salt. Submerge the cleaned octopus, reduce heat, and simmer for 45-60 minutes until tender. Remove and cool, then cut into smaller sections.

Prepare the Marinade:
In a small bowl, whisk together 3 tablespoons olive oil, lemon juice, lemon zest, minced garlic, oregano, red pepper flakes (optional), salt, and pepper. Toss the octopus in the marinade and let it sit for 15-30 minutes (or up to 1 hour in the fridge).

Grill the Octopus:
Preheat the grill to medium-high heat (400°F). Lightly oil the grill grates with 1 tablespoon olive oil. Grill the octopus for 3-4 minutes per side until lightly charred.

Serve:
Transfer the grilled octopus to a platter, drizzle with remaining marinade or olive oil, and garnish with parsley. Serve with lemon wedges.

Nutritional Information (Per Serving): Calories: 250 kcal, Protein: 28g, Carbohydrates: 3g, Total Fat: 13g, Saturated Fat: 2g, Fiber: 1g, Cholesterol: 85mg, Sodium: 500mg, Potassium: 400mg.

Baked Swordfish with Olive Tapenade

Prep. time: 10 min | Cook time: 20 min | Serves: 4

Ingredients:

For the Swordfish:
- Swordfish fillets: 4 (6 oz each)
- Olive oil: 2 tablespoons
- Fresh lemon juice: 2 tablespoons
- Garlic: 2 cloves, minced; Salt: 1/2 teaspoon; Black pepper: 1/4 teaspoon
- Dried oregano: 1 teaspoon
- Fresh parsley: 2 tablespoons, chopped; Lemon wedges: For serving

For the Olive Tapenade:
- Kalamata olives: 1/2 cup, pitted
- Capers: 2 tablespoons, drained
- Fresh parsley: 2 tablespoons, chopped
- Garlic: 1 clove, minced; Olive oil: 2 tablespoons; Fresh lemon juice: 1 tablespoon; Red pepper flakes: 1/4 teaspoon (optional, for heat)
- Salt: 1/4 teaspoon (or to taste)
- Black pepper: 1/4 teaspoon

Directions:

Preheat the Oven:
Preheat the oven to 400°F (200°C). Line a baking sheet with parchment paper or lightly grease with olive oil.

Prepare the Swordfish:
Pat the swordfish fillets dry. Rub both sides with olive oil, minced garlic, lemon juice, salt, black pepper, and dried oregano. Place the fillets on the prepared baking sheet and bake for 15-20 minutes until the fish is opaque and flakes easily with a fork.

Make the Olive Tapenade:
In a food processor or by hand, combine Kalamata olives, capers, parsley, minced garlic, olive oil, lemon juice, red pepper flakes (optional), salt, and black pepper. Pulse until coarsely chopped.

Assemble the Dish:
Once the swordfish is done, spoon olive tapenade over each fillet. Garnish the dish with fresh parsley and serve with lemon wedges for an extra burst of citrus.

Nutritional Information (Per Serving): Calories: 380 kcal, Protein: 35g, Carbohydrates: 5g, Total Fat: 22g, Saturated Fat: 3g, Fiber: 2g, Cholesterol: 90mg, Sodium: 550mg, Potassium: 750mg.

Grilled Sea Bass with Lemon and Herbs

Prep. time: 15 min | Cook time: 20 min | Serves: 4

Ingredients:

- Sea bass fillets: 4 (about 6 oz each)
- Extra virgin olive oil: 4 tablespoons, divided
- Fresh lemon juice: 2 tablespoons
- Garlic: 3 cloves, minced
- Fresh parsley: 2 tablespoons, chopped
- Fresh thyme or oregano: 1 tablespoon, chopped
- Sea salt: 1 teaspoon
- Black pepper: 1/2 teaspoon
- Red pepper flakes (optional): 1/4 teaspoon
- Lemon slices: for garnish
- Fresh parsley: for garnish
- Optional: 1 tablespoon capers, rinsed and chopped

Directions:

Preheat the Grill: Preheat your grill to medium-high heat (about 375-400°F). Lightly oil the grill grates with olive oil or a grill pan if cooking indoors.

Prepare the Sea Bass: Pat the sea bass fillets dry with a paper towel. Drizzle 2 tablespoons of olive oil and 2 tablespoons of lemon juice over both sides of the fillets. Season the fish with sea salt, black pepper, and optional red pepper flakes. Rub the minced garlic and chopped fresh herbs (parsley and thyme or oregano) evenly over the fillets.

Grill the Sea Bass: Place the fillets skin-side down on the grill. Cook for 6-8 minutes per side, or until the fish is opaque and flakes easily with a fork. While grilling, drizzle the remaining 2 tablespoons of olive oil over the fillets for added moisture.

Optional Capers Addition: If using capers, sprinkle them over the fish during the last minute of grilling for a tangy flavor.

Serve: Once cooked, transfer the sea bass to a serving platter. Garnish with lemon slices and additional fresh parsley.

Nutritional Information (Per Serving): Calories: 280 kcal, Protein: 35g, Carbohydrates: 2g, Fats: 14g (2g saturated fat), Fiber: 1g, Cholesterol: 85mg, Sodium: 460mg, Potassium: 700mg.

Chapter

7

Poultry Recipes

Poultry plays an important role in the Mediterranean diet, offering a lean and versatile source of protein that pairs perfectly with the region's vibrant flavors and wholesome ingredients. Mediterranean poultry dishes are often enhanced with fresh herbs, citrus, olive oil, and spices, resulting in meals that are both satisfying and nutritious. From grilled chicken to slow-cooked stews, the possibilities for creating delicious, healthy meals are endless.

In this section, "Poultry Recipes," you'll find a variety of flavorful dishes that make the most of Mediterranean cooking techniques. Whether you're looking for quick weeknight dinners or something special for a family gathering, these recipes will inspire you to bring the best of Mediterranean cuisine to your table. Each dish highlights the balance between bold flavors and simple, healthy ingredients, ensuring that your poultry meals are both delicious and nutritious.

Garlic Lemon Chicken Thighs

Prep. time: 10 min | Cook time: 25 min | Serves: 4

Ingredients:

- Boneless, skinless chicken thighs: 1 lb (about 4-6 thighs)
- Olive oil: 2 tablespoons
- Garlic: 4 cloves, minced
- Fresh lemon juice: 2 tablespoons (about 1 lemon)
- Lemon zest: 1 teaspoon
- Dried oregano: 1 teaspoon
- Salt: 1/2 teaspoon
- Black pepper: 1/4 teaspoon
- Fresh parsley: 2 tablespoons, chopped (for garnish)
- Lemon wedges: for serving

Directions:

Marinate the Chicken:

In a small bowl, whisk together olive oil, minced garlic, lemon juice, lemon zest, dried oregano, salt, and black pepper.

Place the chicken thighs in a resealable plastic bag or shallow dish. Pour the marinade over the chicken, making sure each piece is well-coated. Let it marinate in the refrigerator for at least 15-30 minutes (you can also marinate for up to 2 hours for more flavor).

Cook the Chicken: Heat a large skillet over medium-high heat. Add 1 tablespoon of olive oil and sear the chicken thighs for 4-5 minutes on each side until golden brown and cooked through (internal temperature should reach 165°F/75°C).

Garnish and Serve:

Once the chicken is cooked, remove from heat and let it rest for 5 minutes.

Garnish with freshly chopped parsley and serve with lemon wedges.

Serving Suggestions:

This dish pairs well with a simple side of roasted vegetables, couscous, or a fresh salad.

Nutritional Information (Per Serving): Calories: 280 kcal, Protein: 25g, Carbohydrates: 2g, Total Fat: 18g, Saturated Fat: 4g, Fiber: 1g, Cholesterol: 105mg, Sodium: 450mg, Potassium: 320mg.

Lemon and Oregano Grilled Chicken Breast

Prep. time: 10 min (plus 30 minutes marinating time) | Cook time: 12 min | Serves: 4

Ingredients:

For the Chicken Marinade:
- Chicken breasts: 4 (about 6 oz each)
- Olive oil: 3 tablespoons
- Fresh lemon juice: 3 tablespoons (about 1 large lemon)
- Lemon zest: 1 teaspoon
- Garlic: 3 cloves, minced
- Dried oregano: 2 teaspoons
- Fresh parsley: 2 tablespoons, chopped (optional)
- Salt: 1/2 teaspoon
- Black pepper: 1/4 teaspoon
- Red pepper flakes: 1/4 teaspoon (optional, for heat)

Directions:

Prepare the Marinade:

In a medium bowl, whisk together olive oil, lemon juice, lemon zest, garlic, oregano, parsley (optional), salt, black pepper, and red pepper flakes. Place the chicken breasts in a resealable bag or shallow dish, pour the marinade over, and refrigerate for at least 30 minutes (up to 4 hours for stronger flavor).

Preheat the Grill:

Preheat your grill or grill pan to medium-high heat (about 400°F). Lightly oil the grates if using a grill.

Grill the Chicken:

Remove the chicken from the marinade, allowing excess to drip off. Grill for 5-6 minutes per side, or until the internal temperature reaches 165°F (74°C) and the chicken is golden with a slight char. Let the chicken rest for 5 minutes.

Serve:

Slice the chicken and garnish with parsley and lemon wedges if desired. Serve immediately.

Nutritional Information (Per Serving): Calories: 280 kcal, Protein: 35g, Carbohydrates: 2g, Total Fat: 14g, Saturated Fat: 2g, Fiber: 1g, Cholesterol: 85mg, Sodium: 350mg, Potassium: 450mg.

Chicken Piccata with Capers and Lemon

Prep. time: 10 min | Cook time: 15 min | Serves: 4

Ingredients:

- Boneless, skinless chicken breasts: 4 (about 6 oz each)
- Olive oil: 3 tablespoons (divided)
- Whole wheat flour: 1/4 cup (for dredging)
- Salt: 1/2 teaspoon
- Black pepper: 1/4 teaspoon
- Garlic: 2 cloves, minced
- Chicken broth: 1/2 cup (low-sodium)
- Fresh lemon juice: 1/4 cup (about 1 large lemon)
- Capers: 2 tablespoons, drained
- Fresh parsley: 2 tablespoons, chopped (for garnish)
- Lemon slices: For garnish (optional)

Directions:

Prepare the Chicken: Place each chicken breast between plastic wrap and pound to an even 1/2 inch thickness. Season with salt and pepper, then dredge in whole wheat flour, shaking off the excess.

Cook the Chicken:

Heat 2 tablespoons of olive oil in a skillet over medium-high heat. Sear the chicken for 3-4 minutes per side until golden and cooked through. Transfer to a plate and keep warm.

Make the Lemon-Caper Sauce:

In the same skillet, add 1 tablespoon of olive oil and minced garlic. Sauté for 1 minute until fragrant. Add chicken broth and lemon juice, scraping up browned bits. Simmer for 2-3 minutes until slightly reduced. Stir in the capers and cook for 1 more minute.

Combine and Serve:

Return the chicken to the skillet, spooning the sauce over the top. Simmer for 2 minutes to absorb the flavors. Transfer to a serving plate, pour the sauce over, and garnish with parsley and lemon slices. Serve immediately.

Nutritional Information (Per Serving): Calories: 320 kcal, Protein: 30g, Carbohydrates: 12g, Total Fat: 16g, Saturated Fat: 2g, Fiber: 2g, Cholesterol: 80mg, Sodium: 470mg, Potassium: 550mg.

Baked Chicken with Olives and Tomatoes

Prep. time: 10 min | Cook time: 35 min | Serves: 4

Ingredients:

- Bone-in, skinless chicken thighs or breasts: 4 (about 1 1/2 lbs)
- Olive oil: 2 tablespoons
- Garlic: 3 cloves, minced
- Cherry tomatoes: 1 1/2 cups, halved
- Kalamata olives: 1/2 cup, pitted and halved
- Fresh lemon juice: 2 tablespoons
- Fresh oregano: 1 tablespoon, chopped (or 1 teaspoon dried oregano); Fresh thyme: 1 tablespoon, chopped (or 1 teaspoon dried thyme)
- Red pepper flakes: 1/4 teaspoon (optional, for heat)
- Salt: 1/2 teaspoon
- Black pepper: 1/4 teaspoon
- Fresh parsley: 2 tablespoons, chopped (for garnish)
- Lemon slices: For serving (optional)

Directions:

Preheat the Oven:

Preheat your oven to 400°F (200°C).

Prepare the Chicken and Vegetables:

Pat chicken thighs or breasts dry and season with salt, black pepper, and red pepper flakes (optional). In a bowl, toss cherry tomatoes, Kalamata olives, minced garlic, oregano, thyme, and lemon juice. Drizzle with 1 tablespoon of olive oil and toss to coat.

Assemble the Dish:

Place the seasoned chicken in a baking dish or ovenproof skillet. Spoon the tomato and olive mixture over and around the chicken. Drizzle the remaining tablespoon of olive oil on top.

Bake the Chicken:

Bake for 35-40 minutes until the chicken reaches 165°F (74°C) and the skin is golden and crispy. Cover with foil if browning too quickly.

Garnish and Serve: Let the chicken rest for 5 minutes. Garnish with fresh parsley and serve with lemon slices.

Nutritional Information (Per Serving): Calories: 320 kcal, Protein: 32g, Carbohydrates: 6g, Total Fat: 18g, Saturated Fat: 3g, Fiber: 2g, Cholesterol: 110mg, Sodium: 520mg, Potassium: 500mg.

Roasted Chicken Thighs with Garlic and Rosemary

Prep. time: 10 min | Cook time: 35 min | Serves: 4

Ingredients:

- Bone-in, skin-on chicken thighs: 4 (about 1 1/2 lbs)
- Olive oil: 3 tablespoons
- Garlic: 4 cloves, minced
- Fresh rosemary: 2 tablespoons, chopped (or 1 tablespoon dried rosemary)
- Lemon zest: 1 teaspoon
- Salt: 1/2 teaspoon
- Black pepper: 1/4 teaspoon
- Red pepper flakes: 1/4 teaspoon (optional for heat)
- Fresh lemon juice: 2 tablespoons (about 1 lemon)
- Fresh parsley: 2 tablespoons, chopped (for garnish, optional)

Directions:

Preheat the Oven:
Preheat your oven to 400°F (200°C). Line a baking dish or roasting pan with parchment paper or lightly grease with ol ive oil.

Season the Chicken:
In a small bowl, mix olive oil, minced garlic, chopped rosemary, lemon zest, salt, black pepper, and red pepper flakes (optional). Pat chicken thighs dry, then rub the seasoning mixture all over, including under the skin.

Roast the Chicken:
Place the chicken thighs skin-side up in the prepared dish. Drizzle with lemon juice. Roast for 35-40 minutes until golden and crispy, and the **internal temperature** reaches 165°F (74°C). For extra crispy skin, broil for the last 2-3 minutes.

Garnish and Serve:
Let the chicken rest for 5 minutes. Garnish with fresh parsley if desired and serve.

Nutritional Information (Per Serving): Calories: 350 kcal, Protein: 26g, Carbohydrates: 3g, Total Fat: 26g, Saturated Fat: 5g, Fiber: 1g, Cholesterol: 120mg, Sodium: 450mg, Potassium: 350mg.

Grilled Chicken with Feta and Olive Tapenade

Prep. time: 15 min | Marinating Time: 30 minutes (optional) | Cook time: 15 min(for grilling) | Serves: 4

Ingredients:

For the Grilled Chicken: Boneless, skinless chicken breasts: 4 (about 6 oz each); Olive oil: 3 tablespoons; Fresh lemon juice: 2 tablespoons; Garlic: 2 cloves, minced; Fresh oregano: 1 tablespoon, chopped (or 1 teaspoon dried); Salt: 1/2 teaspoon; Black pepper: 1/4 teaspoon

For the Olive Tapenade: Kalamata olives: 1/2 cup, pitted and finely chopped; Garlic: 1 clove, minced; Olive oil: 2 tablespoons; Capers: 1 tablespoon, drained; Fresh parsley: 2 tablespoons, chopped; Fresh lemon juice: 1 tablespoon; Red pepper flakes: 1/4 teaspoon (optional); Salt: 1/4 teaspoon; Black pepper: 1/4 teaspoon

For Garnish: Feta cheese: 1/4 cup, crumbled; Fresh parsley: 2 tablespoons

Directions:

Marinate the Chicken (Optional):
In a small bowl, whisk together olive oil, lemon juice, minced garlic, oregano, salt, and black pepper. Place the chicken in a shallow dish or resealable bag, pour the marinade over, and refrigerate for 30 minutes to 2 hours.

Prepare the Olive Tapenade:
In a medium bowl, combine chopped Kalamata olives, capers, parsley, garlic, olive oil, lemon juice, red pepper flakes (optional), salt, and black pepper. Set aside.

Grill the Chicken:
Preheat the grill or grill pan to medium-high heat. Lightly oil the grates. Grill the chicken for 5-7 minutes per side until it reaches an internal temperature of 165°F (74°C). Let it rest for 5 minutes.

Assemble the Dish:
Place grilled chicken on a serving platter and top with olive tapenade. Garnish with crumbled feta cheese and fresh parsley or basil.

Nutritional Information (Per Serving): Calories: 370 kcal, Protein: 35g, Carbohydrates: 4g, Total Fat: 23g, Saturated Fat: 6g, Fiber: 2g, Cholesterol: 95mg, Sodium: 520mg, Potassium: 500mg.

Mediterranean Chicken Stir-Fry with Peppers

Prep. time: 10 min | Cook time: 15 min | Serves: 4

Ingredients:

- Boneless, skinless chicken breasts: 1 1/2 lbs, sliced into thin strips
- Olive oil: 3 tablespoons, divided
- Garlic: 3 cloves, minced
- Red bell pepper: 1, thinly sliced
- Yellow bell pepper: 1, thinly sliced
- Green bell pepper: 1, thinly sliced
- Red onion: 1 medium, thinly sliced
- Cherry tomatoes: 1 cup, halved
- Ground cumin: 1 teaspoon
- Dried oregano: 1 teaspoon
- Paprika: 1/2 teaspoon
- Salt: 1/2 teaspoon (or to taste)
- Black pepper: 1/4 teaspoon
- Fresh parsley: 2 tablespoons, chopped (for garnish)
- Fresh lemon juice: 2 tablespoons (about 1 lemon)

Directions:

Prep the Chicken and Vegetables:
In a bowl, toss sliced chicken with 1 tablespoon olive oil, cumin, oregano, paprika, salt, and black pepper. Thinly slice red, yellow, and green bell peppers, red onion, and halve the cherry tomatoes.

Cook the Chicken:
Heat 1 tablespoon olive oil in a skillet over medium-high heat. Add the seasoned chicken in a single layer and cook for 4-5 minutes until golden and cooked through (165°F/74°C). Remove and set aside.

Cook the Vegetables:
In the same skillet, add 1 tablespoon olive oil. Sauté the sliced peppers and onion for 5-7 minutes until softened but still vibrant. Stir in cherry tomatoes and garlic, cooking for 1-2 more minutes.

Combine and Serve:
Return the chicken to the skillet, stir, and cook for 1-2 minutes to heat through. Drizzle with lemon juice and stir. Serve with fresh parsley garnish.

Nutritional Information (Per Serving): Calories: 360 kcal, Protein: 35g, Carbohydrates: 12g, Total Fat: 19g, Saturated Fat: 3g, Fiber: 4g, Cholesterol: 85mg, Sodium: 430mg, Potassium: 700mg.

Chicken and Quinoa with Lemon Dressing

Prep. time: 10 min | Cook time: 25 min | Serves: 4

Ingredients:

For the Chicken and Quinoa:
Boneless, skinless chicken breasts: 1 1/2 lbs (cut into bite-sized pieces); Quinoa: 1 cup, uncooked (rinsed); Water or chicken broth: 2 cups; Olive oil: 2 tablespoons (divided); Garlic: 2 cloves, minced; Cherry tomatoes: 1 cup, halved; Cucumber: 1 medium, diced; Fresh parsley: 1/4 cup, chopped; Black pepper: 1/4 teaspoon; Fresh basil: 2 tablespoons, chopped (optional); Salt: 1/2 teaspoon.

For the Lemon Dressing:
Olive oil: 3 tablespoons; Fresh lemon juice: 3 tablespoons; Lemon zest: 1 teaspoon; Garlic: 1 clove, minced Honey: 1 teaspoon (optional); Dijon mustard: 1 teaspoon; Salt: 1/4 teaspoon; Black pepper: 1/4 teaspoon.

Directions:

Cook the Quinoa:
In a saucepan, combine rinsed quinoa with 2 cups of water or chicken broth. Bring to a boil, reduce heat, cover, and simmer for 15 minutes until the liquid is absorbed. Fluff with a fork and set aside.

Cook the Chicken:
Heat 1 tablespoon of olive oil in a skillet over medium-high heat. Add bite-sized chicken pieces, season with salt and pepper, and cook for 5-7 minutes until golden and cooked through (165°F/74°C). Set aside.

Prepare the Lemon Dressing:
In a small bowl or jar, whisk together olive oil, lemon juice, lemon zest, minced garlic, honey (optional), Dijon mustard, salt, and black pepper. Adjust seasoning as needed.

Assemble the Dish:
In a large bowl, combine cooked quinoa, sautéed chicken, cherry tomatoes, cucumber, parsley, and basil (optional). Drizzle with lemon dressing and toss gently to combine. Adjust seasoning, garnish with fresh herbs or lemon wedges, and serve.

Nutritional Information (Per Serving): Calories: 410 kcal, Protein: 38g, Carbohydrates: 32g, Total Fat: 18g, Saturated Fat: 2.5g, Fiber: 6g, Cholesterol: 85mg, Sodium: 450mg, Potassium: 700mg.

Stuffed Chicken Breasts with Spinach and Feta

Prep. time: 15 min | Cook time: 25 min | Serves: 4

Ingredients:

For the Chicken:
- Boneless, skinless chicken breasts: 4 (about 6 oz each)
- Olive oil: 2 tablespoons (divided)
- Garlic: 3 cloves, minced
- Fresh spinach: 3 cups, chopped (or 1 cup frozen spinach, thawed and drained)
- Feta cheese: 1/2 cup, crumbled
- Fresh lemon juice: 2 tablespoons
- Fresh oregano: 1 tablespoon, chopped (or 1 teaspoon dried oregano)
- Salt: 1/2 teaspoon
- Black pepper: 1/4 teaspoon
- Toothpicks: For securing the chicken breasts

Directions:

Prepare the Chicken:
Butterfly each chicken breast by slicing horizontally to create a pocket, without cutting all the way through. Season both sides with salt and black pepper.

Make the Spinach and Feta Stuffing:
Heat 1 tablespoon olive oil in a skillet over medium heat. Sauté minced garlic for 1 minute, then add spinach and cook for 2-3 minutes until wilted. In a bowl, combine spinach, feta, oregano, and lemon juice. Add optional sun-dried tomatoes, basil, or olives for extra flavor.

Stuff the Chicken:
Spoon the spinach-feta mixture into the chicken pockets and secure with toothpicks.

Cook the Chicken:
Preheat the oven to 375°F (190°C). Sear the stuffed chicken breasts in 1 tablespoon olive oil for 2-3 minutes per side until golden brown. Transfer the skillet to the oven and bake for 15-20 minutes until the chicken reaches 165°F (74°C). Remove the chicken from the oven and allow it to rest for 5 minutes. Remove the toothpicks before serving.

Nutritional Information (Per Serving): Calories: 350 kcal, Protein: 35g, Carbohydrates: 4g, Total Fat: 20g, Saturated Fat: 6g, Fiber: 2g, Cholesterol: 90mg, Sodium: 580mg, Potassium: 600mg.

Chicken with Artichokes and Sun-Dried Tomatoes

Prep. time: 10 min | Cook time: 25 min | Serves: 4

Ingredients:

- Boneless, skinless chicken breasts: 4 (about 1 1/2 lbs)
- Olive oil: 3 tablespoons
- Garlic: 3 cloves, minced
- Artichoke hearts: 1 can (14 oz), drained and quartered
- Sun-dried tomatoes: 1/2 cup, chopped (oil-packed, drained)
- Chicken broth: 1/2 cup (low sodium)
- Fresh lemon juice: 2 tablespoons
- Fresh parsley: 2 tablespoons, chopped
- Fresh basil: 1 tablespoon, chopped (optional)
- Dried oregano: 1 teaspoon
- Salt: 1/2 teaspoon
- Black pepper: 1/4 teaspoon
- Red pepper flakes: 1/4 teaspoon (optional for heat)

Directions:

Prepare the Chicken:
Pat chicken breasts dry and season with salt, black pepper, and oregano. Heat 2 tablespoons of olive oil in a skillet over medium-high heat. Sear the chicken for 5-6 minutes per side until golden and cooked through (165°F/74°C). Remove and set aside.

Cook the Vegetables:
In the same skillet, add 1 tablespoon of olive oil. Sauté minced garlic for 1 minute until fragrant. Stir in artichoke hearts and sun-dried tomatoes, cooking for 2-3 minutes until heated through.

Make the Sauce:
Pour in chicken broth and lemon juice. Bring to a simmer and cook for 3-4 minutes until slightly reduced.

Combine and Serve:
Return the chicken to the skillet and spoon the sauce over. Cook for 2-3 more minutes to meld flavors. Garnish with fresh parsley and basil, if desired. Serve immediately.

Nutritional Information (Per Serving): Calories: 360 kcal, Protein: 35g, Carbohydrates: 8g, Total Fat: 20g, Saturated Fat: 3g, Fiber: 4g, Cholesterol: 90mg, Sodium: 480mg, Potassium: 650mg.

Lemon and Garlic Chicken Drumsticks

Prep. time: 10 min (plus 30 minutes for marinating) | Cook time: 35 min | Serves: 4

Ingredients:

- Chicken drumsticks: 8 (about 2 lbs)
- Olive oil: 3 tablespoons
- Fresh lemon juice: 1/4 cup (about 1 large lemon)
- Lemon zest: 1 teaspoon
- Garlic: 4 cloves, minced
- Dried oregano: 1 teaspoon
- Fresh thyme: 1 tablespoon, chopped (or 1 teaspoon dried thyme)
- Salt: 1/2 teaspoon
- Black pepper: 1/4 teaspoon
- Red pepper flakes: 1/4 teaspoon (optional for a bit of heat)
- Fresh parsley: 2 tablespoons, chopped (for garnish)

Directions:

Prepare the Marinade:
In a large bowl, whisk together olive oil, lemon juice, lemon zest, minced garlic, oregano, thyme, salt, black pepper, and red pepper flakes (optional).

Marinate the Chicken:
Add chicken drumsticks to the marinade, tossing to coat evenly. Cover and refrigerate for at least 30 minutes or up to 2 hours for deeper flavor.

Preheat the Oven:
Preheat the oven to 400°F (200°C) and line a baking sheet with parchment paper or lightly grease it with olive oil.

Roast the Chicken:
Place the marinated drumsticks on the baking sheet in a single layer. Roast for 35-40 minutes, turning halfway through, until golden and cooked through (165°F/74°C). For crispy skin, broil for the last 2-3 minutes.

Garnish and Serve: Let the chicken rest for 5 minutes, then garnish with freshly chopped parsley before serving.

Nutritional Information (Per Serving): Calories: 350 kcal, Protein: 30g, Carbohydrates: 2g, Total Fat: 24g, Saturated Fat: 5g, Fiber: 1g, Cholesterol: 130mg, Sodium: 420mg, Potassium: 350mg.

Chicken with Orzo and Roasted Vegetables

Prep. time: 10 min | Cook time: 25 min | Serves: 4

Ingredients:

For the Chicken:
- Boneless, skinless chicken breasts: 4 (about 5-6 oz each)
- Olive oil: 2 tablespoons
- Garlic cloves, minced: 2
- Lemon, juice and zest: 1
- Dried oregano: 1 teaspoon
- Salt: to taste
- Black pepper: to taste

For the Orzo and Vegetables:
- Orzo (or other small pasta): 1 cup
- Chicken broth (or water): 2 cups
- Red bell pepper, diced: 1
- Zucchini, diced: 1
- Olive oil: 1 tablespoon
- Salt: to taste
- Black pepper: to taste

Directions:

Prepare the Vegetables: Preheat the oven to 400°F (200°C).
Toss the diced red bell pepper and zucchini with 1 tablespoon olive oil, salt, and pepper. Spread the vegetables evenly on a baking sheet and roast for 20-25 minutes, until tender and slightly browned.

Cook the Chicken: In a small bowl, whisk together 2 tablespoons olive oil, minced garlic, lemon juice and zest, dried oregano, salt, and pepper.
Heat a skillet over medium heat and cook the chicken breasts for 6-7 minutes per side until golden brown and fully cooked (internal temperature should reach 165°F/75°C). Let the chicken rest for 5 minutes before slicing.

Cook the Orzo: In a medium pot, bring the chicken broth to a boil. Add the orzo, reduce heat to a simmer, and cook for 8-10 minutes until tender. Drain any excess liquid and season with salt and pepper to taste.

Assemble the Dish:
Divide the orzo onto plates, top with sliced chicken, and roasted vegetables.

Nutritional Information (Per Serving): Calories: 420 kcal, Protein: 33g, Carbohydrates: 40g, Fats: 14g (2g saturated), Fiber: 4g, Cholesterol: 85mg, Sodium: 600mg, Potassium: 780mg.

Chapter
8
Meat Recipes

Meat recipes in the Mediterranean diet are all about balance, focusing on quality over quantity. While meat is enjoyed in moderation, it is often prepared with fresh herbs, spices, and olive oil, creating dishes that are both flavorful and health-conscious. Mediterranean meat dishes frequently incorporate lean cuts of lamb, beef, and pork, paired with seasonal vegetables and grains to deliver a wholesome and satisfying meal.

In this section, "Meat Recipes," you'll discover a range of Mediterranean-inspired dishes that showcase the richness of the region's culinary heritage. From slow-cooked stews to grilled meats, these recipes offer a variety of ways to enjoy meat while staying true to the principles of Mediterranean cooking. Whether you're preparing a special occasion feast or a simple family dinner, these recipes will bring depth of flavor and nutritious ingredients to your table.

Ground Beef and Rice Skillet

Prep. time: 10 min | Cook time: 25 min | Serves: 4

Ingredients:

- Ground beef (85% lean): 1 lb
- Olive oil: 2 tablespoons
- Onion: 1 small, diced
- Garlic: 3 cloves, minced
- Cooked white or brown rice: 2 cups
- Canned diced tomatoes: 1 can (14.5 oz), drained
- Dried oregano: 1 teaspoon
- Ground cumin: 1 teaspoon
- Salt: 1/2 teaspoon
- Black pepper: 1/4 teaspoon
- Fresh parsley: 2 tablespoons, chopped (for garnish)
- Fresh lemon wedges: for serving

Directions:

Cook the Ground Beef:

In a large skillet, heat 1 tablespoon of olive oil over medium heat. Add the ground beef and cook, breaking it apart with a wooden spoon, until browned (about 5-7 minutes). Drain excess fat if necessary.

Sauté the Aromatics:

In the same skillet, push the beef to one side and add the remaining tablespoon of olive oil. Add the diced onion and minced garlic. Sauté for 3-4 minutes until softened.

Add the Tomatoes and Spices:

Stir the diced tomatoes, oregano, cumin, salt, and black pepper into the skillet. Cook for another 2-3 minutes to allow the flavors to combine.

Add the Rice: Stir in the cooked rice until everything is evenly mixed and heated through, about 3-4 minutes.

Serve: Remove from heat and garnish with fresh parsley. Serve with lemon wedges on the side for extra brightness.

Nutritional Information (Per Serving): Calories: 350 kcal, Protein: 20g, Carbohydrates: 30g, Total Fat: 15g, Saturated Fat: 5g, Fiber: 2g, Cholesterol: 60mg, Sodium: 600mg, Potassium: 400mg.

Beef Kofta with Garlic and Cumin

Prep. time: 15 min | Cook time: 15 min | Serves: 4

Ingredients:

For the Kofta:
- Ground beef (preferably lean): 1 lb
- Red onion: 1/2 medium, finely chopped
- Garlic: 3 cloves, minced
- Fresh parsley: 1/4 cup, chopped
- Ground cumin: 1 teaspoon
- Ground coriander: 1 teaspoon
- Paprika: 1/2 teaspoon
- Ground cinnamon: 1/4 teaspoon
- Salt: 1/2 teaspoon
- Black pepper: 1/4 teaspoon
- Olive oil: 1 tablespoon (for brushing)

Customizable Elements:
- Add fresh cilantro or mint for a more herbaceous flavor.
- Substitute ground beef with ground lamb or turkey for variation.

Directions:

Prepare the Kofta Mixture:

In a large bowl, mix ground beef, finely chopped red onion, minced garlic, parsley, cumin, coriander, paprika, cinnamon, salt, and black pepper until well combined. Shape the mixture into 8 oval patties around skewers or into small patties/logs. Refrigerate for 10-15 minutes to firm up.

Cook the Kofta:

Preheat your grill or skillet over medium-high heat and brush with olive oil. Cook the kofta for 4-5 minutes per side, turning occasionally, until browned and cooked through (160°F/71°C). Avoid overcooking to keep them moist.

Serve:

Let the kofta rest for a couple of minutes, then serve immediately with your favorite sides and sauces.

Nutritional Information (Per Serving): Calories: 280 kcal, Protein: 25g, Carbohydrates: 4g, Total Fat: 18g, Saturated Fat: 6g, Fiber: 1g, Cholesterol: 75mg, Sodium: 450mg, Potassium: 400mg.

Grilled Steak with Lemon and Herb Marinade

Prep. time: 10 min (plus 30 minutes to marinate) | Cook time: 12 min | Serves: 4

Ingredients:

For the Steak and Marinade:
- Steak (sirloin, ribeye, or flank steak): 1 1/2 lbs
- Olive oil: 1/4 cup
- Fresh lemon juice: 1/4 cup
- Lemon zest: 1 teaspoon
- Garlic: 3 cloves, minced
- Fresh oregano: 1 tablespoon, chopped (or 1 teaspoon dried oregano); Fresh rosemary: 1 tablespoon, chopped (or 1 teaspoon dried rosemary)
- Fresh thyme: 1 tablespoon, chopped (or 1 teaspoon dried thyme)
- Salt: 1/2 teaspoon
- Black pepper: 1/4 teaspoon
- Red pepper flakes: 1/4 teaspoon (optional, for heat)

Directions:

Prepare the Marinade:

In a small bowl, whisk together olive oil, lemon juice, lemon zest, minced garlic, oregano, rosemary, thyme, salt, black pepper, and red pepper flakes (optional). Place the steak in a shallow dish or resealable bag and pour the marinade over it. Marinate in the refrigerator for at least 30 minutes, up to 2 hours for more flavor.

Grill the Steak:

Preheat your grill or grill pan to medium-high heat and lightly oil the grates. Remove the steak from the marinade and discard the excess. Grill the steak for 4-5 minutes per side for medium-rare (135°F) or adjust to your preferred doneness.

Serve:

Let the steak rest for 5 minutes, then slice against the grain and serve immediately with your favorite side dishes.

Nutritional Information (Per Serving): Calories: 350 kcal, Protein: 28g, Carbohydrates: 3g, Total Fat: 25g, Saturated Fat: 7g, Fiber: 1g, Cholesterol: 80mg, Sodium: 340mg, Potassium: 450mg.

Lamb Chops with Rosemary and Garlic

Prep. time: 10 min (plus 30 minutes to marinate) | Cook time: 10 min | Serves: 4

Ingredients:

- Lamb chops (rib or loin): 8 small chops (about 1 1/2 lbs)
- Olive oil: 3 tablespoons
- Garlic: 4 cloves, minced
- Fresh rosemary: 2 tablespoons, chopped (or 1 tablespoon dried rosemary)
- Fresh lemon juice: 1 tablespoon
- Salt: 1/2 teaspoon
- Black pepper: 1/4 teaspoon
- Red pepper flakes: 1/4 teaspoon (optional, for heat)

Directions:

Marinate the Lamb Chops (Optional):

In a small bowl, whisk together olive oil, minced garlic, chopped rosemary, lemon juice, salt, black pepper, and red pepper flakes (optional). Place the lamb chops in a dish or resealable bag, pour the marinade over them, and refrigerate for 30 minutes to 2 hours for enhanced flavor. If short on time, skip the marinade.

Sear the Lamb Chops:

Heat a skillet or grill pan over medium-high heat and add olive oil. Remove lamb chops from the marinade and sear for 3-4 minutes per side for medium-rare, or 4-5 minutes per side for medium (135°F for medium-rare, 145°F for medium).

Serve:

Let the lamb chops rest for 5 minutes, then serve on a platter. Optionally, garnish with rosemary or lemon wedges.

Nutritional Information (Per Serving): Calories: 420 kcal, Protein: 32g, Carbohydrates: 3g, Total Fat: 32g, Saturated Fat: 12g, Fiber: 1g, Cholesterol: 95mg, Sodium: 350mg, Potassium: 420mg.

Pork Tenderloin with Lemon and Thyme

Prep. time: 10 min (plus 30 minutes to marinate) | Cook time: 20 min | Serves: 4

Ingredients:

- Pork tenderloin: 1 lb (trimmed of any excess fat and silver skin)
- Olive oil: 3 tablespoons
- Fresh lemon juice: 2 tablespoons (about 1 large lemon)
- Lemon zest: 1 teaspoon
- Garlic: 3 cloves, minced
- Fresh thyme: 2 tablespoons, chopped (or 1 tablespoon dried thyme)
- Salt: 1/2 teaspoon
- Black pepper: 1/4 teaspoon
- Red pepper flakes: 1/4 teaspoon (optional, for heat)

Directions:

Marinate the Pork Tenderloin:

In a small bowl, whisk together olive oil, lemon juice, lemon zest, minced garlic, thyme, salt, black pepper, and red pepper flakes (optional). Place the pork tenderloin in a resealable bag or shallow dish, pour the marinade over, and refrigerate for at least 30 minutes (up to 2 hours for stronger flavor).

Cook the Pork Tenderloin:

Preheat the oven to 400°F (200°C) and heat an oven-safe skillet over medium-high heat. Remove the pork from the marinade, discard the excess, and sear it in the skillet for 2-3 minutes per side until browned.

Roast the Pork:

Transfer the skillet to the oven and roast for 12-15 minutes, or until the pork reaches an internal temperature of 145°F (63°C). Let it rest for 5-10 minutes before slicing to retain the juices.

Nutritional Information (Per Serving): Calories: 290 kcal, Protein: 28g, Carbohydrates: 3g, Total Fat: 18g, Saturated Fat: 3g, Fiber: 1g, Cholesterol: 85mg, Sodium: 350mg, Potassium: 450mg.

Beef Skewers with Grilled Vegetables

Prep. time: 10 min (plus 20 minutes to marinate) | Cook time: 12 min | Serves: 4

Ingredients:

- Beef sirloin or flank steak: 1 lb, cut into 1-inch cubes
- Olive oil: 3 tablespoons
- Fresh lemon juice: 2 tablespoons
- Garlic: 2 cloves, minced
- Zucchini: 1, sliced into rounds
- Red bell pepper: 1, cut into large pieces
- Red onion: 1, cut into wedges
- Salt: 1/2 teaspoon
- Black pepper: 1/4 teaspoon
- Fresh herbs (optional): thyme, oregano, or parsley for garnish

Directions:

Marinate the Beef:

In a bowl, whisk together olive oil, lemon juice, garlic, salt, and pepper. Add beef cubes, toss to coat, and refrigerate for 20 minutes.

Prepare the Vegetables:

Toss zucchini, red bell pepper, and red onion with olive oil, salt, and pepper.

Assemble the Skewers:

Thread marinated beef and vegetables onto skewers, alternating between them.

Grill the Skewers:

Preheat a grill or grill pan over medium-high heat and lightly oil the grates. Grill the skewers for 3-4 minutes per side, turning occasionally, until the beef reaches your desired doneness (about 130°F for medium-rare).

Serve:

Let the skewers rest for a couple of minutes, then garnish with fresh herbs, if desired.

Nutritional Information (Per Serving): Calories: 340 kcal, Protein: 28g, Carbohydrates: 8g, Total Fat: 22g, Saturated Fat: 6g, Fiber: 2g, Cholesterol: 70mg, Sodium: 320mg, Potassium: 600mg.

Greek-Style Baked Meatballs with Feta

Prep. time: 10 min | Cook time: 20 min | Serves: 4

Ingredients:

- Ground beef or lamb: 1 lb (lean)
- Feta cheese: 1/2 cup, crumbled
- Egg: 1 large
- Garlic: 2 cloves, minced
- Fresh parsley: 2 tablespoons, chopped
- Dried oregano: 1 teaspoon
- Salt: 1/2 teaspoon
- Black pepper: 1/4 teaspoon
- Olive oil: 1 tablespoon (for greasing the pan or drizzling on top)

Directions:

Preheat the Oven:

Preheat your oven to 400°F (200°C) and line a baking sheet with parchment paper or lightly grease it with olive oil.

Mix the Ingredients:

In a large bowl, combine ground beef or lamb, crumbled feta, egg, minced garlic, parsley, oregano, salt, and pepper. Mix until just combined, avoiding over-mixing.

Shape the Meatballs:

Form the mixture into 1 1/2-inch meatballs (about 16-18 total) and arrange them on the baking sheet with space in between.

Bake the Meatballs:

Drizzle or spray the meatballs with olive oil. Bake for 20-25 minutes until golden brown and cooked through (160°F/71°C internal temperature).

Serving Suggestions:

Serve with whole wheat pita bread or quinoa. Pair with a Greek salad or roasted vegetables for a complete meal. Add a side of tzatziki sauce for dipping.

Nutritional Information (Per Serving): Calories: 330 kcal, Protein: 27g, Carbohydrates: 2g, Total Fat: 24g, Saturated Fat: 9g, Fiber: 0g, Cholesterol: 120mg, Sodium: 550mg, Potassium: 380mg.

Lamb Stew with Olives and Tomatoes

Prep. time: 15 min | Cook time: 1.5 - 2 hours | Serves: 4

Ingredients:

- Lamb stew meat (shoulder or leg): 1 1/2 lbs, cubed
- Olive oil: 2 tablespoons
- Onion: 1 medium, diced
- Garlic: 3 cloves, minced
- Canned diced tomatoes: 1 can (14.5 oz); Chicken or beef broth (low sodium): 1 cup
- Green or black olives: 1/2 cup, pitted and halved
- Red wine (optional): 1/2 cup
- Fresh rosemary: 1 tablespoon, chopped (or 1 teaspoon dried)
- Fresh thyme: 1 tablespoon, chopped (or 1 teaspoon dried)
- Bay leaf: 1; Salt: 1/2 teaspoon
- Black pepper: 1/4 teaspoon
- Red pepper flakes: 1/4 teaspoon (optional, for heat)

Directions:

Prepare and Brown the Lamb: In a large Dutch oven, heat olive oil over medium-high heat. Season the lamb cubes with salt and pepper, then brown them in batches, about 2-3 minutes per side. Remove the lamb and set aside.

Sauté the Aromatics: In the same pot, cook diced onion for 3-4 minutes until softened. Add minced garlic and cook for 1 more minute.

Build the Stew: Deglaze the pot with red wine (optional), scraping up any brown bits, and let it simmer for 2-3 minutes. Stir in canned tomatoes, broth, rosemary, thyme, and a bay leaf. Return the browned lamb to the pot.

Simmer the Stew: Bring the stew to a simmer, reduce heat to low, cover, and cook for 1.5 - 2 hours, stirring occasionally, until the lamb is tender and the flavors meld.

Add Olives and Finish: Stir in halved olives 15 minutes before the stew is done and cook uncovered to thicken the sauce.

Serve: Remove the bay leaf, adjust seasoning, and garnish with fresh herbs if desired. Serve without delay.

Nutritional Information (Per Serving): Calories: 400 kcal, Protein: 30g, Carbohydrates: 10g, Total Fat: 25g, Saturated Fat: 8g, Fiber: 3g, Cholesterol: 90mg, Sodium: 680mg, Potassium: 650mg.

Pork Souvlaki with Tzatziki and Pita Bread

Prep. time: 10 min | Cook time: 12 min | Serves: 4

Ingredients:

For the Pork Souvlaki:
- Pork tenderloin: 1 lb, cut into 1-inch cubes; Olive oil: 2 tablespoons
- Fresh lemon juice: 2 tablespoons
- Garlic: 3 cloves, minced
- Dried oregano: 1 teaspoon
- Fresh thyme: 1 teaspoon (or 1/2 teaspoon dried); Salt: 1/2 teaspoon
- Black pepper: 1/4 teaspoon

For the Tzatziki Sauce:
- Plain Greek yogurt: 1 cup
- Cucumber: 1/2 medium, grated and drained; Garlic: 1 clove, minced
- Fresh dill: 1 tablespoon, chopped
- Fresh lemon juice: 1 tablespoon
- Olive oil: 1 tablespoon; Salt: 1/4 teaspoon; Black pepper: 1/4 teaspoon

Whole wheat pita bread: 4 rounds, warmed

Directions:

Marinate the Pork:
In a medium bowl, whisk together olive oil, lemon juice, garlic, oregano, thyme, salt, and pepper. Add pork cubes, toss to coat, cover, and refrigerate for at least 30 minutes (up to 2 hours for more flavor).

Make the Tzatziki Sauce:
Grate the cucumber and squeeze out excess liquid. In a bowl, mix Greek yogurt, grated cucumber, minced garlic, dill, lemon juice, olive oil, salt, and pepper until smooth. Refrigerate until serving.

Grill the Pork Souvlaki:
Preheat a grill or grill pan over medium-high heat. Thread marinated pork onto skewers. Grill for 3-4 minutes per side, turning occasionally, until cooked through (145°F).

Serve:
Warm the pita bread on the grill or in a skillet for 1-2 minutes. Serve the grilled pork with pita bread and tzatziki sauce.

Nutritional Information (Per Serving): Calories: 420 kcal, Protein: 35g, Carbohydrates: 30g, Total Fat: 18g, Saturated Fat: 5g, Fiber: 4g, Cholesterol: 80mg, Sodium: 600mg, Potassium: 600mg.

Grilled Lamb Burgers with Feta and Mint

Prep. time: 10 min | Cook time: 12 min | Serves: 4

Ingredients:

- Ground lamb: 1 lb
- Feta cheese: 1/2 cup, crumbled
- Fresh mint: 2 tablespoons, chopped
- Fresh parsley: 2 tablespoons, chopped
- Garlic: 2 cloves, minced
- Red onion: 1/4 cup, finely chopped
- Ground cumin: 1 teaspoon
- Salt: 1/2 teaspoon
- Black pepper: 1/4 teaspoon
- Olive oil: 1 tablespoon (for brushing the grill or skillet)

Directions:

Prepare the Burger Mixture:
In a large bowl, combine ground lamb, crumbled feta, mint, parsley, minced garlic, red onion, cumin, salt, and pepper. Mix gently and form into 4 equal-sized patties, about 1/2 inch thick.

Grill the Lamb Burgers:
Preheat the grill or grill pan to medium-high and lightly brush with olive oil. Grill the patties for 4-5 minutes per side, or until they reach 160°F for medium. Avoid pressing down to retain juices.

Serve:
Let the burgers rest for 3-5 minutes. Serve on whole wheat buns, pita bread, or lettuce wraps, or pair with tzatziki on the side.

Nutritional Information (Per Serving): Calories: 400 kcal, Protein: 26g, Carbohydrates: 2g, Total Fat: 32g, Saturated Fat: 12g, Fiber: 1g, Cholesterol: 100mg, Sodium: 550mg, Potassium: 450mg.

Beef and Barley Stew with Fresh Herbs

Prep. time: 15 min | Cook time: 1.5 to 2 hours | Serves: 4

Ingredients:

- Beef stew meat (chuck or round): 1 lb, cubed
- Olive oil: 2 tablespoons
- Onion: 1 medium, chopped
- Carrots: 2, sliced
- Celery: 2 stalks, sliced
- Garlic: 3 cloves, minced
- Pearl barley: 1/2 cup
- Low-sodium beef broth: 4 cups
- Diced tomatoes (canned): 1 can (14.5 oz); Fresh rosemary: 1 tablespoon, chopped (or 1 teaspoon dried)
- Fresh thyme: 1 tablespoon, chopped (or 1 teaspoon dried)
- Bay leaf: 1; Salt: 1/2 teaspoon
- Black pepper: 1/4 teaspoon
- Fresh parsley: 2 tablespoons, chopped (for garnish)

Directions:

Prepare the Beef:
Heat 1 tablespoon of olive oil in a large pot or Dutch oven over medium-high heat. Season beef cubes with salt and pepper. Add beef to the pot and brown on all sides, about 3-4 minutes per side. Remove the beef and set aside.

Sauté the Vegetables:
In the same pot, add remaining olive oil. Sauté chopped onion, carrots, and celery for 5-7 minutes until softened. Add minced garlic and cook for 1 more minute until fragrant.

Add the Broth and Herbs:
Pour in beef broth and diced tomatoes, scraping up any browned bits. Stir in barley, rosemary, thyme, and bay leaf.

Simmer the Stew: Return browned beef to the pot. Bring to a boil, then reduce heat to low, cover, and simmer for 1.5 to 2 hours until beef is tender and barley is cooked. Stir occasionally, adding more broth or water if needed.

Finish and Serve: Remove the bay leaf. Adjust seasoning with salt and pepper as needed. Garnish with fresh parsley and serve hot.

Nutritional Information (Per Serving): Calories: 400 kcal, Protein: 30g, Carbohydrates: 30g, Total Fat: 16g, Saturated Fat: 5g, Fiber: 7g, Cholesterol: 75mg, Sodium: 500mg, Potassium: 700mg.

Mediterranean Spiced Pork Chops with Olives

Prep. time: 10 min | Cook time: 20 min | Serves: 4

Ingredients:

- Bone-in or boneless pork chops: 4 (about 1 inch thick)
- Olive oil: 2 tablespoons
- Garlic: 3 cloves, minced
- Ground cumin: 1 teaspoon
- Ground coriander: 1 teaspoon
- Smoked paprika: 1 teaspoon
- Fresh lemon juice: 2 tablespoons
- Chicken or vegetable broth: 1/2 cup (low sodium); Green or black olives: 1/2 cup, pitted and halved
- Fresh rosemary: 1 tablespoon, chopped (or 1 teaspoon dried)
- Fresh thyme: 1 tablespoon, chopped (or 1 teaspoon dried)
- Salt: 1/2 teaspoon
- Black pepper: 1/4 teaspoon
- Fresh parsley: 2 tablespoons, chopped (for garnish)

Directions:

Prepare the Pork Chops: Pat pork chops dry with a paper towel. In a small bowl, mix cumin, coriander, smoked paprika, salt, and black pepper. Rub the spice mixture evenly over both sides of the pork chops.

Sear the Pork Chops: Heat 1 tablespoon olive oil in a skillet over medium-high heat. Sear the pork chops for 3-4 minutes per side until golden brown. Remove and set aside.

Sauté the Garlic and Herbs:
Lower the heat to medium and add the remaining tablespoon of olive oil. Sauté minced garlic for 1 minute, then stir in chopped rosemary and thyme.

Simmer with Broth and Olives: Add chicken or vegetable broth, lemon juice, and olives to the skillet. Return the pork chops, nestling them into the broth. Simmer uncovered for 5-7 minutes, spooning the broth and olives over the pork chops, until they reach an internal temperature of 145°F (63°C).

Garnish and Serve:
Remove the pork chops from the heat and let rest for a few minutes. Garnish with fresh parsley and serve.

Nutritional Information (Per Serving): Calories: 320 kcal, Protein: 28g, Carbohydrates: 4g, Total Fat: 20g, Saturated Fat: 6g, Fiber: 1g, Cholesterol: 75mg, Sodium: 600mg, Potassium: 500mg.

Lamb and Quinoa Meatballs with Yogurt Sauce

Prep. time: 15 min | Cook time: 25 min | Serves: 4

Ingredients:

For the Meatballs:
- Ground lamb: 1 lb
- Cooked quinoa: 1/2 cup
- Garlic: 2 cloves, minced
- Red onion: 1/4 cup, finely chopped
- Fresh parsley: 2 tablespoons, chopped
- Ground cumin: 1 teaspoon
- Ground coriander: 1 teaspoon
- Black pepper: 1/4 teaspoon
- Olive oil: 1 tablespoon (for greasing the pan); Salt: 1/2 teaspoon

For the Yogurt Sauce:
- Plain Greek yogurt: 1 cup
- Cucumber: 1/2, grated and drained
- Garlic: 1 clove, minced
- Lemon juice: 1 tablespoon
- Fresh dill: 1 tablespoon, chopped
- Salt: 1/4 teaspoon
- Olive oil: 1 tablespoon

Directions:

Prepare the Meatball Mixture:

In a large bowl, mix ground lamb, cooked quinoa, garlic, red onion, parsley, cumin, coriander, salt, and pepper. Gently combine and shape into 16-18 small meatballs.

Cook the Meatballs:

Oven Method: Preheat the oven to 400°F (200°C). Lightly grease a baking sheet and arrange the meatballs. Bake for 18-20 minutes until browned and cooked through.

Skillet Method: Heat olive oil in a skillet over medium heat. Cook the meatballs for 8-10 minutes, turning occasionally, until browned and fully cooked.

Prepare the Yogurt Sauce:

In a small bowl, combine Greek yogurt, grated cucumber, garlic, lemon juice, dill, and salt. Stir in olive oil until smooth. Refrigerate until serving.

Serve:

Serve the meatballs with yogurt sauce on the side or drizzled on top. Garnish with fresh herbs if desired.

Nutritional Information (Per Serving): Calories: 370 kcal, Protein: 28g, Carbohydrates: 15g, Total Fat: 22g, Saturated Fat: 8g, Fiber: 3g, Cholesterol: 75mg, Sodium: 540mg, Potassium: 500mg.

Beef Shawarma with Tahini Dressing

Prep. time: 15 min (plus 30 minutes marinating) | Cook time: 20 min | Serves: 4

Ingredients:

For the Beef Shawarma:
- Beef sirloin or flank steak: 1 lb, thinly sliced; Olive oil: 2 tablespoons
- Garlic: 3 cloves, minced
- Ground cumin: 1 teaspoon
- Ground coriander: 1 teaspoon
- Ground cinnamon: 1/2 teaspoon
- Ground paprika: 1 teaspoon
- Ground turmeric: 1/2 teaspoon
- Salt: 1/2 teaspoon; Black pepper: 1/4 teaspoon; Lemon juice: 2 tablespoons

For the Tahini Dressing:
- Tahini: 1/4 cup; Fresh lemon juice: 2 tablespoons; Garlic: 1 clove, minced
- Water: 2-3 tablespoons (to thin the dressing); Olive oil: 1 tablespoon
- Salt: 1/4 teaspoon; Fresh parsley: 1 tablespoon, chopped (for garnish)

Directions:

Marinate the Beef:

In a bowl, mix olive oil, garlic, cumin, coriander, cinnamon, paprika, turmeric, salt, pepper, and lemon juice. Add sliced beef, toss to coat, and marinate in the fridge for at least 30 minutes (up to 2 hours for more flavor).

Cook the Beef:

Heat a skillet or grill pan over medium-high heat. Cook the marinated beef in batches for 3-4 minutes per side, until browned and cooked through. Set aside.

Make the Tahini Dressing:

In a small bowl, whisk together tahini, lemon juice, garlic, olive oil, and salt. Gradually add water, 1 tablespoon at a time, until the desired consistency is reached. Set aside.

Assemble and Serve:

Serve the beef shawarma with the tahini dressing drizzled on top. Optionally, garnish with fresh parsley.

Nutritional Information (Per Serving): Calories: 380 kcal, Protein: 28g, Carbohydrates: 8g, Total Fat: 26g, Saturated Fat: 6g, Fiber: 2g, Cholesterol: 75mg, Sodium: 450mg, Potassium: 550mg.

Lamb Kebabs with Mint and Yogurt Sauce

Prep. time: 15 min (plus 30 minutes marinating) | Cook time: 12 min | Serves: 4

Ingredients:

For the Lamb Kebabs:
- Ground lamb: 1 lb
- Garlic: 3 cloves, minced
- Red onion: 1/4 cup, finely chopped
- Ground cumin: 1 teaspoon
- Ground coriander: 1 teaspoon
- Ground cinnamon: 1/2 teaspoon
- Fresh parsley: 2 tablespoons, chopped
- Fresh mint: 2 tablespoons, chopped
- Olive oil: 1 tablespoon; Salt: 1/2 teaspoon; Black pepper: 1/4 teaspoon
- Lemon juice: 1 tablespoon

For the Mint Yogurt Sauce:
- Plain Greek yogurt: 1 cup
- Fresh mint: 2 tablespoons, finely chopped; Fresh lemon juice: 1 tablespoon; Garlic: 1 clove, minced;
- Salt: 1/4 teaspoon; Olive oil: 1 tablespoon

Directions:

Prepare the Lamb Kebab Mixture:

In a large bowl, mix ground lamb, minced garlic, red onion, cumin, coriander, cinnamon, parsley, mint, olive oil, salt, pepper, and lemon juice. Gently combine and form into 8-10 kebab-shaped patties or roll onto skewers.

Marinate the Lamb: Cover the lamb kebabs and refrigerate for at least 30 minutes to meld the flavors.

Cook the Lamb Kebabs:

Grill Method: Preheat the grill to medium-high heat. Grill the kebabs for 4-5 minutes per side until browned and cooked through.

Skillet Method: Heat olive oil in a skillet over medium-high heat and cook the kebabs for 4-5 minutes per side until browned.

Prepare the Mint Yogurt Sauce:

In a small bowl, combine Greek yogurt, chopped mint, lemon juice, minced garlic, salt, and olive oil. Stir until smooth and creamy. Refrigerate until serving.

Serve: Serve the lamb kebabs with mint yogurt sauce drizzled on top or on the side.

Nutritional Information (Per Serving): Calories: 350 kcal, Protein: 28g, Carbohydrates: 7g, Total Fat: 24g, Saturated Fat: 8g, Fiber: 1g, Cholesterol: 75mg, Sodium: 450mg, Potassium: 450mg.

Mediterranean Meatballs with Tomato Sauce

Prep. time: 10 min | Cook time: 25 min | Serves: 4

Ingredients:

For the Meatballs:
- Ground beef or lamb: 1 lb
- Garlic: 2 cloves, minced
- Fresh parsley: 2 tablespoons, chopped
- Ground cumin: 1 teaspoon
- Salt: 1/2 teaspoon
- Black pepper: 1/4 teaspoon
- Olive oil: 1 tablespoon (for cooking)

For the Tomato Sauce:
- Canned crushed tomatoes: 1 can (14.5 oz)
- Garlic: 1 clove, minced
- Olive oil: 1 tablespoon
- Dried oregano: 1 teaspoon
- Salt: 1/2 teaspoon
- Black pepper: 1/4 teaspoon

Directions:

Prepare the Meatball Mixture:

In a bowl, combine ground beef or lamb, garlic, parsley, cumin, salt, and pepper. Mix well and form into small meatballs (about 1 1/2 inches in diameter).

Cook the Meatballs:

Heat 1 tablespoon olive oil in a skillet over medium heat. Cook the meatballs for 3-4 minutes per side until browned all over. Remove and set aside.

Make the Tomato Sauce:

In the same skillet, add 1 tablespoon olive oil and minced garlic. Sauté for 1 minute until fragrant. Add crushed tomatoes, oregano, salt, and pepper. Stir and simmer for 5-7 minutes.

Simmer the Meatballs in the Sauce:

Return the browned meatballs to the skillet with the sauce. Cover and simmer for 10 minutes until the meatballs are cooked through.

Serve:

Serve hot with whole wheat pasta, quinoa, or a side of veggies.

Nutritional Information (Per Serving): Calories: 320 kcal, Protein: 22g, Carbohydrates: 10g, Total Fat: 22g, Saturated Fat: 6g, Fiber: 3g, Sodium: 550mg, Potassium: 600mg.

Chapter

9

Vegetable Recipes

Vegetables are the heart of the Mediterranean diet, offering a rainbow of colors, flavors, and nutrients in every dish. Mediterranean cooking celebrates the natural goodness of seasonal vegetables, combining them with olive oil, herbs, and spices to create meals that are both vibrant and nourishing. Whether roasted, grilled, or lightly sautéed, vegetables take center stage, providing a delicious and wholesome foundation for everyday meals.

In this section, "Vegetable Recipes," you'll explore a variety of creative and flavorful ways to prepare vegetables. From simple salads and side dishes to hearty mains, these recipes highlight the versatility of vegetables in Mediterranean cuisine. Perfect for vegetarians and anyone looking to add more plant-based meals to their diet, these dishes bring the best of Mediterranean flavors to your table, packed with nutrition and taste.

Chickpea and Spinach Stew

Prep. time: 10 min | Cook time: 20 min | Serves: 4

Ingredients:

- Olive oil: 2 tablespoons
- Onion: 1 small, diced
- Garlic: 3 cloves, minced
- Canned chickpeas: 1 can (15 oz), drained and rinsed
- Fresh spinach: 4 cups, packed
- Canned diced tomatoes: 1 can (14.5 oz), drained
- Vegetable broth: 1 cup
- Dried oregano: 1 teaspoon
- Ground cumin: 1 teaspoon
- Salt: 1/2 teaspoon
- Black pepper: 1/4 teaspoon
- Lemon juice: 1 tablespoon (optional, for extra brightness)
- Fresh parsley: 2 tablespoons, chopped (for garnish)

Directions:

Sauté the Aromatics:

In a large skillet, heat the olive oil over medium heat. Add the diced onion and cook for 3-4 minutes until softened. Stir in the minced garlic and cook for another minute until fragrant.

Add Chickpeas and Tomatoes:

Add the chickpeas, diced tomatoes, and vegetable broth to the skillet. Stir in the oregano, cumin, salt, and black pepper. Bring the mixture to a simmer and cook for 5-7 minutes to allow the flavors to meld.

Add Spinach:

Gradually stir in the spinach and cook for another 2-3 minutes until wilted.

Finish with Lemon Juice (Optional):

Stir in the lemon juice for extra brightness. Taste and adjust seasoning if needed.

Serve:

Garnish with freshly chopped parsley and serve immediately. This stew pairs wonderfully with whole grain bread, couscous, or over rice for a complete meal.

Nutritional Information (Per Serving): Calories: 240 kcal, Protein: 8g, Carbohydrates: 30g, Total Fat: 10g, Saturated Fat: 1.5g, Fiber: 8g, Cholesterol: 0mg, Sodium: 550mg, Potassium: 500mg.

Roasted Cauliflower with Tahini and Pine Nuts

Prep. time: 10 min | Cook time: 25 min | Serves: 4

Ingredients:

- Cauliflower: 1 medium head, cut into florets
- Olive oil: 2 tablespoons
- Ground cumin: 1 teaspoon
- Salt: 1/2 teaspoon
- Black pepper: 1/4 teaspoon
- Pine nuts: 1/4 cup, toasted

For the Tahini Sauce:
- Tahini: 1/4 cup
- Fresh lemon juice: 2 tablespoons
- Garlic: 1 clove, minced
- Water: 2-3 tablespoons (to thin the sauce)
- Salt: 1/4 teaspoon
- Olive oil: 1 tablespoon

Directions:

Preheat the Oven:

Preheat your oven to 425°F (220°C). Line a baking sheet with parchment paper or foil.

Prepare the Cauliflower: In a large bowl, toss cauliflower florets with olive oil, ground cumin, salt, and pepper until evenly coated.

Roast the Cauliflower:

Spread the cauliflower in a single layer on the baking sheet. Roast for 25-30 minutes, turning once halfway through, until golden brown and tender.

Toast the Pine Nuts: While the cauliflower roasts, toast pine nuts in a dry skillet over medium heat for 2-3 minutes, stirring frequently, until lightly browned. Set aside.

Make the Tahini Sauce:

In a small bowl, whisk together tahini, lemon juice, minced garlic, olive oil, and salt. Gradually add water, 1 tablespoon at a time, until smooth and pourable.

Assemble the Dish: Drizzle the tahini sauce over the roasted cauliflower. Sprinkle with toasted pine nuts and garnish with fresh herbs if desired.

Nutritional Information (Per Serving): Calories: 230 kcal, Protein: 5g, Carbohydrates: 13g, Total Fat: 18g, Saturated Fat: 2g, Fiber: 4g, Sodium: 350mg, Potassium: 500mg.

Grilled Zucchini with Lemon and Olive Oil

Prep. time: 5 min | Cook time: 10 min | Serves: 4

Ingredients:

- Zucchini: 4 medium, sliced lengthwise into 1/4-inch thick slices
- Olive oil: 2 tablespoons
- Fresh lemon juice: 1 tablespoon
- Garlic: 1 clove, minced
- Salt: 1/2 teaspoon
- Black pepper: 1/4 teaspoon
- Fresh parsley or basil: 2 tablespoons, chopped (optional)

Optional Customizations:

- Add a pinch of red pepper flakes for heat.
- Sprinkle with grated Parmesan cheese for extra flavor.
- Use fresh thyme or rosemary instead of parsley for a different herb profile.

Directions:

Preheat the Grill:
Preheat a grill or grill pan to medium-high heat.

Prepare the Zucchini:
In a large bowl, toss zucchini slices with olive oil, lemon juice, garlic, salt, and black pepper until evenly coated.

Grill the Zucchini:
Place the zucchini slices on the preheated grill. Grill for 3-4 minutes per side until tender with grill marks, but still retaining some texture.

Garnish and Serve:
Transfer the zucchini to a serving platter. Garnish with fresh parsley or basil, and optionally drizzle with more olive oil or lemon juice. Serve immediately.

Nutritional Information (Per Serving): Calories: 80 kcal, Protein: 2g, Carbohydrates: 6g, Total Fat: 7g, Saturated Fat: 1g, Fiber: 2g, Cholesterol: 0mg, Sodium: 180mg, Potassium: 350mg.

Stuffed Bell Peppers with Quinoa and Feta

Prep. time: 15 min | Cook time: 35 min | Serves: 4

Ingredients:

- Bell peppers: 4 large (any color)
- Quinoa: 1 cup, uncooked
- Olive oil: 1 tablespoon
- Red onion: 1/2 medium, finely chopped
- Garlic: 2 cloves, minced
- Diced tomatoes: 1 can (14.5 oz), drained
- Feta cheese: 1/2 cup, crumbled
- Fresh parsley: 2 tablespoons, chopped
- Fresh oregano or basil: 1 tablespoon, chopped (optional)
- Salt: 1/2 teaspoon
- Black pepper: 1/4 teaspoon
- Lemon juice: 1 tablespoon
- Pine nuts: 2 tablespoons, toasted (optional)

Directions:

Cook the Quinoa: Rinse quinoa under cold water. In a saucepan, combine quinoa with 2 cups of water. Bring to a boil, reduce heat to low, cover, and simmer for 15 minutes until tender and water is absorbed. Fluff with a fork and set aside.

Prepare the Bell Peppers: Preheat the oven to 375°F (190°C). Cut the tops off the bell peppers, remove seeds and membranes, and set aside.

Prepare the Filling: Heat olive oil in a skillet over medium heat. Sauté red onion and garlic for 3-4 minutes until softened. Stir in cooked quinoa, diced tomatoes, feta, parsley, oregano (optional), salt, and pepper. Remove from heat, then add lemon juice and toasted pine nuts (if using).

Stuff the Bell Peppers: Spoon the quinoa mixture into the bell peppers. Place stuffed peppers in a baking dish with about 1/4 inch of water in the bottom.

Bake the Peppers: Cover the dish with foil and bake for 30 minutes. Remove the foil and bake for an additional 5-10 minutes until the peppers are tender and slightly browned. **Serve:** Let the peppers cool slightly. Garnish with extra parsley or a sprinkle of feta, if desired, and serve.

Nutritional Information (Per Serving): Calories: 300 kcal, Protein: 10g, Carbohydrates: 35g, Total Fat: 12g, Saturated Fat: 4g, Fiber: 6g, Cholesterol: 15mg, Sodium: 480mg, Potassium: 650mg.

Ratatouille with Fresh Herbs and Olive Oil

Prep. time: 15 min | Cook time: 35 min | Serves: 4

Ingredients:

- Eggplant: 1 medium, diced
- Zucchini: 2 medium, diced
- Bell peppers: 2 (any color), diced
- Yellow onion: 1 medium, diced
- Garlic: 3 cloves, minced
- Tomatoes: 3 medium, chopped (or 1 can diced tomatoes, drained)
- Olive oil: 3 tablespoons
- Fresh thyme: 2 teaspoons (or 1 teaspoon dried)
- Fresh basil: 2 tablespoons, chopped
- Fresh parsley: 2 tablespoons, chopped
- Salt: 1/2 teaspoon
- Black pepper: 1/4 teaspoon
- Optional: Red pepper flakes (1/4 teaspoon) for heat

Directions:

Prepare the Vegetables:
Preheat the oven to 375°F (190°C). Dice the eggplant, zucchini, bell peppers, and onion. Mince the garlic.

Sauté the Vegetables: Heat 2 tablespoons of olive oil in an oven-safe skillet or Dutch oven over medium heat. Sauté the onion and garlic for 3-4 minutes until softened. Add eggplant, zucchini, and bell peppers, cooking for 5-7 minutes until slightly browned.

Add Tomatoes and Herbs: Stir in chopped tomatoes, thyme, salt, and pepper. Simmer for 5 minutes to combine the flavors.

Bake the Ratatouille:
Drizzle the remaining tablespoon of olive oil over the vegetables. Transfer the skillet to the oven and bake, uncovered, for 20-25 minutes until tender and slightly caramelized.

Finish with Fresh Herbs:
Remove from the oven and stir in fresh basil and parsley. Adjust seasoning if needed.

Serve:
Serve warm as a side dish or over couscous, quinoa, or crusty whole-grain bread.

Nutritional Information (Per Serving): Calories: 180 kcal, Protein: 4g, Carbohydrates: 18g, Total Fat: 10g, Saturated Fat: 1.5g, Fiber: 6g, Cholesterol: 0mg, Sodium: 240mg, Potassium: 700mg.

Roasted Eggplant with Garlic and Parsley

Prep. time: 10 min | Cook time: 30 min | Serves: 4

Ingredients:

- Eggplant: 2 medium, cut into 1-inch cubes
- Olive oil: 3 tablespoons
- Garlic: 3 cloves, minced
- Fresh parsley: 2 tablespoons, chopped
- Salt: 1/2 teaspoon
- Black pepper: 1/4 teaspoon
- Fresh lemon juice: 1 tablespoon (optional)

Optional Customizations:
- Add 1/2 teaspoon of cumin or smoked paprika for additional flavor.
- Sprinkle with red pepper flakes for a hint of heat.
- Substitute parsley with fresh basil or cilantro for variety.

Directions:

Preheat the Oven:
Preheat your oven to 400°F (200°C) and line a baking sheet with parchment paper.

Prepare the Eggplant:
Place cubed eggplant in a bowl, drizzle with olive oil, and season with salt and pepper. Toss until evenly coated.

Roast the Eggplant:
Spread the eggplant in a single layer on the baking sheet. Roast for 25-30 minutes, turning once halfway through, until golden brown and tender.

Add Garlic and Finish:
In the last 5 minutes of roasting, sprinkle minced garlic over the eggplant to infuse flavor. Roast for the remaining 5 minutes.

Garnish and Serve:
Transfer the eggplant to a serving dish, drizzle with lemon juice (optional), and sprinkle with fresh parsley. Serve warm.

Nutritional Information (Per Serving): Calories: 120 kcal, Protein: 2g, Carbohydrates: 10g, Total Fat: 9g, Saturated Fat: 1.5g, Fiber: 4g, Cholesterol: 0mg, Sodium: 200mg, Potassium: 400mg.

Sautéed Spinach with Garlic and Lemon

Prep. time: 5 min | Cook time: 5 min | Serves: 4

Ingredients:

- Fresh spinach: 10 oz (about 6 cups)
- Olive oil: 2 tablespoons
- Garlic: 3 cloves, thinly sliced or minced
- Fresh lemon juice: 1 tablespoon
- Salt: 1/4 teaspoon
- Black pepper: 1/4 teaspoon
- Lemon zest: 1 teaspoon (optional)
- Red pepper flakes: 1/4 teaspoon (optional, for a bit of heat)

Optional Customizations:

- Add pine nuts or slivered almonds for crunch.
- Substitute spinach with Swiss chard or kale.
- Garnish with fresh herbs like parsley or basil for added flavor.

Directions:

Prepare the Ingredients:
Wash and pat dry the spinach. Thinly slice or mince the garlic.

Sauté the Garlic:
Heat olive oil in a large skillet over medium heat. Add garlic and sauté for about 1 minute, until fragrant but not browned.

Add the Spinach:
Add the spinach to the skillet, tossing to coat with the garlic and olive oil. Sauté for 2-3 minutes, stirring frequently, until wilted and bright green.

Finish with Lemon:
Remove from heat and drizzle with fresh lemon juice. Season with salt, black pepper, and optional red pepper flakes and lemon zest. Toss to combine.

Serve: Serve warm, garnished with extra lemon zest or fresh herbs if desired.

Serving Suggestions: Pair with grilled chicken, fish, or lamb for a balanced meal. Serve alongside a Mediterranean grain like quinoa, couscous, or farro. Add it as a filling for a whole grain wrap or pita with hummus for a light lunch.

Nutritional Information (Per Serving): Calories: 80 kcal, Protein: 2g, Carbohydrates: 5g, Total Fat: 7g, Saturated Fat: 1g, Fiber: 2g, Cholesterol: 0mg, Sodium: 150mg, Potassium: 470mg.

Mediterranean Stuffed Mushrooms with Feta

Prep. time: 10 min | Cook time: 20 min | Serves: 4

Ingredients:

- Large mushrooms (like cremini or button): 12-16 (stems removed)
- Feta cheese: 1/2 cup, crumbled
- Garlic: 2 cloves, minced
- Olive oil: 2 tablespoons
- Red onion: 1/4 cup, finely chopped
- Fresh parsley: 2 tablespoons, chopped
- Fresh oregano or thyme: 1 tablespoon, chopped (or 1 teaspoon dried)
- Panko breadcrumbs (optional): 1/4 cup (for extra crunch)
- Salt: 1/4 teaspoon
- Black pepper: 1/4 teaspoon
- Lemon juice: 1 tablespoon
- Pine nuts (optional): 2 tablespoons, toasted

Directions:

Preheat the Oven: Preheat your oven to 375°F (190°C) and line a baking sheet with parchment paper or lightly grease with olive oil.

Prepare the Mushrooms: Remove the stems from the mushrooms and set aside. Clean the mushroom caps with a damp cloth and place them on the prepared baking sheet.

Prepare the Filling: Finely chop the mushroom stems. Heat 1 tablespoon of olive oil in a skillet over medium heat, then sauté the chopped stems, garlic, and red onion for 3-4 minutes until softened. Stir in crumbled feta, parsley, oregano, breadcrumbs (optional), salt, and pepper.

Stuff the Mushrooms: Spoon the feta mixture into each mushroom cap, pressing gently. Drizzle with the remaining 1 tablespoon of olive oil.

Bake the Mushrooms: Bake for 15-20 minutes until the mushrooms are tender and the stuffing is golden brown.

Garnish and Serve:
Drizzle with fresh lemon juice and sprinkle with toasted pine nuts (optional). Garnish with parsley or fresh herbs before serving.

Nutritional Information (Per Serving): Calories: 180 kcal, Protein: 6g, Carbohydrates: 9g, Total Fat: 14g, Saturated Fat: 4g, Fiber: 2g, Cholesterol: 15mg, Sodium: 350mg, Potassium: 400mg.

Grilled Asparagus with Olive Oil and Lemon Zest

Prep. time: 5 min | Cook time: 10 min | Serves: 4

Ingredients:

- Fresh asparagus: 1 lb (trim the tough ends)
- Olive oil: 2 tablespoons
- Lemon zest: 1 teaspoon
- Fresh lemon juice: 1 tablespoon
- Salt: 1/4 teaspoon
- Black pepper: 1/4 teaspoon
- Garlic (optional): 1 clove, minced
- Red pepper flakes (optional): 1/4 teaspoon (for a bit of heat)
- Fresh parsley or basil: 2 tablespoons, chopped (optional garnish)

Directions:

Prepare the Asparagus:
Rinse and trim the woody ends of the asparagus spears. Pat dry.

Preheat the Grill:
Preheat your grill or grill pan to medium-high heat.

Season the Asparagus:
In a large bowl, toss the asparagus with olive oil, minced garlic (optional), salt, and black pepper.

Grill the Asparagus:
Place the asparagus in a single layer on the grill. Grill for 3-4 minutes per side, turning occasionally, until tender and lightly charred.

Finish with Lemon:
Once off the grill, drizzle with fresh lemon juice and sprinkle with lemon zest. Optionally, add red pepper flakes for heat and garnish with parsley or basil.

Serve:
Serve immediately as a side dish or pair with a Mediterranean-inspired protein.

Nutritional Information (Per Serving): Calories: 90 kcal, Protein: 3g, Carbohydrates: 6g, Total Fat: 7g, Saturated Fat: 1g, Fiber: 3g, Cholesterol: 0mg, Sodium: 150mg, Potassium: 280mg.

Spaghetti Squash with Olive Tapenade

Prep. time: 10 min | Cook time: 40 min | Serves: 4

Ingredients:

For the Spaghetti Squash:
- Spaghetti squash: 1 medium (about 2-3 lbs)
- Olive oil: 2 tablespoons
- Salt: 1/2 teaspoon
- Black pepper: 1/4 teaspoon

For the Olive Tapenade:
- Kalamata olives (pitted): 1/2 cup
- Green olives (pitted): 1/2 cup
- Capers: 1 tablespoon, rinsed
- Garlic: 1 clove, minced
- Olive oil: 2 tablespoons
- Lemon juice: 1 tablespoon
- Fresh parsley: 2 tablespoons, chopped
- Red pepper flakes: 1/4 teaspoon (optional)
- Black pepper: 1/4 teaspoon

Directions:

Prepare the Spaghetti Squash:
Preheat your oven to 400°F (200°C). Cut the squash in half lengthwise, scoop out the seeds, and drizzle with olive oil, salt, and pepper. Place cut side down on a baking sheet lined with parchment paper and roast for 35-40 minutes until tender.

Make the Olive Tapenade:
While the squash roasts, prepare the tapenade. In a food processor, combine Kalamata and green olives, capers, garlic, olive oil, lemon juice, parsley, red pepper flakes (optional), and black pepper. Pulse until finely chopped but slightly chunky.

Shred the Spaghetti Squash:
Once roasted, let the squash cool for a few minutes. Use a fork to scrape the inside, creating spaghetti-like strands. Transfer to a bowl.

Assemble the Dish: Toss the squash with the olive tapenade until well combined. Adjust seasoning with salt, pepper, or lemon juice as needed.

Serve: Serve warm, garnished with fresh parsley or red pepper flakes if desired.

Nutritional Information (Per Serving): Calories: 180 kcal, Protein: 3g, Carbohydrates: 14g, Total Fat: 14g, Saturated Fat: 2g, Fiber: 4g, Cholesterol: 0mg, Sodium: 450mg, Potassium: 400mg.

Baked Sweet Potatoes with Greek Yogurt and Chives

Prep. time: 5 min | Cook time: 45 min | Serves: 4

Ingredients:

- Sweet potatoes: 4 medium (about 1 lb each)
- Greek yogurt (plain, full-fat or low-fat): 1 cup
- Olive oil: 2 tablespoons
- Fresh chives: 2 tablespoons, finely chopped
- Salt: 1/2 teaspoon
- Black pepper: 1/4 teaspoon
- Garlic powder (optional): 1/4 teaspoon
- Lemon zest (optional): 1 teaspoon

Optional Customizations:
- Add a sprinkle of paprika or cumin for extra warmth.
- Top with crumbled feta or toasted pine nuts for added texture and flavor.

Directions:

Preheat the Oven:
Preheat your oven to 400°F (200°C). Line a baking sheet with parchment paper or foil.
Prepare the Sweet Potatoes: Wash and dry the sweet potatoes. Pierce each a few times with a fork to allow steam to escape.
Bake the Sweet Potatoes: Place the sweet potatoes on the prepared baking sheet. Bake for 45-50 minutes until tender when pierced with a fork.
Prepare the Yogurt Topping:
While the sweet potatoes bake, mix Greek yogurt with 1 tablespoon of olive oil, salt, pepper, and garlic powder (optional). Stir until smooth.
Assemble the Dish:
Once the sweet potatoes are baked, let them cool slightly before slicing open. Fluff the insides with a fork and drizzle with the remaining tablespoon of olive oil. Top with a dollop of the yogurt mixture, fresh chives, and lemon zest (optional).
Serve:
Serve immediately as a side dish or main course with a salad or grilled vegetables.

Nutritional Information (Per Serving): Calories: 280 kcal, Protein: 6g, Carbohydrates: 45g, Total Fat: 8g, Saturated Fat: 2g, Fiber: 7g, Cholesterol: 5mg, Sodium: 320mg, Potassium: 950mg.

Roasted Brussels Sprouts with Balsamic Glaze

Prep. time: 10 min | Cook time: 30 min | Serves: 4

Ingredients:

- Brussels sprouts: 1 lb, trimmed and halved
- Olive oil: 2 tablespoons
- Balsamic vinegar: 2 tablespoons
- Honey (or maple syrup for a vegan option): 1 tablespoon
- Salt: 1/2 teaspoon
- Black pepper: 1/4 teaspoon
- Garlic powder (optional): 1/2 teaspoon
- Red pepper flakes (optional): 1/4 teaspoon for heat
- Fresh parsley or thyme (optional garnish): 2 tablespoons, chopped

Optional Customizations:
Add toasted almonds or pine nuts for crunch. Sprinkle with grated Parmesan cheese for extra richness. Use lemon zest and juice for a citrusy variation.

Directions:

Preheat the Oven:
Preheat your oven to 400°F (200°C). Line a baking sheet with parchment paper or lightly grease with olive oil.
Prepare the Brussels Sprouts: In a large bowl, toss halved Brussels sprouts with olive oil, salt, pepper, and garlic powder (optional) until evenly coated.
Roast the Brussels Sprouts:
Spread the Brussels sprouts cut side down in a single layer on the baking sheet. Roast for 25-30 minutes, flipping halfway through, until crispy and golden brown.
Make the Balsamic Glaze: While roasting, prepare the balsamic glaze by simmering balsamic vinegar and honey (or maple syrup) in a small saucepan over medium heat for 5-6 minutes, until slightly thickened. Remove from heat.
Finish the Brussels Sprouts: Drizzle the balsamic glaze over the roasted Brussels sprouts and toss gently to coat. Optionally, add red pepper flakes for heat and garnish with fresh parsley or thyme.
Serve: Serve warm as a side dish or part of a Mediterranean-inspired meal.

Nutritional Information (Per Serving): Calories: 140 kcal, Protein: 3g, Carbohydrates: 18g, Total Fat: 7g, Saturated Fat: 1g, Fiber: 4g, Cholesterol: 0mg, Sodium: 320mg, Potassium: 400mg.

Mediterranean Vegetable Stir-Fry with Garlic

Prep. time: 10 min | Cook time: 10 min | Serves: 4

Ingredients:

- Olive oil: 2 tablespoons
- Garlic: 3 cloves, minced
- Zucchini: 2 medium, sliced into rounds or half-moons
- Red bell pepper: 1, thinly sliced
- Yellow bell pepper: 1, thinly sliced
- Cherry tomatoes: 1 cup, halved
- Red onion: 1/2 medium, thinly sliced
- Fresh spinach: 2 cups
- Fresh parsley: 2 tablespoons, chopped
- Salt: 1/2 teaspoon
- Black pepper: 1/4 teaspoon
- Dried oregano: 1 teaspoon
- Lemon juice: 1 tablespoon
- Feta cheese (optional): 1/4 cup, crumbled

Directions:

Prepare the Vegetables:
Wash and chop the vegetables. Slice the zucchini, bell peppers, cherry tomatoes, and onion.

Heat the Skillet:
Heat 2 tablespoons of olive oil in a large skillet over medium heat. Add minced garlic and sauté for 30 seconds until fragrant.

Cook the Vegetables:
Add bell peppers, zucchini, and red onion to the skillet. Cook for 5-6 minutes, stirring occasionally, until softened but still crisp. Add cherry tomatoes and spinach, stirring for 2-3 minutes until spinach wilts and tomatoes soften.

Season and Finish:
Season the stir-fry with salt, black pepper, dried oregano, and lemon juice. Stir and cook for 1-2 more minutes until flavors combine.

Serve: Remove from heat, stir in fresh parsley, and optionally sprinkle with crumbled feta before serving.

Nutritional Information (Per Serving): Calories: 150 kcal, Protein: 4g, Carbohydrates: 15g, Total Fat: 9g, Saturated Fat: 1.5g, Fiber: 5g, Cholesterol: 0mg (add 20mg if feta is used), Sodium: 350mg, Potassium: 550mg.

Baked Zucchini Fries with Lemon Aioli

Prep. time: 15 min | Cook time: 20 min | Serves: 4

Ingredients:

For the Zucchini Fries:
- Zucchini: 2 medium, cut into 3-inch sticks; Olive oil: 2 tablespoons
- Panko breadcrumbs: 1/2 cup
- Parmesan cheese (optional): 1/4 cup, grated; Garlic powder: 1/2 teaspoon
- Dried oregano: 1 teaspoon
- Salt: 1/2 teaspoon
- Black pepper: 1/4 teaspoon
- Egg: 1 large, beaten

For the Lemon Aioli:
- Greek yogurt: 1/2 cup
- Mayonnaise: 2 tablespoons
- Fresh lemon juice: 1 tablespoon
- Lemon zest: 1 teaspoon
- Garlic: 1 clove, minced
- Olive oil: 1 teaspoon
- Salt: 1/4 teaspoon
- Black pepper: 1/4 teaspoon

Directions:

Preheat the Oven:
Preheat your oven to 425°F (220°C). Line a baking sheet with parchment paper or lightly grease with olive oil.

Prepare the Zucchini Fries: Cut the zucchini into sticks about 3 inches long and 1/2 inch thick. In a bowl, mix Panko breadcrumbs, Parmesan (if using), garlic powder, oregano, salt, and black pepper.

Coat the Zucchini: Dip each zucchini stick in beaten egg, then coat with the breadcrumb mixture, pressing to ensure it sticks. Place the coated zucchini on the prepared baking sheet.

Bake the Zucchini Fries: Drizzle or spray with olive oil for crispiness. Bake for 20-25 minutes, turning halfway through, until golden brown and crispy.

Make the Lemon Aioli: While the zucchini fries bake, whisk together Greek yogurt, mayonnaise, lemon juice, lemon zest, garlic, olive oil, salt, and black pepper in a small bowl until smooth.

Serve: Serve the crispy zucchini fries hot with lemon aioli on the side for dipping.

Nutritional Information (Per Serving): Calories: 190 kcal, Protein: 7g, Carbohydrates: 17g, Total Fat: 11g, Saturated Fat: 3g, Fiber: 3g, Cholesterol: 45mg, Sodium: 380mg, Potassium: 350mg.

Grilled Eggplant Rolls with Feta and Spinach

Prep. time: 15 min | Cook time: 12 min | Serves: 4

Ingredients:

- Eggplant: 2 medium, sliced lengthwise into 1/4-inch thick slices
- Olive oil: 2 tablespoons
- Fresh spinach: 2 cups, chopped
- Feta cheese: 1/2 cup, crumbled
- Garlic: 2 cloves, minced
- Fresh parsley: 2 tablespoons, chopped
- Fresh dill (optional): 1 tablespoon, chopped
- Lemon juice: 1 tablespoon
- Salt: 1/2 teaspoon
- Black pepper: 1/4 teaspoon
- Red pepper flakes (optional): 1/4 teaspoon for a hint of heat

Optional Customizations:

Add sun-dried tomatoes or roasted red peppers to the filling for extra flavor. Substitute feta with goat cheese or ricotta for a creamier filling.

Directions:

Prepare the Eggplant:

Preheat the grill or grill pan to medium-high heat. Brush both sides of the eggplant slices with olive oil and season with salt and pepper.

Grill the Eggplant: Grill the eggplant slices for 3-4 minutes per side, until tender with grill marks. Remove and set aside.

Prepare the Filling:

In a skillet over medium heat, sauté minced garlic in 1 tablespoon of olive oil for 1 minute until fragrant. Add chopped spinach and cook for 2-3 minutes until wilted. Remove from heat and stir in crumbled feta, parsley, dill (optional), lemon juice, and red pepper flakes.

Assemble the Rolls:

Lay each grilled eggplant slice flat. Place 1-2 tablespoons of the spinach and feta mixture at one end, then roll tightly around the filling. Secure with a toothpick if necessary.

Serve: Arrange the rolls on a platter and drizzle with extra olive oil and lemon juice. Garnish with parsley or dill if desired.

Nutritional Information (Per Serving): Calories: 180 kcal, Protein: 6g, Carbohydrates: 10g, Total Fat: 14g, Saturated Fat: 4g, Fiber: 4g, Cholesterol: 15mg, Sodium: 320mg, Potassium: 600mg.

Moroccan Spiced Carrots with Olive Oil and Mint

Prep. time: 10 min | Cook time: 30 min | Serves: 4

Ingredients:

- Carrots: 1 lb, peeled and sliced into 1/4-inch rounds
- Olive oil: 2 tablespoons
- Ground cumin: 1 teaspoon
- Ground coriander: 1 teaspoon
- Ground cinnamon: 1/2 teaspoon
- Ground paprika (sweet or smoked): 1/2 teaspoon
- Salt: 1/2 teaspoon
- Black pepper: 1/4 teaspoon
- Fresh lemon juice: 1 tablespoon
- Fresh mint: 2 tablespoons, chopped
- Fresh parsley (optional): 1 tablespoon, chopped
- Red pepper flakes (optional): 1/4 teaspoon for a hint of heat

Directions:

Preheat the Oven:

Preheat your oven to 400°F (200°C). Line a baking sheet with parchment paper or lightly grease with olive oil.

Prepare the Carrots:

In a large bowl, toss sliced carrots with olive oil, cumin, coriander, cinnamon, paprika, salt, and black pepper until evenly coated.

Roast the Carrots:

Spread the carrots in a single layer on the baking sheet. Roast for 25-30 minutes, stirring halfway, until tender and slightly caramelized.

Finish with Lemon and Mint:

Transfer the roasted carrots to a serving bowl. Drizzle with fresh lemon juice and sprinkle with chopped mint and parsley. Toss gently to combine.

Serve:

Serve warm, garnished with red pepper flakes if desired.

Nutritional Information (Per Serving): Calories: 120 kcal, Protein: 1g, Carbohydrates: 14g, Total Fat: 7g, Saturated Fat: 1g, Fiber: 4g, Cholesterol: 0mg, Sodium: 320mg, Potassium: 380mg.

Chapter 10

Desserts

Desserts in the Mediterranean diet are a celebration of natural sweetness and simplicity. Rather than relying on heavy creams or excess sugar, Mediterranean desserts often highlight fruits, nuts, and honey, creating a light yet satisfying end to a meal. These desserts balance indulgence with wholesome ingredients, offering flavors that are as nutritious as they are delicious.

In this section, "Desserts," you'll find a selection of sweet treats that reflect the Mediterranean approach to healthy indulgence. From fruit-based dishes to baked goods infused with olive oil and nuts, these recipes are designed to satisfy your sweet tooth while staying true to the principles of balanced, natural eating. Whether for a special occasion or a simple weekday treat, these desserts will bring a touch of Mediterranean sweetness to your table.

Baked Pears with Honey and Walnuts

Prep. time: 10 min | Cook time: 25 min | Serves: 4

Ingredients:

- Pears: 4 (ripe but firm), halved and cored
- Honey: 2 tablespoons
- Walnuts: 1/4 cup, chopped
- Cinnamon: 1/2 teaspoon
- Fresh lemon juice: 1 tablespoon
- Extra virgin olive oil: 1 tablespoon
- Greek yogurt: for serving (optional)

Directions:

Preheat the Oven:
Preheat your oven to 375°F (190°C).

Prepare the Pears:
Arrange the pear halves cut-side up in a baking dish. Drizzle with olive oil and lemon juice.

Top the Pears:
In a small bowl, mix the chopped walnuts with cinnamon. Spoon the mixture into the center of each pear half, then drizzle the pears with honey.

Bake the Pears:
Bake in the preheated oven for 20-25 minutes, or until the pears are tender and golden.

Serve:
Serve warm, optionally with a dollop of Greek yogurt for added creaminess.

Nutritional Information (Per Serving): Calories: 190 kcal, Protein: 2g, Carbohydrates: 28g, Total Fat: 8g, Saturated Fat: 1g, Fiber: 4g, Cholesterol: 0mg, Sodium: 5mg, Potassium: 200mg.

Greek Yogurt with Honey and Walnuts

Prep. time: 5 min | Cook time: None | Serves: 2

Ingredients:

- Greek yogurt (plain, full-fat or low-fat): 1 cup
- Honey: 2 tablespoons
- Walnuts: 1/4 cup, chopped and lightly toasted
- Ground cinnamon (optional): 1/4 teaspoon
- Fresh mint leaves (optional garnish)

Optional Customizations:
- Add a drizzle of lemon or orange zest for a citrusy twist.
- Use almonds, pistachios, or hazelnuts instead of walnuts.
- Top with fresh berries, figs, or pomegranate seeds for extra flavor and color.

Directions:

Prepare the Ingredients:
Lightly toast chopped walnuts in a skillet over medium heat for 2-3 minutes if desired, to enhance flavor.

Assemble the Yogurt:
Divide Greek yogurt between two serving bowls.

Add the Honey and Walnuts:
Drizzle 1 tablespoon of honey over each bowl and sprinkle toasted walnuts on top.

Finish with Cinnamon (Optional):
For extra warmth, sprinkle a pinch of cinnamon over the yogurt and honey.

Garnish and Serve:
Optionally, garnish with fresh mint leaves for color and serve immediately.

Serving Suggestions:
Serve as a light dessert or healthy breakfast. Pair with fresh fruit like figs, berries, or banana slices. Enjoy as a post-workout snack to replenish protein and healthy fats.

Nutritional Information (Per Serving): Calories: 220 kcal, Protein: 10g, Carbohydrates: 21g, Total Fat: 12g, Saturated Fat: 2g, Fiber: 2g, Cholesterol: 10mg, Sodium: 55mg, Potassium: 250mg.

Sun-Kissed Citrus Salad

Prep. time: 10 min | Cook time: None | Serves: 4

Ingredients:

- Oranges: 2 large, peeled and thinly sliced into rounds; Grapefruit: 1 large, peeled and segmented
- Mandarins: 2 small, peeled and separated into segments
- Pomegranate seeds: 1/2 cup
- Fresh mint leaves: 2 tablespoons, finely chopped
- Honey or agave syrup: 2 tablespoons (optional for extra sweetness)
- Fresh lemon juice: 1 tablespoon
- Olive oil (extra virgin, optional): 1 teaspoon; Sea salt: a pinch (optional)

Optional Customizations:
- Sprinkle a dash of cinnamon or cardamom for a hint of spice. Add a handful of toasted almonds or pistachios for a crunchy texture. Top with a dollop of Greek yogurt.

Directions:

Prepare the Citrus Fruits:
Peel and slice the oranges into thin rounds. Peel and segment the grapefruit and mandarins, removing any seeds.

Arrange the Fruit:
In a large serving bowl or platter, arrange the orange slices, grapefruit segments, and mandarin pieces in an overlapping pattern.

Add Pomegranate Seeds and Mint: Sprinkle the pomegranate seeds evenly over the citrus fruits, followed by the finely chopped mint leaves.

Make the Dressing:
In a small bowl, whisk together the honey (or agave syrup), fresh lemon juice, and a light drizzle of extra virgin olive oil (if using). Add a pinch of sea salt to enhance the flavors.

Dress the Salad: Drizzle the dressing evenly over the citrus salad. Gently toss to combine all the ingredients without breaking the citrus pieces.

Serve: Serve immediately or chill in the refrigerator for 15 minutes to allow the flavors to meld. Garnish with a few extra mint leaves before serving.

Nutritional Information (Per Serving): Calories: 130 kcal, Protein: 1g, Carbohydrates: 31g, Total Fat: 1.5g, Saturated Fat: 0g, Fiber: 5g, Cholesterol: 0mg, Sodium: 5mg, Potassium: 350mg.

Lemon Yogurt Mousse with a Hint of Vanilla

Prep. time: 10 min | Chilling Time: 1 hours | Cook time: None | Serves: 4

Ingredients:

- Greek yogurt (plain, full-fat or low-fat): 2 cups
- Fresh lemon juice: 3 tablespoons
- Lemon zest: 1 tablespoon
- Honey: 3 tablespoons (or to taste)
- Vanilla extract: 1 teaspoon
- Heavy cream: 1/2 cup, whipped to soft peaks; Fresh mint leaves (optional for garnish)
- Berries (such as blueberries or raspberries) for garnish

Optional Customizations:
- Substitute honey with agave syrup or maple syrup for a vegan-friendly option (if using dairy-free yogurt).
- Add a pinch of ground cinnamon or nutmeg. Mix in some chopped nuts (like almonds or pistachios) for extra texture.

Directions:

Prepare the Yogurt Mixture:
In a large bowl, whisk together the Greek yogurt, fresh lemon juice, lemon zest, honey, and vanilla extract until smooth and well combined.

Whip the Cream:
In a separate bowl, whip the heavy cream using a hand mixer or a whisk until soft peaks form.

Fold the Ingredients Together:
Gently fold the whipped cream into the yogurt mixture using a spatula. Be careful not to overmix; the goal is to keep the mousse light and airy.

Chill the Mousse:
Spoon the mousse into individual serving glasses or bowls. Cover and refrigerate for at least 1 hour to allow the flavors to meld and the texture to firm up slightly.

Serve:
Before serving, garnish with fresh mint leaves and a handful of berries for a burst of color and added freshness.

Nutritional Information (Per Serving): Calories: 180 kcal, Protein: 7g, Carbohydrates: 22g, Total Fat: 7g, Saturated Fat: 4g, Fiber: 0g, Cholesterol: 20mg, Sodium: 45mg, Potassium: 170mg.

Chocolate Avocado Mousse with a Hint of Mint

Prep. time: 10 min | Chilling Time: 15 minutes | Cook time: None | Serves: 4

Ingredients:

- Ripe avocados: 2 medium-sized
- Unsweetened cocoa powder: 1/4 cup
- Honey or maple syrup: 3 tablespoons (or to taste);
- Vanilla extract: 1 teaspoon
- Fresh mint leaves: 2 tablespoons, finely chopped (plus extra for garnish)
- Almond milk (or any plant-based milk): 1/4 cup
- Dark chocolate chips (optional for garnish): 2 tablespoons
- Sea salt: a pinch

Optional Customizations:

- Substitute honey with agave syrup for a vegan-friendly option. Add a pinch of cinnamon or chili powder for a spicy twist. Sprinkle with crushed nuts (like almonds or pistachios).

Directions:

Blend the Ingredients:

In a food processor or blender, combine the ripe avocados, unsweetened cocoa powder, honey (or maple syrup), vanilla extract, chopped mint leaves, almond milk, and a pinch of sea salt.

Process Until Smooth:

Blend the ingredients on high until the mixture is smooth and creamy, scraping down the sides as needed. Taste and adjust sweetness if desired.

Chill the Mousse:

Transfer the mousse into individual serving bowls or glasses. Cover and refrigerate for at least 15 minutes to allow the flavors to meld and the mousse to set.

Serve:

Before serving, garnish with fresh mint leaves and a sprinkle of dark chocolate chips for added flavor and texture.

Nutritional Information (Per Serving): Calories: 210 kcal, Protein: 3g, Carbohydrates: 25g, Total Fat: 14g, Saturated Fat: 2g, Fiber: 7g, Cholesterol: 0mg, Sodium: 30mg, Potassium: 420mg.

Easy Chia Seed Pudding with Berries

Prep. time: 5 min | Chilling Time: 2 hours | Cook time: None | Serves: 4

Ingredients:

- Chia seeds: 1/2 cup; Almond milk (or any plant-based milk): 2 cups
- Honey or maple syrup: 2 tablespoons (or to taste);
- Vanilla extract: 1 teaspoon
- Mixed berries (such as strawberries, blueberries, raspberries): 1 cup, fresh or frozen
- Nuts or seeds (optional for garnish): 2 tablespoons, chopped
- Fresh mint leaves (optional for garnish): a few leaves

Optional Customizations:

- Substitute honey with agave syrup for a vegan-friendly option.
- Add a pinch of cinnamon or nutmeg for a warm, spicy flavor.
- Top with a drizzle of dark chocolate or sprinkle of coconut flakes.

Directions:

Combine the Ingredients:

In a medium bowl, whisk together the chia seeds, almond milk, honey (or maple syrup), and vanilla extract until well combined.

Mix Well:

Let the mixture sit for 5 minutes, then whisk again to prevent clumping. This ensures that the chia seeds are evenly distributed in the liquid.

Chill the Pudding:

Cover the bowl with plastic wrap or transfer the mixture to individual serving containers. Refrigerate for at least 2 hours, or overnight, until the chia seeds have absorbed the liquid and the pudding has thickened.

Prepare the Topping: Before serving, gently mix the fresh or frozen berries in a small bowl. If using frozen berries, let them thaw slightly.

Serve: Spoon the chia seed pudding into serving bowls or glasses. Top with a generous portion of mixed berries, and garnish with chopped nuts or seeds and fresh mint leaves if desired.

Nutritional Information (Per Serving): Calories: 180 kcal, Protein: 6g, Carbohydrates: 23g, Total Fat: 9g, Saturated Fat: 1g, Fiber: 10g, Cholesterol: 0mg, Sodium: 90mg, Potassium: 280mg.

Olive Oil Cake with Lemon Zest

Prep. time: 15 min | Cook time: 40 min | Serves: 8

Ingredients:

- All-purpose flour: 1 1/2 cups
- Baking powder: 1 1/2 teaspoons
- Salt: 1/4 teaspoon
- Granulated sugar: 3/4 cup
- Eggs: 3 large
- Extra virgin olive oil: 1/2 cup
- Whole milk (or almond milk): 1/2 cup
- Fresh lemon zest: 1 tablespoon (from about 1 lemon)
- Fresh lemon juice: 2 tablespoons
- Vanilla extract: 1 teaspoon
- Powdered sugar (optional, for dusting)

Optional Customizations:
Add 1/2 teaspoon of almond extract for a subtle nutty flavor. Use orange zest and juice instead of lemon for an orange-flavored cake.

Directions:

Preheat the Oven:
Preheat your oven to 350°F (175°C). Grease an 8-inch round cake pan and line the bottom with parchment paper.
Prepare the Dry Ingredients: In a medium bowl, whisk together flour, baking powder, and salt.
Mix the Wet Ingredients:
In a large bowl, whisk sugar and eggs for 2-3 minutes until pale and thick. Gradually whisk in olive oil. Stir in milk, lemon zest, lemon juice, and vanilla extract.
Combine the Wet and Dry Ingredients: Gently fold the dry ingredients into the wet mixture until just combined. Avoid overmixing.
Bake the Cake:
Pour the batter into the prepared pan and smooth the top. Bake for 40-45 minutes, or until a toothpick comes out clean and the top is golden.
Cool and Serve: Let the cake cool for 10 minutes in the pan, then transfer to a wire rack to cool completely. Optionally, dust with powdered sugar before serving.

Nutritional Information (Per Serving): Calories: 290 kcal, Protein: 5g, Carbohydrates: 38g, Total Fat: 13g, Saturated Fat: 2g, Fiber: 1g, Cholesterol: 60mg, Sodium: 140mg, Potassium: 100mg.

Tiramisu with Espresso and Mascarpone

Prep. time: 20 min | Chilling Time: 4 hours or overnight | Cook time: None | Serves: 8

Ingredients:

For the Tiramisu:
- Ladyfinger cookies (savoiardi): 24 pieces; Freshly brewed espresso (or strong coffee): 1 1/2 cups, cooled
- Mascarpone cheese: 8 oz (1 cup)
- Greek yogurt (plain, full-fat or low-fat): 1/2 cup (optional)
- Honey or maple syrup: 1/4 cup (or sugar); Vanilla extract: 1 teaspoon
- Cocoa powder: 2 tablespoons
- Dark chocolate (optional for garnish): 1/4 cup, shaved

For the Cream Mixture:
- Eggs: 3 large (separated)
- Sugar: 1/4 cup (divided between yolks and whites)
- Mascarpone cheese: 8 oz (1 cup)
- Greek yogurt: 1/2 cup (optional, for lighter cream)

Directions:

Prepare the Espresso: Brew espresso or strong coffee and let it cool to room temperature. Optionally, add a tablespoon of coffee liqueur for extra flavor.
Prepare the Mascarpone Cream: In a bowl, whisk egg yolks and half the sugar until pale and creamy (about 2-3 minutes). Add mascarpone and Greek yogurt (optional), whisking until smooth. In another bowl, beat egg whites with remaining sugar until soft peaks form. Gently fold the egg whites into the mascarpone mixture.
Dip the Ladyfingers: Quickly dip each ladyfinger into the cooled espresso, ensuring they don't get too soggy. Lay half of the soaked ladyfingers in a 9x9-inch baking dish.
Layer the Tiramisu: Spread half of the mascarpone mixture over the soaked ladyfingers. Add another layer of soaked ladyfingers, followed by the remaining mascarpone mixture. **Dust with Cocoa Powder:** Generously dust the top with cocoa powder using a fine-mesh sieve. Optionally, shave dark chocolate over the top.
Chill the Tiramisu: Cover with plastic wrap and refrigerate for at least 4 hours or overnight to set and develop flavors. **Serve:** Before serving, dust with more cocoa powder or garnish with extra shaved dark chocolate.

Nutritional Information (Per Serving): Calories: 260 kcal, Protein: 6g, Carbohydrates: 27g, Total Fat: 13g, Saturated Fat: 7g, Fiber: 1g, Cholesterol: 100mg, Sodium: 80mg, Potassium: 150mg.

Galaktoboureko (Custard-filled Filo Pastry)

Prep. time: 25 min | Cook time: 50 min | Serves: 12

Ingredients:

For the Custard Filling:
- Semolina (fine): 1/2 cup
- Milk (low-fat or whole): 3 cups
- Sugar: 1/2 cup; Eggs: 3 large, beaten
- Vanilla extract: 1 teaspoon
- Butter: 2 tablespoons; Lemon zest: 1 teaspoon; Ground cinnamon (optional): 1/4 teaspoon;

For the Filo Pastry:
- Filo dough: 1 package (16 oz), thawed
- Butter (melted): 1/2 cup (or use a combination of butter and olive oil)

For the Syrup:
- Water: 1 cup; Honey: 1/2 cup
- Sugar: 1/4 cup; Lemon juice: 2 tablespoons; Cinnamon stick: 1
- Orange zest (optional): 1 teaspoon

Directions:

Prepare the Custard and Filo Pastry:
In a medium saucepan, heat the milk and semolina over medium heat, stirring until thickened (5-7 minutes). Remove from heat and gradually stir in the sugar and beaten eggs, whisking constantly. Return to low heat for 2-3 minutes. Add vanilla extract, butter, lemon zest, and cinnamon (optional). Set aside.

Preheat oven to 350°F (175°C) and butter a 9x13-inch baking dish. Layer 8 filo sheets, brushing each with melted butter. Pour the custard over the filo. Add 8 more sheets on top, buttering each, and tuck the edges. Score the top.

Bake for 45-50 minutes until golden and crispy.

Make the Syrup and Finish:
In a saucepan, combine water, honey, sugar, lemon juice, cinnamon stick, and orange zest. Simmer for 8-10 minutes. Remove the cinnamon stick and zest.

Pour the warm syrup over the baked pastry. Let soak for 1 hour before serving.

Nutritional Information (Per Serving): Calories: 280 kcal, Protein: 5g, Carbohydrates: 40g, Total Fat: 12g, Saturated Fat: 7g, Fiber: 1g, Cholesterol: 65mg, Sodium: 140mg, Potassium: 120mg.

Sicilian Cannoli with Sweet Ricotta Filling

Prep. time: 25 min | Chilling Time: 30 minutes | Cook time: 10 min(for frying the shells) | Serves: 12 cannoli

Ingredients:

For the Cannoli Shells:
- All-purpose flour: 1 cup
- Sugar: 1 tablespoon; Unsweetened cocoa powder: 1 tablespoon
- Salt: 1/4 teaspoon; Butter (cold): 1 tablespoon, cut into small pieces
- White wine or apple cider vinegar: 1/4 cup; Olive oil: 1 tablespoon
- Egg white: 1, beaten (for sealing the shells); Olive oil or vegetable oil for frying (if making the shells)

For the Sweet Ricotta Filling:
- Ricotta cheese (whole or part-skim): 2 cups; Powdered sugar: 1/2 cup
- Vanilla extract: 1 teaspoon
- Fresh orange zest: 1 teaspoon
- Mini dark chocolate chips: 1/4 cup
- Pistachios (optional): 1/4 cup, chopped

Directions:

Prepare the Dough for Cannoli Shells:
In a bowl, whisk together flour, sugar, cocoa powder, and salt. Work in cold butter until the mixture resembles coarse crumbs. Add wine (or vinegar) and olive oil, stirring until a dough forms. Knead until smooth, wrap in plastic, and chill for 30 minutes.

Roll and Fry the Shells:
Roll the dough on a floured surface to 1/8 inch thickness. Cut into 4-inch circles, wrap around cannoli molds, and seal with egg white. Heat oil to 350°F (175°C) and fry shells for 2-3 minutes until golden. Drain on paper towels and cool before removing from molds.

Prepare the Ricotta Filling:
Mix ricotta, powdered sugar, and vanilla in a bowl. Stir in orange zest and chocolate chips, then refrigerate for 30 minutes.

Fill and Garnish the Cannoli:
Pipe the ricotta filling into both ends of the cannoli shells. Optionally, dip the ends in chopped pistachios and garnish with orange zest. Dust with powdered sugar before serving.

Nutritional Information (Per Serving): Calories: 220 kcal, Protein: 6g, Carbohydrates: 25g, Total Fat: 10g, Saturated Fat: 5g, Fiber: 2g, Cholesterol: 20mg, Sodium: 80mg, Potassium: 150mg.

Sfogliatella Pastry with Ricotta and Lemon Zest

Prep. time: 45 min | Cook time: 30 min | Chilling Time: 1 hour | Serves: 12

Ingredients:

For the Pastry:
- Pre-made puff pastry sheets (store-bought): 1 package (16 oz), thawed
- Olive oil or melted butter: 1/4 cup (to brush the pastry layers)

For the Ricotta Filling:
- Ricotta cheese (whole or part-skim): 1 cup
- Semolina flour: 1/4 cup
- Sugar: 1/4 cup
- Fresh lemon zest: 1 tablespoon
- Vanilla extract: 1 teaspoon
- Eggs: 1 large
- Ground cinnamon (optional): 1/4 teaspoon
- Orange zest (optional): 1 teaspoon
- Salt: 1/4 teaspoon

Directions:

Prepare the Ricotta Filling:
In a bowl, mix ricotta, semolina flour, sugar, lemon zest, vanilla, cinnamon (optional), and salt. Add the egg and stir until smooth. Refrigerate for at least 1 hour to firm up.

Prepare the Puff Pastry:
Roll out the thawed puff pastry sheets on a floured surface until 1/8 inch thick. Cut into 12 circles (about 4 inches in diameter).

Layer and Shape the Pastry: Stack two or three pastry circles, brushing each with olive oil or butter. Roll the stack into a thin log, then roll it back into a spiral. Flatten slightly and press the edges to form a cone or seashell shape, creating a cavity in the center.

Assemble and Bake:
Fill each pastry cavity with 1-2 tablespoons of the ricotta mixture. Gently seal the edges. Preheat oven to 375°F (190°C) and place pastries on a parchment-lined baking sheet. Brush tops with olive oil or butter and bake for 25-30 minutes until golden and crispy.

Cool and Serve:
Let pastries cool slightly on a wire rack. Dust with powdered sugar before serving.

Nutritional Information (Per Serving): Calories: 210 kcal, Protein: 5g, Carbohydrates: 24g, Total Fat: 10g, Saturated Fat: 4g, Fiber: 1g, Cholesterol: 45mg, Sodium: 150mg, Potassium: 80mg.

Pistachio and Almond Biscotti

Prep. time: 15 min | Cook time: 40 min | Chilling Time: 15 min | Serves: 18-20 biscotti

Ingredients:

- All-purpose flour: 1 1/2 cups
- Almond flour: 1/2 cup
- Baking powder: 1 teaspoon
- Salt: 1/4 teaspoon
- Sugar (or coconut sugar): 1/3 cup
- Large eggs: 2
- Olive oil: 2 tablespoons
- Vanilla extract: 1 teaspoon
- Lemon zest: 1 teaspoon
- Raw pistachios (unsalted): 1/2 cup, roughly chopped
- Almonds (unsalted): 1/2 cup, roughly chopped

Directions:

Preheat the Oven:
Preheat your oven to 350°F (175°C) and line a baking sheet with parchment paper.

Mix the Dry and Wet Ingredients:
In a large bowl, whisk together flour, almond flour, baking powder, salt, and sugar. In a separate bowl, beat eggs, olive oil, vanilla extract, and lemon zest until combined. Gradually mix wet ingredients into the dry mixture to form a sticky dough. Fold in chopped pistachios and almonds.

Shape and Bake: Lightly flour your hands and shape the dough into a 10-12 inch log, about 3 inches wide. Place on the baking sheet and bake for 20-25 minutes, until firm and golden. Let cool for 10-15 minutes.

Slice and Second Bake: Slice the cooled log diagonally into 1/2-inch thick biscotti. Arrange the slices cut-side down on the baking sheet. Bake for another 10-12 minutes, flipping halfway, until crisp and golden.

Cool and Serve: Let the biscotti cool completely on a wire rack to harden before serving.

Nutritional Information (Per Serving): Calories: 120 kcal, Protein: 4g, Carbohydrates: 14g, Total Fat: 6g, Saturated Fat: 1g, Fiber: 2g, Cholesterol: 30mg, Sodium: 60mg, Potassium: 100mg.

Sesame Halva with Honey

Prep. time: 10 min | Cook time: 10 min | Chilling Time: 1 hour | Serves: 12

Ingredients:

- Tahini (sesame paste): 1 cup
- Honey: 1/2 cup
- Vanilla extract: 1 teaspoon
- Salt: 1/8 teaspoon (optional, for balance)
- Toasted sesame seeds: 2 tablespoons (optional for garnish)

Optional Customizations:

- Add chopped pistachios, almonds, or walnuts (1/4 cup) for added crunch.
- Add 1/4 teaspoon ground cinnamon or cardamom.
- Use a combination of honey and maple syrup for a slightly different sweetness profile.
- Stir in dark chocolate chips (1/4 cup) or drizzle melted chocolate over the top.

Directions:

Prepare the Honey Syrup: In a small saucepan, heat the honey over medium-low heat until it reaches a simmer. Stir occasionally and cook for about 3-5 minutes until the honey thickens slightly, but be careful not to let it burn.

Combine the Tahini and Honey:
In a medium bowl, stir the tahini with vanilla extract and salt (if using) until smooth. Gradually pour the warm honey into the tahini, stirring constantly until the mixture is fully combined and starts to thicken. The texture should be smooth and slightly stiff.

Transfer to a Mold: Line a small loaf pan or square dish (approximately 6x6 inches) with parchment paper, allowing the edges to hang over for easy removal.
Pour the tahini-honey mixture into the pan and smooth the top with a spatula.

Garnish and Chill:
Sprinkle the toasted sesame seeds or chopped nuts over the top, if desired.
Cover the halva and refrigerate for at least 1 hour, or until firm and set.

Slice and Serve: Once chilled, remove the halva from the pan by lifting the parchment paper. Slice into small squares or rectangles.

Nutritional Information (Per Serving): Calories: 160 kcal, Protein: 4g, Carbohydrates: 15g, Total Fat: 10g, Saturated Fat: 1.5g, Fiber: 2g, Cholesterol: 0mg, Sodium: 15mg, Potassium: 70mg.

Vanilla Panna Cotta with Fresh Berries

Prep. time: 10 min | Cook time: 5 min | Chilling Time: 4 hours or overnight | Serves: 6

Ingredients:

- Whole milk: 1 cup
- Heavy cream: 1 cup
- Plain Greek yogurt (optional, for a lighter version): 1/2 cup
- Honey or maple syrup: 1/4 cup
- Vanilla extract: 1 teaspoon
- Gelatin powder: 1 packet (about 2 1/4 teaspoons)
- Water: 2 tablespoons (for blooming the gelatin)
- Fresh mixed berries (e.g., strawberries, raspberries, blueberries): 1 cup
- Lemon zest (optional for garnish): 1 teaspoon

Optional Customizations:

- Use almond extract (1/4 teaspoon).
- Add a teaspoon of orange zest to the mixture for a citrusy note.
- Top with toasted nuts.

Directions:

Bloom the Gelatin:
Sprinkle gelatin over 2 tablespoons of water in a small bowl and let sit for 5 minutes to soften.

Heat the Milk and Cream: In a saucepan, warm milk, heavy cream, and honey over medium heat, stirring until honey dissolves. Do not let it boil.

Dissolve the Gelatin: Remove from heat and whisk in bloomed gelatin until fully dissolved. Stir in vanilla extract.

Incorporate Yogurt (Optional): If using Greek yogurt, whisk it into the warm mixture until smooth.

Pour into Molds: Divide the mixture into 6 ramekins or dessert cups. Cool slightly, cover, and refrigerate for at least 4 hours or overnight to set.

Prepare the Berries:
Toss mixed berries with honey or lemon juice for added flavor.

Serve: Run a knife around the edges of the panna cotta and invert onto plates, or serve in the ramekins. Top with berries and garnish with lemon zest if desired.

Nutritional Information (Per Serving): Calories: 200 kcal, Protein: 6g, Carbohydrates: 20g, Total Fat: 10g, Saturated Fat: 6g, Fiber: 1g, Cholesterol: 40mg, Sodium: 50mg, Potassium: 150mg.

Mahalabia (Middle Eastern Milk Pudding)

Prep. time: 5 min | Cook time: 10 min | Chilling Time: 2-3 hours | Serves: 6

Ingredients:

- Whole milk (or almond milk for a dairy-free option): 3 cups
- Cornstarch: 1/4 cup
- Honey or maple syrup: 1/4 cup (or adjust to taste)
- Rosewater or orange blossom water: 1-2 teaspoons (optional)
- Vanilla extract: 1 teaspoon
- Ground cinnamon or ground cardamom: 1/4 teaspoon (optional)
- Crushed pistachios or almonds: 2 tablespoons (for garnish)
- Fresh fruit (such as berries or pomegranate seeds) for garnish (optional)

Directions:

Mix the Cornstarch and Milk: In a medium saucepan, whisk together 1/2 cup of cold milk with the cornstarch until smooth and fully dissolved. This ensures there are no lumps in the pudding.

Heat the Milk Mixture: Add the remaining 2 1/2 cups of milk to the saucepan along with honey (or maple syrup). Stir continuously over medium heat until the mixture starts to thicken, about 7-8 minutes. Be sure not to let the milk come to a full boil.

Add Flavorings: Once the mixture begins to thicken, remove from the heat. Stir in the vanilla extract and either rosewater or orange blossom water, as well as any optional spices like cinnamon or cardamom for added flavor. Whisk well to combine.

Pour and Chill: Pour the mahalabia mixture into individual serving bowls or ramekins. Let the pudding cool to room temperature, then cover and refrigerate for at least 2-3 hours, or until fully set.

Garnish and Serve: Before serving, garnish the mahalabia with crushed pistachios, almonds, or fresh fruit like pomegranate seeds or berries. A sprinkle of ground cinnamon or a drizzle of honey can also add extra flavor.

Nutritional Information (Per Serving): Calories: 150 kcal, Protein: 5g, Carbohydrates: 25g, Total Fat: 4g, Saturated Fat: 2g, Fiber: 1g, Cholesterol: 10mg, Sodium: 50mg, Potassium: 180mg.

Kataifi (Shredded Filo Pastry with Nuts)

Prep. time: 20 min | Cook time: 40 min | Chilling Time: 1 hour | Serves: 12

Ingredients:

For the Kataifi Pastry:
- Kataifi (shredded filo pastry): 1 package (about 16 oz)
- Olive oil or melted butter: 1/2 cup
- Walnuts or pistachios (chopped): 1 cup
- Almonds (chopped): 1/2 cup
- Ground cinnamon: 1 teaspoon
- Ground cloves: 1/4 teaspoon (optional)

For the Syrup:
- Water: 1 cup
- Honey: 1/2 cup
- Sugar: 1/4 cup (optional, for a less sweet version, skip this)
- Lemon juice: 1 tablespoon
- Cinnamon stick: 1
- Orange zest: 1 teaspoon (optional)

Directions:

Preheat the Oven: Preheat your oven to 350°F (175°C) and grease a 9x13-inch baking dish with olive oil or melted butter.

Prepare the Nut Filling: In a bowl, mix the chopped walnuts, almonds, ground cinnamon, and ground cloves (if using).

Assemble the Kataifi Rolls: Gently fluff the kataifi pastry. Take a small handful (2-3 tablespoons) and spread into a thin strip. Place 1 tablespoon of the nut mixture at one end, then roll to form a log. Place the rolls in the prepared dish and repeat.

Brush with Olive Oil:
Brush the tops of the kataifi rolls generously with olive oil or melted butter.

Bake the Kataifi: Bake for 35-40 minutes, until golden brown and crispy.

Prepare the Syrup: In a saucepan, combine water, honey, sugar (if using), lemon juice, cinnamon stick, and orange zest. Bring to a boil, reduce heat, and simmer for 8-10 minutes. Remove the cinnamon stick.

Soak the Kataifi: Once baked, pour the warm syrup evenly over the kataifi rolls. Let them absorb the syrup and cool completely for about 1 hour.

Nutritional Information (Per Serving): Calories: 250 kcal, Protein: 4g, Carbohydrates: 30g, Total Fat: 14g, Saturated Fat: 2g, Fiber: 2g, Cholesterol: 0mg, Sodium: 50mg, Potassium: 120mg.

Revani (Greek Semolina Cake with Citrus Syrup)

Prep. time: 15 min | Cook time: 40 min | Chilling Time: 1 hour | Serves: 12

Ingredients:

For the Cake:
- Semolina (fine or coarse): 1 cup
- All-purpose flour: 1/2 cup
- Baking powder: 1 1/2 teaspoons
- Eggs: 3 large; Honey: 1/3 cup
- Olive oil: 1/3 cup
- Greek yogurt: 1/2 cup
- Fresh orange zest: 1 tablespoon
- Vanilla extract: 1 teaspoon
- Ground cinnamon (optional): 1/2 teaspoon

For the Citrus Syrup:
- Water: 1 cup; Honey: 1/3 cup
- Fresh lemon juice: 1/4 cup
- Fresh orange juice: 1/4 cup
- Orange zest: 1 teaspoon
- Lemon zest: 1 teaspoon
- Cinnamon stick: 1

Directions:

Prepare the Cake: Preheat your oven to 350°F (175°C) and grease an 8x8-inch or 9x9-inch baking dish with olive oil. Mix the Dry Ingredients: In a large bowl, whisk together semolina, all-purpose flour, baking powder, and optional cinnamon.

Beat the Wet Ingredients: In another bowl, beat eggs with honey for 2-3 minutes until fluffy. Add olive oil, Greek yogurt, orange zest, and vanilla extract, mixing until smooth.

Combine Wet and Dry Ingredients: Add the wet mixture to the dry ingredients, stirring until just combined. Pour the batter into the prepared dish and smooth the top.

Bake the Cake: Bake for 35-40 minutes until golden and a toothpick comes out clean.

Prepare the Citrus Syrup:

In a saucepan, combine water, honey, lemon juice, orange juice, lemon zest, orange zest, and a cinnamon stick. Boil, reduce heat, and simmer for 8-10 minutes until thickened. Remove the cinnamon stick.

Soak the Cake:

Poke holes in the cake with a skewer, then pour the warm syrup over it. Let the cake absorb the syrup and cool completely before serving.

Nutritional Information (Per Serving): Calories: 210 kcal, Protein: 5g, Carbohydrates: 28g, Total Fat: 10g, Saturated Fat: 2g, Fiber: 1g, Cholesterol: 50mg, Sodium: 50mg, Potassium: 90mg.

Ricotta Cheesecake with Almond Crust

Prep. time: 15 min | Cook time: 50 min | Chilling Time: 1 hour | Serves: 8

Ingredients:

For the Almond Crust:
- Almond flour: 1 1/2 cups
- Honey or maple syrup: 2 tablespoons
- Coconut oil (melted): 2 tablespoons
- Salt: 1/4 teaspoon
- Ground cinnamon (optional): 1/4 teaspoon

For the Ricotta Filling:
- Ricotta cheese: 2 cups (preferably whole-milk ricotta)
- Greek yogurt: 1/2 cup
- Eggs: 3 large
- Honey or maple syrup: 1/4 cup
- Vanilla extract: 1 teaspoon
- Lemon zest: 1 teaspoon
- Almond extract (optional): 1/4 teaspoon

Directions:

Prepare the Almond Crust:

Preheat your oven to 350°F (175°C). Grease a 9-inch springform pan with coconut oil or nonstick spray. In a medium bowl, combine almond flour, honey (or maple syrup), melted coconut oil, salt, and cinnamon (if using). Stir until it resembles wet sand. Press the mixture evenly into the bottom of the pan, smoothing it with the back of a spoon. Bake for 10-12 minutes until lightly golden. Let it cool.

Prepare the Ricotta Filling:

In a large bowl, mix ricotta cheese, Greek yogurt, eggs, honey, vanilla extract, lemon zest, and almond extract (if using). Blend until smooth.

Pour the ricotta filling over the cooled almond crust and spread it evenly.

Bake the Cheesecake: Bake for 35-40 minutes until the center is set but slightly jiggly, and the top is lightly golden.

Cool:

Cool the cheesecake at room temperature for 1 hour, then refrigerate for at least 2 hours or overnight.

Nutritional Information (Per Serving): Calories: 280 kcal, Protein: 11g, Carbohydrates: 15g, Total Fat: 20g, Saturated Fat: 8g, Fiber: 2g, Cholesterol: 120mg, Sodium: 180mg, Potassium: 150mg.

Almond Amaretti Cookies

Prep. time: 10 min | Cook time: 18 min | Serves: 20-24 cookies

Ingredients:

- Almond flour: 2 cups
- Honey or maple syrup: 1/4 cup
- Egg whites: 2 large
- Almond extract: 1/2 teaspoon
- Vanilla extract: 1 teaspoon
- Lemon zest: 1 teaspoon (optional)
- Pinch of salt
- Powdered sugar (for dusting, optional): 2 tablespoons

Optional Customizations:

- Add 1/4 teaspoon ground cinnamon for a warm flavor.
- Use orange zest instead of lemon zest for a citrusy twist.
- Add a tablespoon of cocoa powder for a chocolate version.

Directions:

Preheat your oven to 325°F (165°C) and line a baking sheet with parchment paper.

Whisk the Egg Whites: In a large mixing bowl, whisk the egg whites with a pinch of salt until soft peaks form. This will give the cookies a light, airy texture.

Prepare the Dough: In a separate bowl, combine the almond flour, honey (or maple syrup), almond extract, vanilla extract, and lemon zest (if using). Gently fold the whipped egg whites into the almond mixture until well combined. The dough should be sticky but manageable.

Shape the Cookies: Using a spoon or your hands, scoop about a tablespoon of dough and roll it into a ball. Place the dough balls on the prepared baking sheet, leaving about 1 inch between each cookie. If desired, dust the tops with powdered sugar.

Bake the Cookies: Bake in the preheated oven for 15-18 minutes, or until the tops are golden and slightly cracked. The cookies should be firm to the touch but still soft in the center.

Cool and Serve: Remove the cookies from the oven and let them cool on the baking sheet for a few minutes before transferring them to a wire rack to cool completely.

Nutritional Information (Per Serving): Calories: 90 kcal, Protein: 3g, Carbohydrates: 7g, Total Fat: 6g, Saturated Fat: 0.5g, Fiber: 1g, Cholesterol: 0mg, Sodium: 20mg, Potassium: 20mg.

Sütlaç (Turkish Rice Pudding with Cinnamon)

Prep. time: 5 min | Cook time: 35 min | Chilling Time: 1-2 hours (optional) | Serves: 6

Ingredients:

- Short-grain rice: 1/2 cup
- Water: 1 cup
- Whole milk (or almond milk for dairy-free): 4 cups
- Honey or maple syrup: 1/4 cup (adjust to taste)
- Vanilla extract: 1 teaspoon
- Ground cinnamon: 1 teaspoon (plus extra for garnish)
- Cornstarch: 1 tablespoon (optional, for thickening)
- Pinch of salt

Optional Customizations:

- Add 1/4 teaspoon ground cardamom or nutmeg for extra warmth.
- Use coconut milk for a creamier, dairy-free version.
- Stir in orange zest or lemon zest.

Directions:

Cook the Rice:

In a medium saucepan, combine rice and water. Bring to a boil over medium heat, then reduce to low, cover, and simmer for 10-12 minutes until the water is absorbed and the rice is tender.

Heat the Milk:

Stir in the milk and bring to a simmer over medium heat. Cook, stirring frequently, for 15-20 minutes until the mixture thickens slightly.

Add Sweeteners and Flavorings:

Stir in honey (or maple syrup), vanilla extract, cinnamon, and a pinch of salt. Taste and adjust sweetness if needed.

Optional Thickening:

If desired, dissolve cornstarch in a tablespoon of cold water and stir into the pudding. Cook for another 3-5 minutes until thickened.

Serve or Chill: Once at your preferred consistency, remove from heat. Serve warm or chill in the fridge for 1-2 hours.

Nutritional Information (Per Serving): Calories: 180 kcal, Protein: 6g, Carbohydrates: 30g, Total Fat: 5g, Saturated Fat: 3g, Fiber: 1g, Cholesterol: 15mg, Sodium: 60mg, Potassium: 160mg.

Apple and Almond Crisp

Prep. time: 15 min | Cook time: 30 min | Serves: 6

Ingredients:

For the Filling:
- Apples: 4 medium, peeled, cored, and sliced
- Honey: 2 tablespoons
- Lemon juice: 1 tablespoon
- Cinnamon: 1 teaspoon

For the Topping:
- Almond flour: 1/2 cup
- Rolled oats: 1/2 cup
- Chopped almonds: 1/4 cup
- Olive oil: 2 tablespoons
- Honey: 2 tablespoons
- Cinnamon: 1/2 teaspoon

Directions:

Preheat the Oven:

Preheat your oven to 350°F (175°C). Grease an 8x8-inch baking dish or pie dish.

Prepare the Filling:

In a large bowl, toss the sliced apples with honey, lemon juice, and cinnamon until evenly coated. Spread the apple mixture evenly in the prepared baking dish.

Make the Topping:

In a separate bowl, combine the almond flour, rolled oats, chopped almonds, cinnamon, olive oil, and honey. Mix until crumbly.

Assemble and Bake:

Sprinkle the topping evenly over the apples. Bake for 25-30 minutes, or until the apples are tender and the topping is golden brown.

Serve:

Serve warm, optionally with a scoop of Greek yogurt or a drizzle of extra honey.

Nutritional Information (Per Serving): Calories: 240 kcal, Protein: 4g, Carbohydrates: 36g, Total Fat: 10g, Saturated Fat: 1.5g, Fiber: 5g, Cholesterol: 0mg, Sodium: 5mg, Potassium: 220mg.

Orange and Almond Cake

Prep. time: 10 min | Cook time: 40 min | Serves: 8

Ingredients:

- Almond flour: 1 1/2 cups
- Eggs: 3 large
- Sugar: 1/2 cup
- Fresh orange juice: 1/4 cup
- Orange zest: 1 tablespoon (from 1 orange)
- Baking powder: 1 teaspoon
- Extra virgin olive oil: 1/4 cup
- Vanilla extract: 1 teaspoon
- Salt: 1/4 teaspoon
- Powdered sugar (optional): for dusting

Directions:

Preheat the Oven:

Preheat your oven to 350°F (175°C). Grease an 8-inch round cake pan and line the bottom with parchment paper.

Mix the Wet Ingredients:

In a large bowl, whisk together the eggs, sugar, olive oil, fresh orange juice, orange zest, and vanilla extract until well combined.

Add the Dry Ingredients:

Stir in the almond flour, baking powder, and salt until the batter is smooth.

Bake the Cake:

Pour the batter into the prepared cake pan and spread it evenly. Bake for 35-40 minutes, or until a toothpick inserted in the center comes out clean.

Cool and Serve:

Allow the cake to cool in the pan for 10 minutes, then transfer it to a wire rack to cool completely. Dust with powdered sugar before serving if desired.

Nutritional Information (Per Serving): Calories: 250 kcal, Protein: 7g, Carbohydrates: 18g, Total Fat: 17g, Saturated Fat: 2g, Fiber: 3g, Cholesterol: 55mg, Sodium: 120mg, Potassium: 80mg.

Introduction to the 30-Day Mediterranean Meal Plan

Welcome to your 30-day Mediterranean meal plan! This plan is designed to help you embrace the healthy, flavorful, and balanced lifestyle of the Mediterranean diet. With a focus on whole foods, fresh ingredients, and vibrant flavors, this meal plan will guide you through a month of delicious meals that are not only satisfying but also nourishing for your body.

How to Use This Meal Plan

1. **Balanced Nutrition**: Each day in this meal plan includes three meals (breakfast, lunch, and dinner) and a dessert, with two dishes served at each main meal. The plan is carefully crafted to ensure a balance of protein, healthy fats, and carbohydrates, helping to keep your energy levels stable throughout the day.

2. **Flexibility and Variety**: Feel free to swap meals between days according to your personal preferences or dietary needs. The Mediterranean diet is all about enjoying a wide variety of foods, so don't hesitate to make adjustments based on what you have available or what you enjoy most.

3. **Portion Control**: While this plan provides guidelines for a balanced diet, it's important to listen to your body's hunger cues. You can adjust portion sizes to better align with your energy needs, especially if you're engaging in regular physical activity or aiming for specific health goals.

4. **Ingredient Substitutions**: If you have allergies or dietary restrictions, you can substitute ingredients without compromising the Mediterranean spirit of the dishes. For example, replace dairy-based ingredients with plant-based alternatives or choose gluten-free grains like quinoa or rice.

5. **Meal Prep Tips**: To make your week smoother, consider preparing certain components of your meals in advance. Chopping vegetables, cooking grains, or making sauces ahead of time can save you valuable minutes during busy days and help you stay on track.

6. **Stay Hydrated**: Hydration plays a key role in the Mediterranean lifestyle. Aim to drink plenty of water throughout the day, and if you like, enjoy herbal teas or a glass of red wine occasionally, as is common in traditional Mediterranean cultures.

7. **Enjoy the Process**: The Mediterranean diet is more than just a way of eating—it's a way of life that emphasizes enjoying your meals with friends and family. Take the time to savor each bite, appreciate the flavors, and share these delicious dishes with your loved ones whenever possible.

30-Day Mediterranean Meal Plan

Day 1

Breakfast:
Mediterranean Veggie Omelet with Feta
Greek Yogurt with Honey, Almonds, and Berries
Lunch:
Classic Greek Salad with Feta and Olives
Grilled Steak with Lemon and Herb Marinade
Dinner:
Grilled Salmon with Lemon and Capers
Avocado and Tomato Salad with Lemon Dressing
Dessert: Ricotta Cheesecake with Almond Crust
Nutritional Information (approximate):
Calories: 2,160 kcal, Protein: 103g
Carbohydrates: 218g, Total Fat: 110g

Day 2

Breakfast:
Greek Pita Wrap with Egg, Spinach, and Feta
Tahini Banana Smoothie with Sesame Seeds
Lunch:
Mediterranean Chicken Stir-Fry with Peppers
Ratatouille with Fresh Herbs and Olive Oil
Dinner:
Shrimp Scampi with Garlic and Olive Oil
Orzo with Spinach and Pine Nuts
Dessert: Chocolate Avocado Mousse with a Hint of Mint
Nutritional Information (approximate):
Calories: 2,170 kcal, Protein: 104g
Carbohydrates: 230g, Total Fat: 110g

Day 3

Breakfast:
Overnight Oats with Dried Fruits and Seeds
Egg Muffins with Spinach, Feta, and Oregano
Lunch:
Tuscan White Bean Soup with Kale
Greek-Style Baked Meatballs with Feta
Dinner:
Lemon and Oregano Grilled Chicken Breast
Grilled Zucchini with Lemon and Olive Oil
Dessert: Orange and Almond Cake
Nutritional Information (approximate):
Calories: 2,150 kcal, Protein: 104g
Carbohydrates: 220g, Total Fat: 108g

Day 4

Breakfast:
Spinach and Sundried Tomato Frittata
Whole Grain Pancakes with Pomegranate Syrup
Lunch:
Quinoa Salad with Lemon Vinaigrette
Greek-Style Baked Meatballs with Feta
Dinner:
Chicken Piccata with Capers and Lemon
Cucumber, Tomato, and Red Onion Salad
Dessert: Vanilla Panna Cotta with Fresh Berries
Nutritional Information (approximate):
Calories: 2,150 kcal, Protein: 101g
Carbohydrates: 225g, Total Fat: 106g

Day 5

Breakfast:
Avocado Toast with Olive Oil & Cherry Tomatoes
Almond & Orange Smoothie with Chia Seeds
Lunch:
Baked Swordfish with Olive Tapenade
Farro with Sun-Dried Tomatoes and Basil
Dinner:
Beef Kofta with Garlic and Cumin
Spinach Salad with Pomegranate and Feta
Dessert: Tiramisu with Espresso and Mascarpone
Nutritional Information (approximate):
Calories: 2,180 kcal, Protein: 102g
Carbohydrates: 229g, Total Fat: 108g

Day 6

Breakfast:
Shakshuka with Fresh Herbs and Crumbled Feta
Mediterranean Bruschetta with Tomatoes and Basil
Lunch:
Hearty Lentil and Vegetable Soup
Mediterranean Brown Rice with Roasted Garlic
Dinner:
Grilled Octopus with Lemon and Oregano
Avocado and Tomato Salad with Lemon Dressing
Dessert: Galaktoboureko (Custard-filled Filo Pastry)
Nutritional Information (approximate):
Calories: 2,060 kcal, Protein: 94g
Carbohydrates: 215g, Total Fat: 101g

Day 7

Breakfast:
  Smoked Salmon and Cream Cheese Bagel
  Greek Yogurt with Honey, Almonds and Berries
Lunch:
  Avocado and Tomato Salad with Lemon Dressing
  Beef Skewers with Grilled Vegetables
Dinner:
  Baked Cod with Tomatoes and Olives
  Cucumber, Tomato, and Red Onion Salad
Dessert: Sicilian Cannoli with Sweet Ricotta Filling
Nutritional Information (approximate):
  Calories: 2,110 kcal, Protein: 100,5g
  Carbohydrates: 129g, Total Fat: 98g

Day 8

Breakfast:
  Spinach and Sundried Tomato Frittata
  Tahini Banana Smoothie with Sesame Seeds
Lunch:
  Spiced Moroccan Chickpea and Carrot Stew
  Farro with Sun-Dried Tomatoes and Basil
Dinner:
  Roasted Chicken Thighs with Garlic and Rosemary
  Ratatouille with Fresh Herbs and Olive Oil
Dessert: Lemon Yogurt Mousse with a Hint of Vanilla
Nutritional Information (approximate):
  Calories: 2,180 kcal, Protein: 98g
  Carbohydrates: 224g, Total Fat: 110g

Day 9

Breakfast:
  Whole Grain Pancakes with Pomegranate Syrup
  Zucchini and Olive Oil Breakfast Loaf
Lunch:
  Spinach Salad with Pomegranate and Feta
  Lamb Stew with Olives and Tomatoes
Dinner:
  Grilled Sardines with Olive Oil and Parsley
  Mediterranean Barley with Lemon and Olive Oil
Dessert: Easy Chia Seed Pudding with Berries
Nutritional Information (approximate):
  Calories: 2,060 kcal, Protein: 98g
  Carbohydrates: 220g, Total Fat: 105g

Day 10

Breakfast:
  Scrambled Eggs with Roasted Peppers and Olives
  Almond & Orange Smoothie with Chia Seeds
Lunch:
  Pork Tenderloin with Lemon and Thyme
  Warm Potato Salad with Capers and Olive Oil
Dinner:
  Grilled Sea Bass with Lemon and Herbs
  Couscous Salad with Sun-Dried Tomatoes and Parsley
Dessert: Mahalabia (Middle Eastern Milk Pudding)
Nutritional Information (approximate):
  Calories: 2,150 kcal, Protein: 96g,
  Carbohydrates: 220g, Total Fat: 110g

Day 11

Breakfast:
  Mediterranean Veggie Omelet with Feta
  Whole Grain Pancakes with Pomegranate Syrup
Lunch:
  Beef Shawarma with Tahini Dressing
  Cucumber, Tomato, and Red Onion Salad
Dinner:
  Lemon and Garlic Chicken Drumsticks
  Roasted Brussels Sprouts with Balsamic Glaze
Dessert: Pistachio and Almond Biscotti
Nutritional Information (approximate):
  Calories: 2,180 kcal, Protein: 105g,
  Carbohydrates: 225g, Total Fat: 112g

Day 12

Breakfast:
  Shakshuka with Fresh Herbs and Crumbled Feta
  Zucchini and Olive Oil Breakfast Loaf
Lunch:
  Grilled Lamb Burgers with Feta and Mint
  Spinach Salad with Pomegranate and Feta
Dinner:
  Baked Tilapia with Garlic and Herbs
  Mediterranean Vegetable Stir-Fry with Garlic
Dessert: Sesame Halva with Honey
Nutritional Information (approximate):
  Calories: 2,140 kcal, Protein: 102g,
  Carbohydrates: 220g, Total Fat: 109g

Day 13

Breakfast:
  Tahini Banana Smoothie with Sesame Seeds
  Egg Muffins with Spinach, Feta, and Oregano
Lunch:
  Mediterranean Spiced Pork Chops with Olives
  Grilled Zucchini with Lemon and Olive Oil
Dinner:
  Seafood Paella with Saffron
  Avocado and Tomato Salad with Lemon Dressing
Dessert: Sfogliatella Pastry with Ricotta and Lemon Zest
Nutritional Information (approximate):
  Calories: 2,170 kcal, Protein: 105g,
  Carbohydrates: 230g, Total Fat: 115g

Day 14

Breakfast:
  Avocado Toast with Olive Oil & Cherry Tomatoes
  Almond & Orange Smoothie with Chia Seeds
Lunch:
  Chicken and Quinoa with Lemon Dressing
  Roasted Beet Salad with Goat Cheese and Walnuts
Dinner:
  Grilled Sardines with Olive Oil and Parsley
  Farro with Sun-Dried Tomatoes and Basil
Dessert: Revani (Greek Semolina Cake with Citrus Syrup)
Nutritional Information (approximate):
  Calories: 2,160 kcal, Protein: 100g,
  Carbohydrates: 226g, Total Fat: 110g

Day 15

Breakfast:
  Breakfast Tacos with Hummus and Veggies
  Greek Yogurt with Honey, Almonds, and Berries
Lunch:
  Chicken Piccata with Capers and Lemon
  Bulgur Wheat Salad with Cucumber and Mint
Dinner:
  Baked Trout with Lemon and Fresh Herbs
  Grilled Vegetable Salad with Balsamic Glaze
Dessert: Almond Amaretti Cookies
Nutritional Information (approximate):
  Calories: 2,150 kcal, Protein: 105g,
  Carbohydrates: 218g, Total Fat: 110g

Day 16

Breakfast:
  Mediterranean Bruschetta with Tomatoes and Basil
  Almond & Orange Smoothie with Chia Seeds
Lunch:
  Saffron-Infused Mediterranean Seafood Stew
  Whole Wheat Spaghetti with Olive Oil and Garlic
Dinner:
  Lemon and Garlic Chicken Drumsticks
  Spinach Salad with Pomegranate and Feta
Dessert: Kataifi (Shredded Filo Pastry with Nuts)
Nutritional Information (approximate):
  Calories: 2,180 kcal, Protein: 102g,
  Carbohydrates: 225g, Total Fat: 108g

Day 17

Breakfast:
  Zucchini and Olive Oil Breakfast Loaf
  Tahini Banana Smoothie with Sesame Seeds
Lunch:
  Grilled Lamb Kebabs with Mint and Yogurt Sauce
  Warm Potato Salad with Capers and Olive Oil
Dinner:
  Baked Cod with Tomatoes and Olives
  Mediterranean Barley with Lemon and Olive Oil
Dessert: Vanilla Panna Cotta with Fresh Berries
Nutritional Information (approximate):
  Calories: 2,140 kcal, Protein: 104g,
  Carbohydrates: 230g, Total Fat: 109g

Day 18

Breakfast:
  Scrambled Eggs with Roasted Peppers and Olives
  Whole Grain Pancakes with Pomegranate Syrup
Lunch:
  Hearty Lentil and Vegetable Soup
  Farro Salad with Grilled Zucchini and Feta
Dinner:
  Grilled Salmon with Lemon and Capers
  Roasted Brussels Sprouts with Balsamic Glaze
Dessert: Mahalabia (Middle Eastern Milk Pudding)
Nutritional Information (approximate):
  Calories: 2,170 kcal, Protein: 98g,
  Carbohydrates: 220g, Total Fat: 112g

Day 19

Breakfast:
  Shakshuka with Fresh Herbs and Crumbled Feta
  Almond & Orange Smoothie with Chia Seeds
Lunch:
  Pork Souvlaki with Tzatziki and Pita Bread
  White Bean and Arugula Salad with Lemon Zest
Dinner:
  Grilled Octopus with Lemon and Oregano
  Orzo with Spinach and Pine Nuts
Dessert: Sütlaç (Turkish Rice Pudding with Cinnamon)
Nutritional Information (approximate):
  Calories: 2,160 kcal, Protein: 100g,
   Carbohydrates: 225g, Total Fat: 110g

Day 20

Breakfast:
  Mediterranean Bruschetta with Tomatoes and Basil
  Tahini Banana Smoothie with Sesame Seeds
Lunch:
  Grilled Chicken with Feta and Olive Tapenade
  Couscous Salad with Sun-Dried Tomatoes and Parsley
Dinner:
  Baked Tilapia with Garlic and Herbs
  Roasted Cauliflower with Tahini and Pine Nuts
Dessert: Apple and Almond Crisp
Nutritional Information (approximate):
  Calories: 2,140 kcal, Protein: 98g,
  Carbohydrates: 220g, Total Fat: 108g

Day 21

Breakfast:
  Spinach and Sundried Tomato Frittata
  Whole Grain Pancakes with Pomegranate Syrup
Lunch:
  Classic Greek Lemon Chicken Soup (Avgolemono)
  Quinoa Salad with Lemon Vinaigrette
Dinner:
  Grilled Sea Bass with Lemon and Herbs
  Grilled Zucchini with Lemon and Olive Oil
Dessert: Ricotta Cheesecake with Almond Crust
Nutritional Information (approximate):
  Calories: 2,150 kcal, Protein: 102g,
  Carbohydrates: 218g, Total Fat: 110g

Day 22

Breakfast:
  Breakfast Tacos with Hummus and Veggies
  Greek Yogurt with Honey, Almonds, and Berries
Lunch:
  Mediterranean Spiced Pork Chops with Olives
  Warm Potato Salad with Capers and Olive Oil
Dinner:
  Grilled Salmon with Lemon and Capers
  Spinach Salad with Pomegranate and Feta
Dessert: Lemon Yogurt Mousse with a Hint of Vanilla
Nutritional Information (approximate):
  Calories: 2,160 kcal, Protein: 100g,
  Carbohydrates: 220g, Total Fat: 112g

Day 23

Breakfast:
  Avocado Toast with Olive Oil & Cherry Tomatoes
  Almond & Orange Smoothie with Chia Seeds
Lunch:
  Spiced Moroccan Chickpea and Carrot Stew
  Farro with Sun-Dried Tomatoes and Basil
Dinner:
  Baked Swordfish with Olive Tapenade
  Grilled Vegetable Salad with Balsamic Glaze
Dessert: Galaktoboureko (Custard-filled Filo Pastry)
Nutritional Information (approximate):
  Calories: 2,170 kcal, Protein: 104g,
  Carbohydrates: 225g, Total Fat: 115g

Day 24

Breakfast:
  Shakshuka with Fresh Herbs and Crumbled Feta
  Zucchini and Olive Oil Breakfast Loaf
Lunch:
  Hearty Lentil and Vegetable Soup
  Mediterranean Barley with Lemon and Olive Oil
Dinner:
  Grilled Octopus with Lemon and Oregano
  Orzo with Spinach and Pine Nuts
Dessert: Sfogliatella Pastry with Ricotta and Lemon Zest
Nutritional Information (approximate):
  Calories: 2,180 kcal, Protein: 102g,
  Carbohydrates: 220g, Total Fat: 110g

Day 25

Breakfast:
  Scrambled Eggs with Roasted Peppers and Olives
  Almond & Orange Smoothie with Chia Seeds
Lunch:
  Beef Shawarma with Tahini Dressing
  Roasted Beet Salad with Goat Cheese and Walnuts
Dinner:
  Mussels with White Wine and Garlic
  Quinoa with Roasted Red Peppers and Feta
Dessert: Pistachio and Almond Biscotti
Nutritional Information (approximate):
  Calories: 2,170 kcal, Protein: 98g,
  Carbohydrates: 218g, Total Fat: 108g

Day 26

Breakfast:
  Mediterranean Veggie Omelet with Feta
  Greek Yogurt with Honey, Almonds, and Berries
Lunch:
  Saffron-Infused Mediterranean Seafood Stew
  Couscous Salad with Sun-Dried Tomatoes and Parsley
Dinner:
  Lemon and Oregano Grilled Chicken Breast
  Grilled Zucchini with Lemon and Olive Oil
Dessert: Revani (Greek Semolina Cake with Citrus Syrup)
Nutritional Information (approximate):
  Calories: 2,160 kcal, Protein: 100g,
  Carbohydrates: 226g, Total Fat: 110g

Day 27

Breakfast:
  Breakfast Bowl with Quinoa and Avocado
  Tahini Banana Smoothie with Sesame Seeds
Lunch:
  Pork Tenderloin with Lemon and Thyme
  Spinach Salad with Pomegranate and Feta
Dinner:
  Grilled Lamb Burgers with Feta and Mint
  Baked Zucchini Fries with Lemon Aioli
Dessert: Orange and Almond Cake
Nutritional Information (approximate):
  Calories: 2,180 kcal, Protein: 105g,
  Carbohydrates: 220g, Total Fat: 108g

Day 28

Breakfast:
  Mediterranean Bruschetta with Tomatoes and Basil
  Whole Grain Pancakes with Pomegranate Syrup
Lunch:
  Tuscan White Bean Soup with Kale
  Farro Salad with Grilled Zucchini and Feta
Dinner:
  Grilled Sardines with Olive Oil and Parsley
  Ratatouille with Fresh Herbs and Olive Oil
Dessert: Vanilla Panna Cotta with Fresh Berries
Nutritional Information (approximate):
  Calories: 2,170 kcal, Protein: 102g,
  Carbohydrates: 230g, Total Fat: 112g

Day 29

Breakfast:
  Spinach and Sundried Tomato Frittata
  Avocado Toast with Olive Oil & Cherry Tomatoes
Lunch:
  Chicken with Orzo and Roasted Vegetables
  Cucumber, Tomato, and Red Onion Salad
Dinner:
  Baked Sea Bass with Tomatoes and Olives
  Mediterranean Stuffed Mushrooms with Feta
Dessert: Sütlaç (Turkish Rice Pudding with Cinnamon)
Nutritional Information (approximate):
  Calories: 2,150 kcal, Protein: 104g,
  Carbohydrates: 220g, Total Fat: 108g

Day 30

Breakfast:
  Shakshuka with Fresh Herbs and Crumbled Feta
  Almond & Orange Smoothie with Chia Seeds
Lunch:
  Classic Greek Lemon Chicken Soup (Avgolemono)
  Warm Potato Salad with Capers and Olive Oil
Dinner:
  Shrimp Scampi with Garlic and Olive Oil
  Grilled Asparagus with Olive Oil and Lemon Zest
Dessert: Kataifi (Shredded Filo Pastry with Nuts)
Nutritional Information (approximate):
  Calories: 2,180 kcal, Protein: 106g,
  Carbohydrates: 228g, Total Fat: 112g

Made in United States
Troutdale, OR
12/29/2024

27390029R10062